Novel Ideas
Mapping Textual Analysis within the Novel

– CHRIS DANIELS –

An environmentally friendly book printed and bound in England by
www.printondemand-worldwide.com

This book is made entirely of chain-of-custody materials

www.fast-print.net/store.php

Novel Ideas – Mapping Textual Analysis within the Novel
Copyright © Chris Daniels 2012

All rights reserved

No part of this book may be reproduced in any form by photocopying or any electronic or mechanical means, including information storage or retrieval systems, without permission in writing from both the copyright owner and the publisher of the book.

ISBN 978-178035-406-4

First published 2012 by
FASTPRINT PUBLISHING
Peterborough, England.

Novel Ideas

Contents

Introduction.   2

Block Diagrams.
People Society and Change.   4-5
Class and Money.   6-7
Perspective.   8-9
Race and Gender.   10-11
Societal, Sexual and Generational Dissonance.   12-13

Essays
People, Society, & Change.   14
Middlemarch. (Eliot, G.)

Class & Money.   49
Germinal. (Zola, E.)
Far from the Madding Crowd. (Hardy, T.)

Perspective.   85
Madame Bovary. (Flaubert, G.)
The Portrait of a Lady. (James, H.)

Race and Gender.   128
The Awakening. (Chopin, K.)
Heart of Darkness. (Conrad, J.)

Societal, Sexual and Generational Dissonance.   160
Dangerous Acquaintances. (De Laclose, C.).
A Vindication of the Rights of Woman. (Wollstonecraft, M.)
Fathers and Sons. (Turgenev, I.)
Selected Stories. (Mansfield, K.)

Introduction

Novel Ideas and the use of Block Diagrams within Literature

Among other things, block diagrams can be a means of dealing with the sheer volume of material that descends on students engaging with English literature at both A-Level and university level courses. For example, a one year 19th. C. literature course run by a university over a considerable number of years comprised of twelve novels, two course material books, an anthology, videos and audio tapes.

The point is does the workload associated with courses, such as the above, take into account the reality of students' lives, especially mature students, who might have work and family commitments over and above the course work involved. With the high cost of a university education, of no matter what stripe, it is in everyone's interest that chosen courses should be completed in an efficient and cost effective manner.

What I have set out to do is to take a wide range of sometimes complex novels written over a period in excess of 200 years by British, Commonwealth, French, American, and Russian authors. These novels also take on important issues of their day that, in most cases, pursue points still relevant in today's world. Such as this can easily be seen by comparing the work of Mary Wollstonecraft in the 1790's with those that followed such as Kate Chopin and even Katherine Mansfield in the 1920s. The idea is to then reduce the content of the essays in question to a still more manageable level by containing the points raised therein on single page block diagrams.

What this form of block diagram does is to give students a more easily retained visual representation of an essay that might comprise of over twelve thousand words relating to complex issues raised in the novels. It also allows students to compare and contrast similarities and differences across the novels chosen, a question frequently asked of students throughout most literature courses and under exam conditions.

If students were to operate this system for themselves it could also help by consolidating literary points brought up throughout the year. In other words this methodology can be used as a template and need not only apply to the novels I have dealt with.

The use of a simpler version of the block diagram is a well tried system of managing excessive amounts of information on major electrical and instrumentation construction projects including petro-chem. plants, oil rigs, power stations etc. Although primarily of use to students throughout a literary degree course the same system could be employed by students on A-level courses as an aid to disciplining their approach to this wide and often complex subject.

The block diagram used in this case for literary purposes is much more comprehensive than a mind map. I have placed the block diagrams separate from the essays but together for ease of reference and comparison. Also, I think that this methodology of dealing with course material reduces somewhat worries over what might have been inadvertently missed out that could have serious consequences at a later date. In my experience this methodology does not get rid of the complexities involved in this subject but rather it can foreground complexities and allow people to reach a position whereby they can deal with them more effectively as they arise.

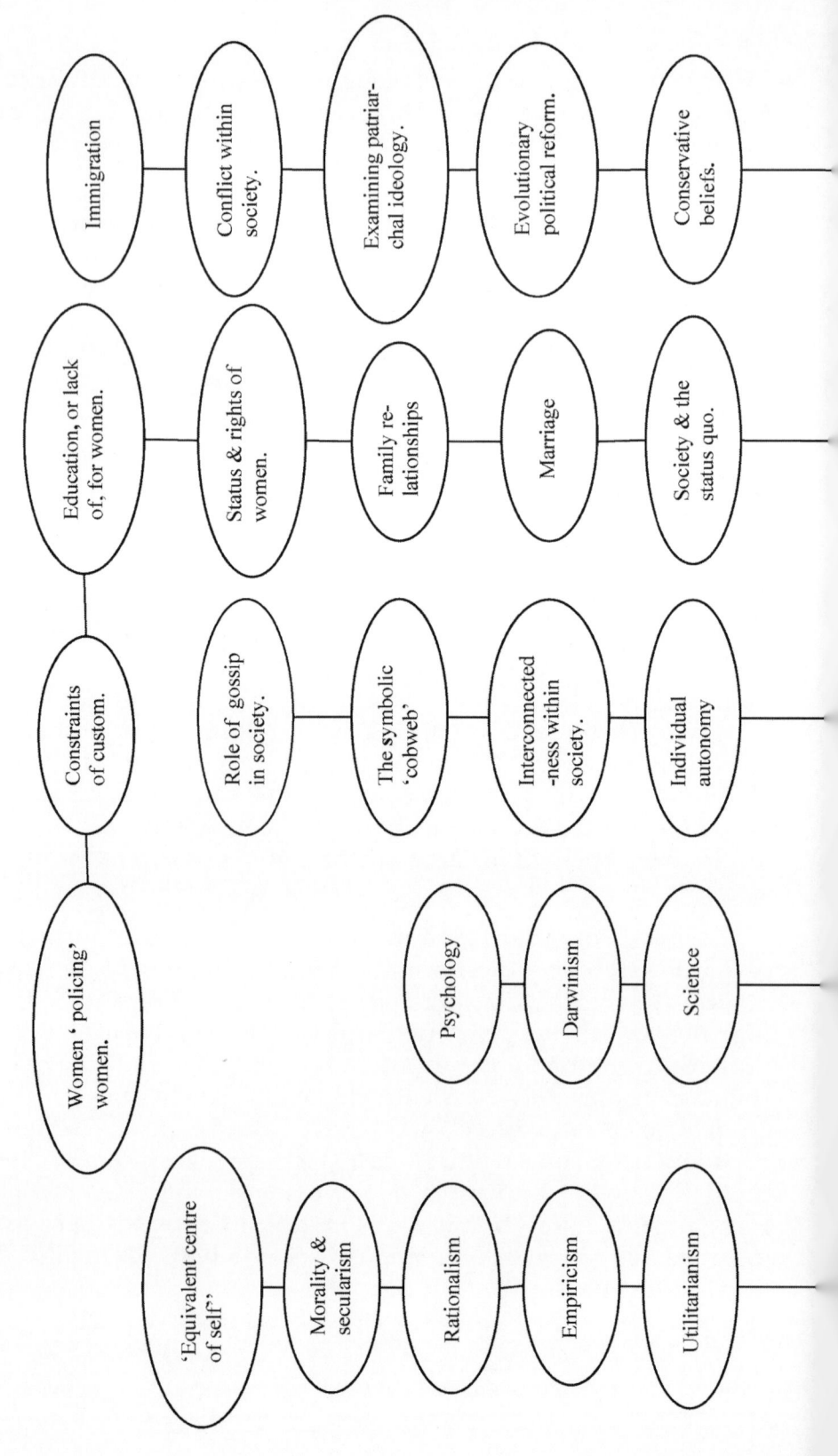

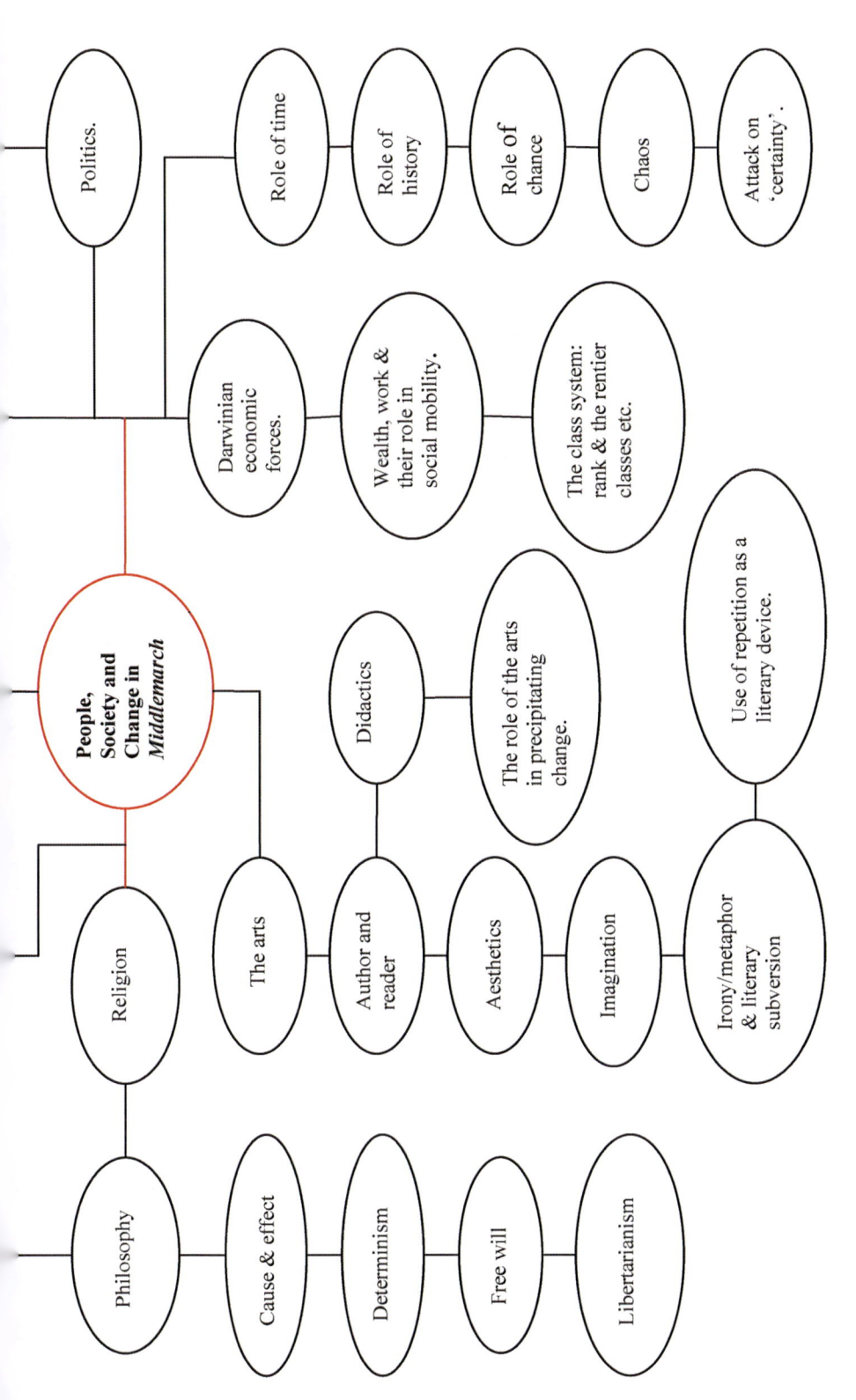

- The importance of work relative to both sexes.
- The role of chance in financial affairs.
- Comparative importance of utilitarianism & religion.
- Darwinism & economic determinism.

- The male's role in the construction of own class identity through appearance.
- Defining women as a sub-species within the lower classes.
- Sexual commodification of women.
- Appearance & its role in misogynistic attitudes towards women.

- Women as a sexual currency/sexual commodification of women.
- The role of class & wealth in the empowerment of women.
- Fecundity, children, sexuality, & class.
- Use of time. i.e. Historical cycles & stasis within society.

- Justification of misogyny, also violence & female subservience.
- Social and cultural conditioning.
- Environmental & human degradation.
- Darwinism & economic determinism.
- Darwinian Theory, inherited traits & free will.

- Defining women as a sub-species within the lower classes.
- Political divisions. i.e. nihilism/anarchism vs. Political & financial co-operation between the workers?
- The conjunction between money, work & class.
- The 'beast' in the tabernacle.

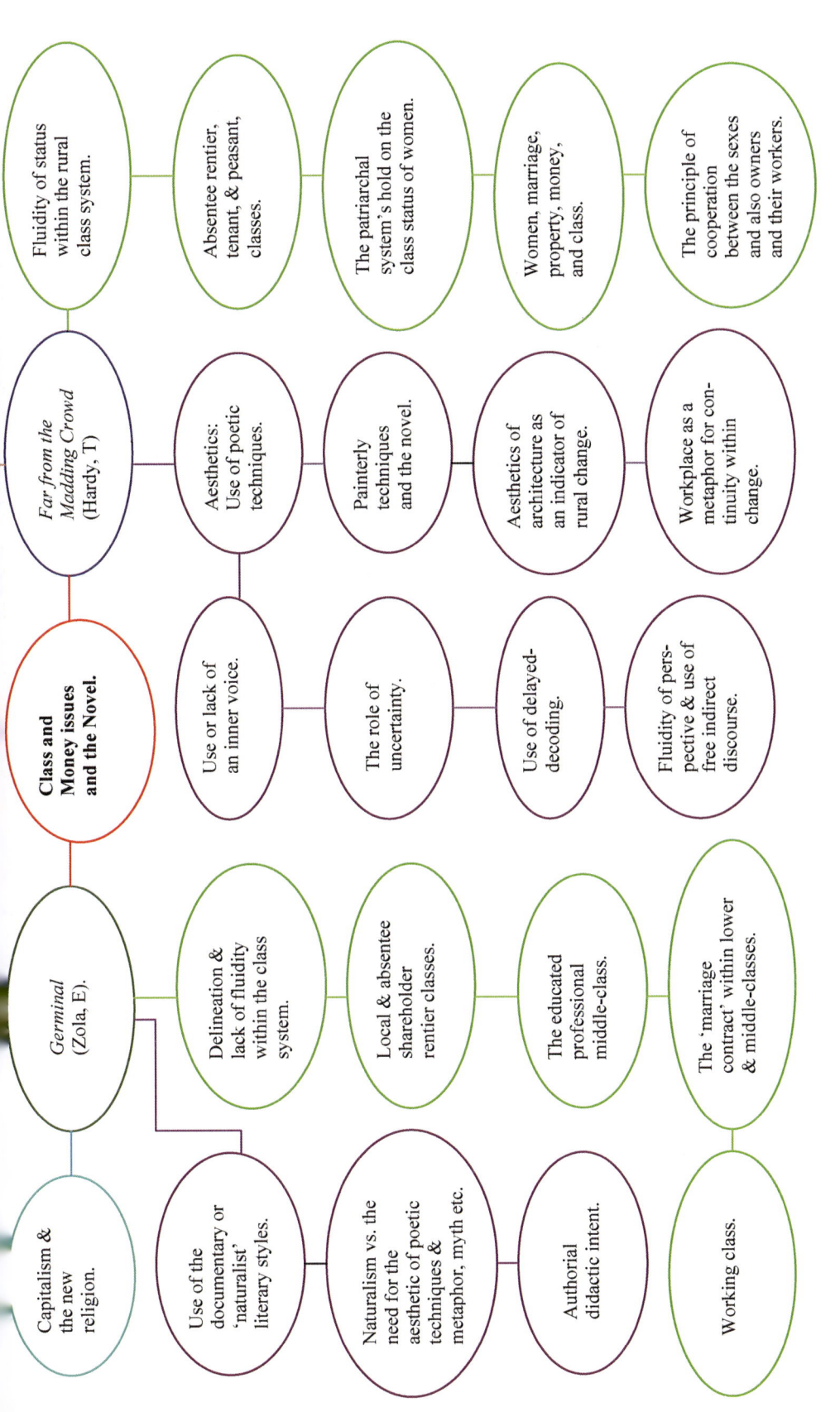

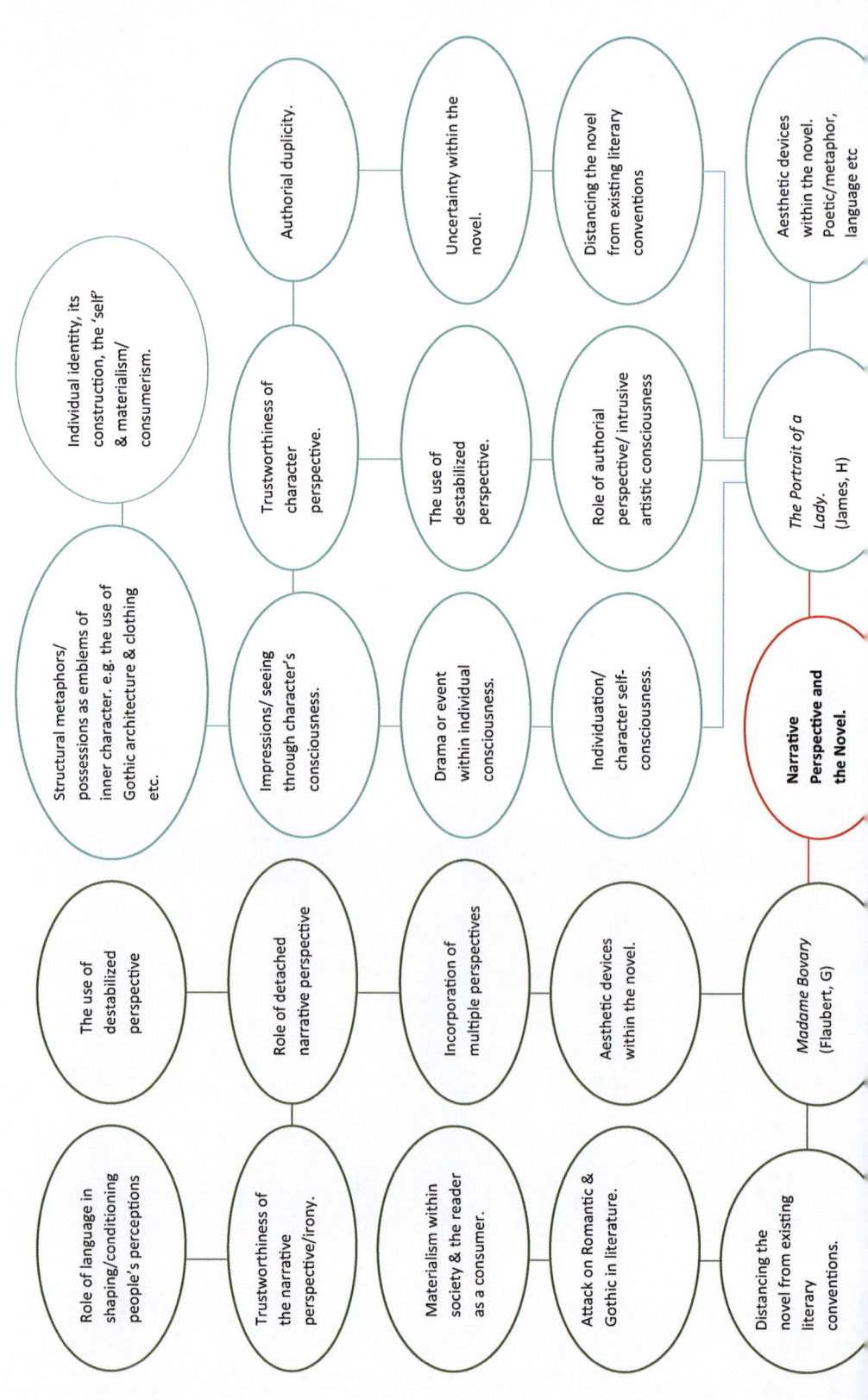

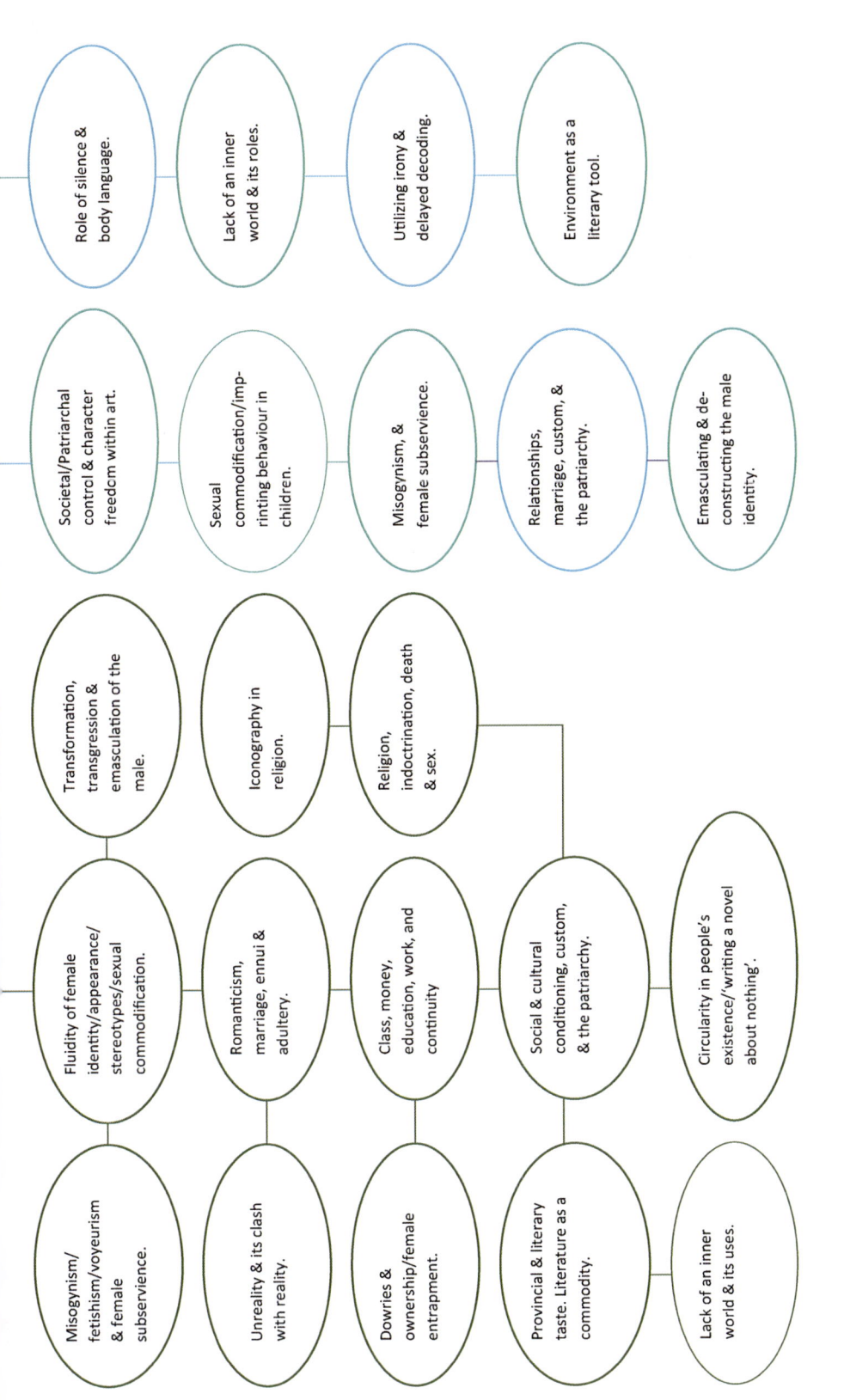

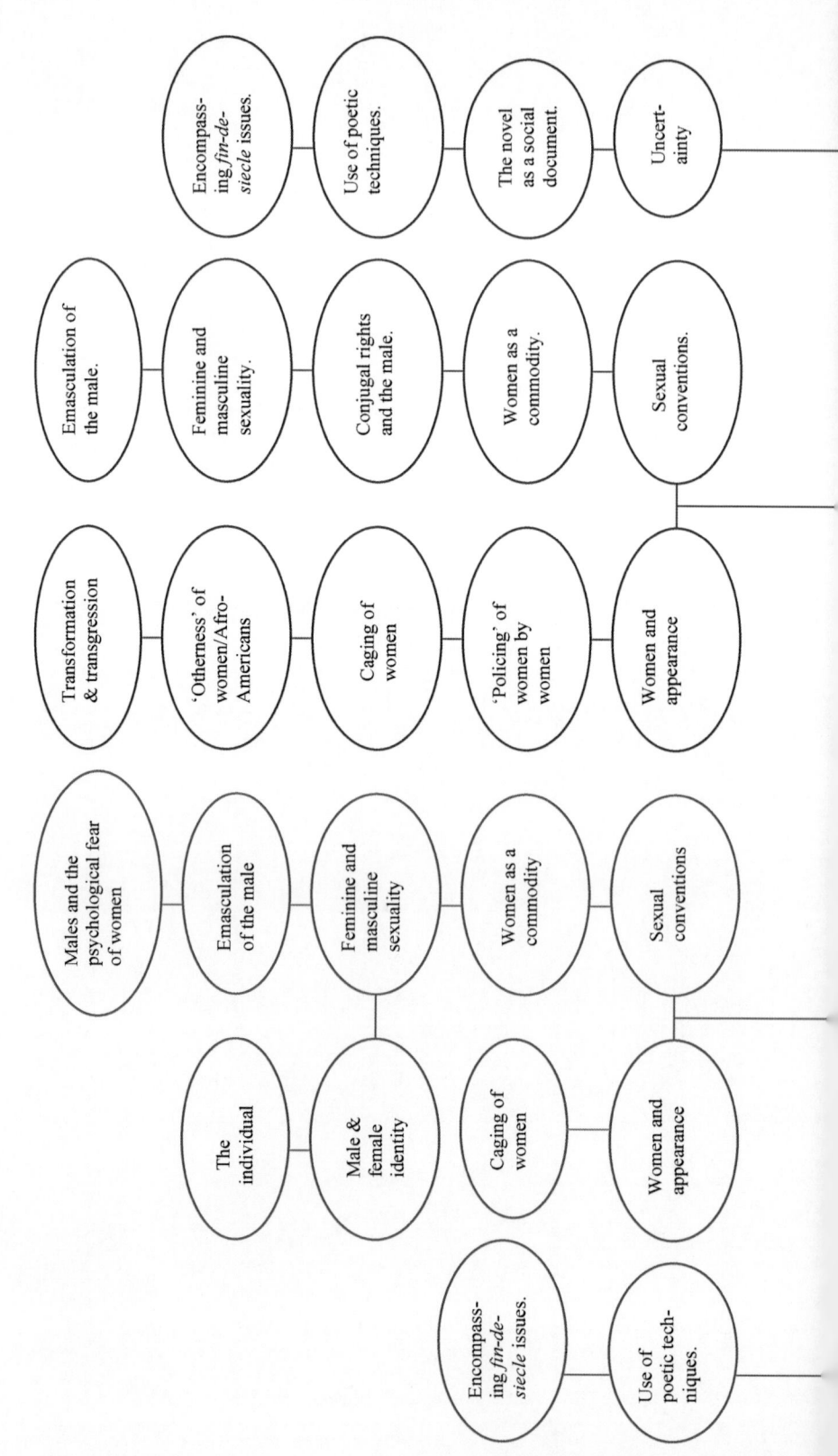

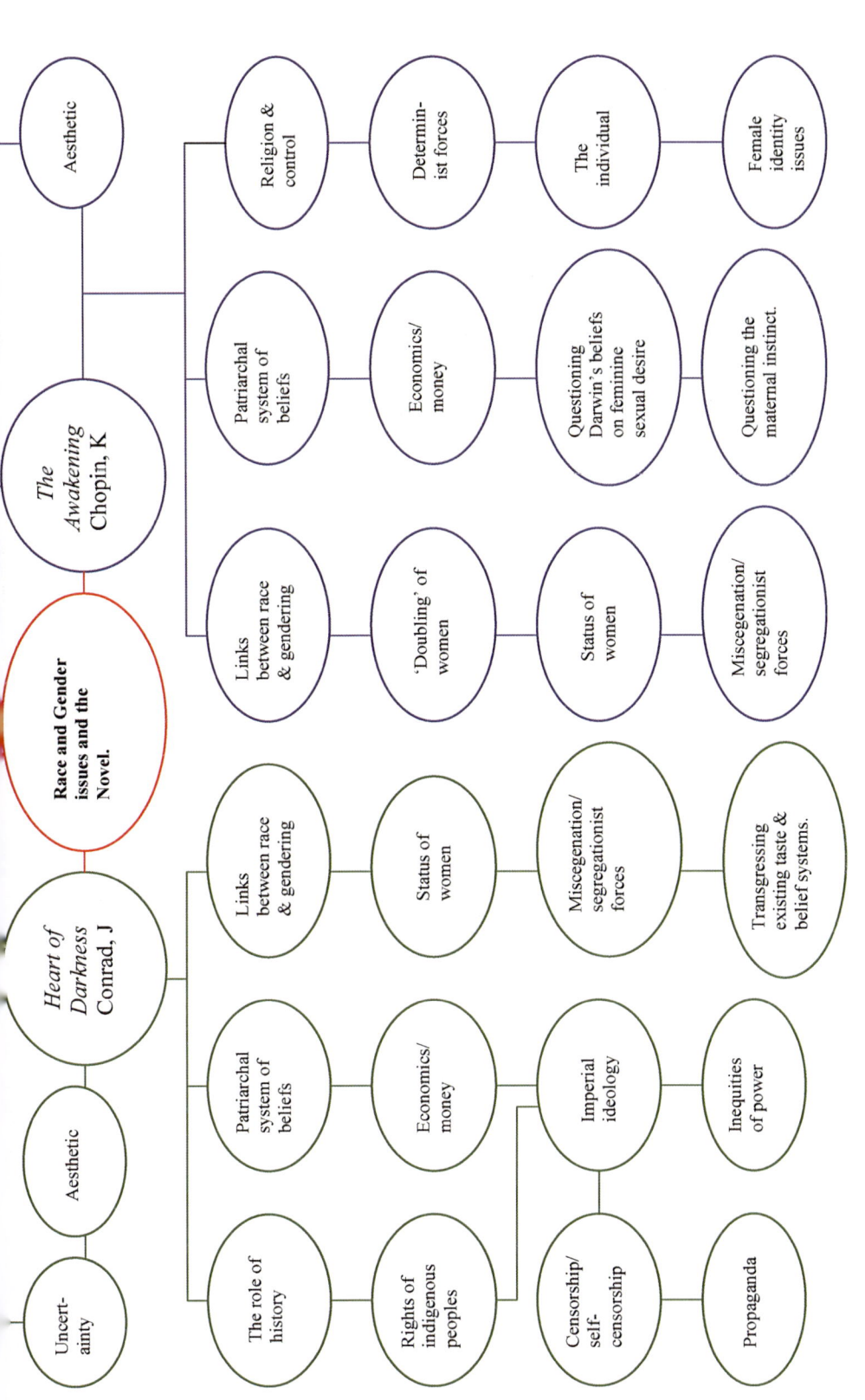

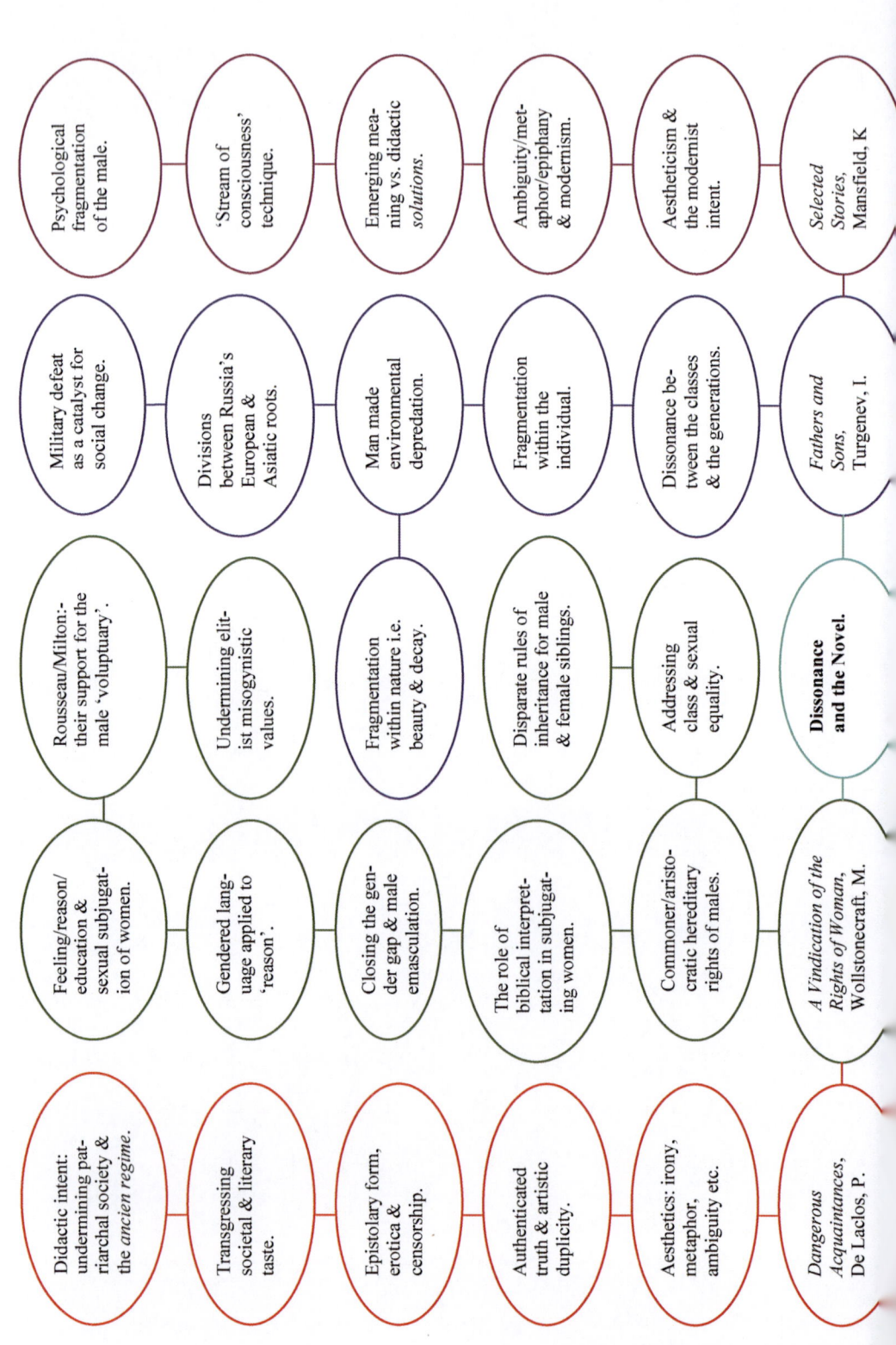

Column 1 (red)

- Women's rights & sexual commodification of women.
- Women 'policing' women: standards & behaviour.
- The role of education & religion in subjugating women.
- Marriage, female choice, sexual ambiguity in women.
- Women & emotion/feeling, perceived lack of reason?

Column 2 (green)

- Inequality of character & 'being' between the sexes.
- Transgressing patriarchal society norms.
- Women/appearance/obedience/duplicity/'policing' of women.
- Sexual commodification of women.
- Prostitution & the single girl/married woman.

Column 3 (green)

- Resistance to the education of women as a norm.
- Sex education for girls, & children in general.
- Women, freedom, & the institution of marriage.
- Use of environment as metaphor for social decay.
- Defects within Scientific Materialism/Nihilism.

Column 4 (blue)

- Didactic intent & uncertainty within the novel.
- Aesthetic needs versus utilitarian beliefs.
- Foreign influence, cultures & national inferiority.
- Feminine qualities as metaphor for modernizing.
- Support for incremental social change.

Column 5 (purple)

- Emasculation of the male e.g. internalized male hysteria.
- Women as a sexual/domestic commodity.
- Questioning class system/feminine & family values.
- Male ownership of women.
- Passive resistance to male authority.

Chapter One

Middlemarch (Eliot, G.) and People, Society, Change.

In Eliot's fictional world of *Middlemarch* [Eliot, G. (1998), Oxford University Press, Oxford. (All references are to this novel unless otherwise stated)] her characters' actions, choices and aspirations cause resonances elsewhere that can sometimes have unforeseen consequences for the individual and those around them. Throughout the work Eliot brings to bear forces as diverse as the political, economic, sociological, philosophical, scientific, artistic and historical that might, working over a period of time, bring about change in both the individual and the society they inhabit. For good or ill she shows us her characters actively helping to create the society that they inhabit, in some cases precipitating change in this society, and that this in turn can institute change in the very individuals/groups involved in these processes. Eliot also makes plain that there are existing forces within society that actively work as a constraint on change. For her the longevity of the more conservative elements of these forces means that they may have some worth, especially as a test by which to measure any newer system of beliefs proposed as the way forward for society. Within *Middlemarch* Eliot confronts each and every philosophical system of belief that she introduces with the world as it exists thus both testing and taking them beyond the realms of abstract theory. In other words this struggle for ascendancy between the different belief systems can be seen as a form of intellectual Darwinism with time being one of the most important tests of their worth.

Also, the work's inclusiveness, content, and a structural openness, encourages her readers to question their own view of the world around them that could, in effect, open them up to a process of change. An example of this is the way the tenets of religion are repeatedly visited through the different characters that in effect hollows out support for religion in general. In fact again with the aid of repetition this same scepticism is also brought to bear on any secular system of beliefs that might replace the moral framework that Christianity provided to her 19th. Century readers. In other words, art itself can play an important role in bringing about change. Eliot also suggests that any radical changes should come about by evolutionary means rather than as a seismic revolutionary shock to society and that it should work from the individual level outwards and then on into society. We the readers are often placed within the skin of the individual characters that are themselves a product of imagination and this gives the work both originality and a psychological dimension. A theme throughout the work is that if we are to pass judgement on the actions, or otherwise, of people we should at least attempt to see the world through their eyes. This can be seen in terms of an awareness of the needs of others that is separate from our own. Although readers may view these in purely psychological terms it also possesses a strand of ethical belief that would take us beyond the religious dogma of the day. Furthermore, Eliot shows us that what appears on the surface as a world of separateness, difference and conflict between, and within, the classes often conceals an underlying organic interconnectedness that stretches throughout the whole of Middlemarch society.

What Eliot sub-titles as *A Study of Provincial Life* opens with an observation on insularity and continuity within Middlemarch's class system that also raises issues surrounding divisions within and without the family in question. The third-person, detached, authorial voice, informs us that Mr Brooke's family had in the past no recourse to 'yard-measuring or parcel-tying forefathers'

(*Middlemarch* p.7) and that in some respects this can be seen to have effectively insulated them from a rapidly changing commercial world of Britain in the 19th. Century. This is set against a 'hereditary strain of Puritan energy' situated in his niece Dorothea, that 'glowed alike through faults and virtues' (p.8). Dorothea's 'Puritan energy' does suggest that she is much more aligned with, and been effected by, the Protestant work ethic of her times than her uncle where this 'energy' was 'clearly in abeyance'. Here Eliot critically juxtaposes the class system's insular hereditary principle with a Darwinian world of commerce and its inherent competitive traits.

Ambiguously, 'Puritan energy' could also allude to the periodic outbreaks of Calvinistic 'enthusiasm' that marred interpretation of religious tenets and caused instability within Protestant Christianity in the 19th. Century. Eliot's use of 'Puritan' raises the idea that the 'virtue' of the Protestant work ethic within society sat side by side with the 'fault' of religious division precipitated by fundamentalist 'enthusiasm' and that these might also exist in the some way within Dorothea. In a sense do these 'faults and virtues', or divisions, within Dorothea merely reflect 'faults and virtues' that exist within the society, and its beliefs, that she inhabits. Also, buried inside Eliot's text is a hint that despite the longevity of the Brooke line, the bundle of characteristics that make up who they are is as much open to chance as any other class in this delineated society and if so what value may be placed on any society structured along these lines. Already there are signs that what Dorothea may or may not do can be subject to inherited traits and this suggests a questioning of any libertarian support for absolute free will on the part of the individual. Eliot is not damning free will but she is putting forward the case for it to be balanced against inherent economic and religious forces that can also be seen as part of a more general determinist world.

Eliot's use of 'energy...glowed...faults' can also be seen in terms of a metaphor for uncontrollable volcanic type forces within Dorothea that may spill over without warning. This emphasizes Eliot's earlier point that Dorothea was 'likely to seek martyrdom, to make retractions, and then to incur martyrdom after all in a quarter where she had not sought it' (p.8). In other words Eliot is again emphasizing the potential for instability within her character and also within what is apparently a stable, wealthy, family environment. But there is also a suggestion that Dorothea, and other women of her class, require outlets and real purpose in their lives that their situation does not allow. Eliot's irony seems to be much more supportive of the niece and this has the effect of drawing the reader onto her side rather than the side of the uncle as head of the family.

Even between Dorothea and her sister Celia we are made aware of differences in character as Dorothea was 'usually spoken of as being remarkably clever' while Celia was seen as having 'more common-sense' (p.7). Eliot is defining differences within the sisters' characters but is also raising the importance of the opinion of people who may not even be connected, socially or otherwise, with the Brooke family. What is 'spoken' by others is an important thread that links Middlemarch's community even where there is no direct connection. The reader is already being made aware of the importance of gossip as a determinist force and how it may shape perceptions of character, even at the risk of possible misinterpretation of the signs that may be available to others. Also, supporters of determinist philosophy would argue that Dorothea's inherited volatile traits are psychological forces that may act against her ability to operate freely. What any individual may inherit is in itself subject to chance as can be seen by Eliot's close examination of three members of the same family. Within a matter of several pages she is already bringing forward issues surrounding religion, class, work, the economic, philosophy, the role of chance and our need to take into account the innate divisions that exist, not only along class lines but also within individuals and their families as well.

Eliot's ironic mocking tone of voice towards Brooke is emphasized when she has Mrs Cadwallader later state that he was incapable of "resolution" (*Middlemarch* p.54) and this further steers her readers towards a more sceptical view of him than the character of Dorothea. Also, although we may see her as more open to change Eliot tells us that in with Dorothea's other characteristics there is also the problem of possessing a 'theoretic' mind. This combination might in fact 'hinder' her marriage prospects, these 'being decided according to custom, by good looks, vanity, and merely canine affection' (p.8). Eliot's irony shows an even-handed approach to her characters but her use of 'theoretic' ambiguously leaves open for her readers whether this is a criticism of Dorothea or Middlemarch society's expectations in a woman. For her readers this adds to the suspicion that young girls should be neither 'remarkably clever' nor 'theoretic' if they are to succeed in Middlemarch's marriage stakes, this being described as being no more than 'her lot'. Also, Eliot's use of 'canine affection' effectively skewers the role of women who may go down this road in relation to men and even any male who might demand it. The importance of appearance, or 'good looks', on the part of women is also subverted by Eliot throughout this piece of condensed irony.

Already there is a suggestion that Dorothea's lack of 'vanity' places her outside of a sense of self that goes with the more egotistical of this world. Through the two sisters Eliot also takes a dig at the education of women when she informs us that 'they had both been educated, since they were about twelve years old' (p.8). These are two girls that are still only in their teenage years and furthermore the extent of their education had been decided on by a 'bachelor uncle and guardian'. Dorothea's naivety is made plain by the fact that she 'retained very childlike ideas about marriage' (p.10). She saw that a 'really delightful marriage must be that where your husband was a sort of father, and could teach you even Hebrew, if you wished it'. What 'really' damns Dorothea's take on marriage is not so much the husband as a supportive 'father' and teacher but the idea of equality inherent in the words 'if you wished it'. Eliot's understated observations leave open for her reader's interpretation such points that for women marriage can be a much more threatening institution than this. Also, we are coaxed towards the idea that this society has left Dorothea without the necessary tools, socially or educationally, to make proper choices in the one thing that she was being steered towards and even groomed for.

Furthermore, we learn that in this society the girls in question are a sexual commodity, with their value depending on their outward appearance and their inner psychological makeup, or ability to show 'canine affection'. Or, as Sally Shuttleworth defines it 'each part of Middlemarch life is related to every other part; individual identity is not only influenced by the larger social organism, it is actively defined by it.' (*The Nineteenth-Century Novel, A Critical Reader* p.291). Shuttleworth also sees this as an 'individual autonomy' that is subject to 'life-processes' that are embedded within Middlemarch society. In fact as stated earlier by Eliot, 'custom' in itself is a straitjacket that can be used very effectively to diminish freedom of action and, as we can see, even women's thought processes. Eliot's view that, '[W]omen were expected to have weak opinions' (*Middlemarch* p.9) is an indication to her readers of her own critical stance towards this element of the constraining nature of 'custom' and here she effectively undermines the continuity inherent in 'custom'. Already readers can adjudge determinist forces as diverse as custom, societal, educational and sexual working on character in such a way as to constrain their actions as individuals.

In her introduction to *Middlemarch* Felicia Bonaparte touches lightly on the influence of such as J. S. Mill on Eliot. She writes that with some reservations Eliot supported his use of 'enlightened self-interest' as a 'basis of the ethical system of his Utilitarian philosophy' (p.xvii). Alluding to Carlyle as an influence on Eliot, Bonaparte later states her worry about utilitarianism was 'that a society so conceived would be not a community but an aggregate of egoists' (p.xxv). Despite this reservation by Eliot we can see that if the way forward is the use of elements of utilitarian philosophy then the nature of the forces it has to deal with that are acting on women can themselves be seen in determinist terms.

Some of the determinist forces acting on the character Dorothea are taken up in an essay by Fred Wilson on the philosophical works of J. S. Mill. Wilson states that 'Mill argued that in the modern age people everywhere, in Britain at least, are being freed from the bondage of custom and unnecessary regulation...Women alone remain tied to a certain role. In fact, society so educates women that they bind themselves' (Extract on John Stuart Mill p.27 from *Stanford Encyclopedia of Philosophy*). He backs this up with a direct quote from Mill's *Subjection of Women* stating that "[M]en hold women in subjection by representing to them meekness, submissiveness, and resignation of all individual will into the hands of a man, as an essential part of sexual attractiveness" (p.27). These expectations on the part of men would strike a chord in Eliot's 19th.Century women readers and the more modern feminist views that followed on. The more obvious flaw of utilitarian 'self-interest' is that it hardly seems credible that men would willingly give up such powers over any woman without a major struggle on the part of women in general. Despite this there are embedded in character, dialogue and plot, some very trenchant elements of Mill's thoughts on the condition of women in 19th. Century Britain, giving Eliot's fiction both a philosophic and a didactic content.

Eliot's characters are set retrospectively in the historical context of a nation in the cusp of change and engaged with reform of the constitution. That they were 'still discussing Mr Peel's late conduct on the Catholic Question' gives her readers an approximate period in which to place the events she is unfolding before them (*Middlemarch* p.9). Eliot's use of 'Question' does suggest to her readers that there are conflicting views with regard to this change, as a nation's constitution may be perceived as web of interconnected checks and balances that could easily be upset. As stated by Bonaparte '[T]he subject of freedom and its limits is a persistent theme in *Middlemarch*' (p.xii). By showing us constraints operating at a national, family and individual level, Eliot herself 'questions' the absolute ability to act freely at either the national level or lower down the order of things. Also, by placing her characters in a historical context Eliot shifts the perspective of individuals, and their actions, to the larger social and national horizon. When viewed forty years later, during a period following the passing of the '2nd. Reform Bill' (p. xlix), and in a more objective fashion, the passing of the '1829: Catholic Emancipation Act' (p.xliii) can be judged by Eliot's readers to be a necessary evolutionary change rather than a seismic change in society.

This experience of managed social change conflicts with some of the fears of individual expectations of the day and shows her late 19th. Century readers how the past can act as a lesson by projecting itself into the present. Through Brooke we are warned that historical movement may not be linear as "history moves in circles" (p.16) and this introduces us to the theme of repetition and cycles. In this case time is an important element in the process of evolving change in the nation's constitution as it allows a considered judgement on the merits of the changes made. This idea of conflict at a family, national, and an individual level, is a theme that keeps cropping up throughout the narrative. That the fabric of society is still intact suggests to Eliot's late 19th. Century readers that their society should be open to changes but through evolutionary rather than revolutionary methods. This suggests to both us and them that her novel is also about the state of the nation. Already readers are being required to interpret language, character, and events, within the text in an even-handed and open-minded fashion. Because of this Ermath rightly states that Eliot's readers are being introduced to 'an outside to every inside, a margin to every system...a plurality of worlds' (*A Critical Reader*, (p.329).

The character of Brooke allows Eliot to bring forward ideas relating to philosophy, science, history, and again the role of time. In dialogue with the more outward looking fellow landowner Chettam he states that "science...it would not do. It leads to everything; you can let nothing alone" (*Middlemarch* p.16). For Brooke's more conservative views science is too open-ended for his taste and the outcome, or effects of change, cannot be easily determined. Dorothea sees the changes necessary as "it is better to spend money in finding out how men can make the most of the land which supports them all, than in keeping dogs and horses only to gallop over it". This she sees as "performing experiments for the good of all". We see that there is conflict within the landowning classes as to the way forward that also spills over into a difference within the Brooke family. If Chettam improves things on his land by, as he sees it, "setting a good pattern of farming among my tenants" (p.15), then it is easy to see Brooke's nervousness in that this may precipitate a call for improvements among his own tenants. Again it is the problem of precipitating changes that bring in train consequences that are difficult to foresee or control.

In this scene Eliot is also portraying two families taking their own decisions as separate entities but at the same time caught up in an interconnected web of cause and effect. That the changes might sound reasonable to some is damned by Brooke when he states "[T]he fact is, human reason may carry you a little too far - over the hedge, in fact" (p.16). Here he is again showing his fears and at the same time taking logic and "reason" to task that is intrinsic to the rationalist philosophical view of the way forward.

Further on we learn that Brooke is reading 'Southey's "Peninsular War" (p.16) making the point that he is both well read and that he should not be taken for a fool. At sixty years of age Brooke and his generation would still remember the effects of the French Revolution and the way that "reason" was carried to extremes, which tipped out of control, eventually leading to both the Terror in France and war across Europe. Only "at one time" did Brooke believe in "human perfectibility" but experience has now taught him otherwise. Again he is making the point that "time" is an important element in exposing any flaws in a particular system of beliefs. The differences within and without the Brooke family over the proposed changes has now become a battle of ideas. Brooke supports the status quo on his property and basis this on his experiences of the past and his worry that "history moves in circles". In opposition to Brooke, and in support of Chettam, Dorothea is propagating the philosophy "the good of all" that is embedded in utilitarianism and is also deprecating the use of land for the purpose of pleasure.

Here she neatly combines the notion of the commercial, through the better use of money and land, with Protestant

Puritanism and its antagonistic attitude towards the pursuit of pleasure for pleasure's sake. Ironically, Dorothea's attitude towards the popular pursuit, among such as the local gentry, of riding to the hounds may have pushed the logic of her argument "over the hedge" and in this case placed Chettam in the same camp as Brooke. This also makes the point that if change has to be instituted then others have to be persuaded of the need for that change and then brought along with it. This is emphasized later with her ringing statement that "I think we deserve to be beaten out of our beautiful houses with a scourge of small cords – all of us who let tenants live in such sties as we see around us." (p.29) In reality it is hard to see members of the rentier classes accepting this without a fight, despite Dorothea's Biblical analogy to Christ forcibly expelling the money changers from the temple. In the light of the lack of "human perfectibility" Eliot herself seems to be wary of the constraints inherent in any philosophical view that may improve the lot of others whether it is in Chettam, Brooke or, as in this case, Dorothea's ability to go a step too far.

By alluding to the role of history, and Brooke's reading matter, Eliot is taking us inside the skin of this character and, in her typically even handed approach, allowing us to see the world through his eyes that opens up readers to a more sympathetic view of the character's beliefs. Also, the author is using history, time, and character, to show her readers that any lurch from one set of beliefs into another has its own dangers thus underlining her support for a more evolutionary approach towards change. Whatever the merits of utilitarian theory the sheer longevity of conservative beliefs that are portrayed to us, through the character Brookes, also has to be taken into account. His experience over time is juxtaposed with Dorothea's youth, inexperience, and lack of a full formal education, that we already know about thus hinting to us to be cautious of her views. Throughout this scene the 'faults and virtues' (p.8) of what are essentially abstract philosophical points of view are being tested against each other by the use of character, dialogue, and plot, that also demands an inclusive and interpretive role on the part of the reader. Eliot can be seen to be counselling caution in the sense that if humans are subject to 'faults and virtues' then any human construct, be it abstract or otherwise, could equally be seen in this light.

Later Eliot also uses Brooke's practical view towards the need for change in attitudes towards Catholicism but she then laces his words with a reason for religion as a means of holding people back. He states that "Catholicism was a fact; and as to refusing an acre of your ground for a Romanist chapel, all men needed the bridal of religion, which, properly speaking, was the dread of a Hereafter" (*Middlemarch* p.18). Brooke the conservative was only allowing change when it was already a "fact" and his linking of "bridal" with fear or "dread of a Hereafter" is a much more telling point for Eliot's 19th. Century readers. Religion is, in his view, a necessity to slow or even stop unwanted change and is driven by a "dread" of something that can neither be proved nor disproved. For Eliot's readers the "dread" is a purely psychological cause but its effect is an equally psychological "bridal" that they can now see as capable of holding back society in general. This point is emphasized by Eliot when she speaks of Dorothea and '[T]he intensity of her religious disposition, the coercion it exercised over her life.' (p.26) Here we see that some people can be shackled or coerced by nothing more than internalized determinist forces based on religious beliefs. But, ambiguously, by the use of 'disposition' is Eliot placing the reason for this 'coercion' at the feet of Darwinian inherited traits. This would also raise the question, is there an inherent advantage for humanity in having such a set of beliefs even if only for the discipline it places on a society or as Brook puts it 'the bridal of religion'?

Here Eliot again uses the word 'theoretic' to describe Dorothea's nature only this time it is much more closely tied in with religion. Her 'theoretic' mind is neither leavened by experience nor by education. In fact we are directly informed that she is 'struggling in the bonds of a narrow teaching'. As in the use of 'bridal' we now have 'coercion' and 'bonds' to add to the description of people mired in struggles but in the case of Dorothea Eliot points the finger at the basic problem of her 'narrow teaching'. We also know that this young girl possessed ambition through 'her desire to make her life greatly effective' (p.26), that she was wealthy, and that she had the leisure time to improve herself. This points up for Eliot's readers a bleak outlook in life for the majority of 19th. Century women who did not possess these same advantages. Dorothea may get involved in good works but any inkling that she should have a public and professional existence is strangled by means of her 'narrow teaching' and gender. The under use of feminine talents, the lack of a proper, and broader, education for women to prepare them for the world as it exists, are issues that we find cropping up at various moments within the novel.

Later in the work Eliot further undermines religious beliefs by her portrait of the clergyman Casaubon as being closed off from the world through his intellectual pursuit of the 'Key to all Mythologies' (p.58). Dorothea had seen his 'great work' as being 'of attractively labyrinthine extent' (p.22). In contrast to this she sees her own existence being 'hemmed in by a social life which seemed nothing but a labyrinth of petty courses' (p.26). There is a suggestion of duality in the metaphorical labyrinth as both are trapped, one in his intellectual work and the other in a social straightjacket. The overarching 'bridal of religion' that acts on 'all men' is seen here to be working in tandem with, in Casaubon's case, a self-imposed force working at an individual level and, in the case of Dorothea, it is much more general societal forces as well that are seen to be acting on her. In literary terms Eliot's 19th. Century readers could relate to Dorothea's stunted aspirations in a realist sense but if Casaubon is in effect mired in a 'labyrinth' it is also clear that in this case it is of his own making. From a feminist perspective, we already know that even if Dorothea were to throw off the shackles of 'her religious disposition' there would still be plenty enough 'coercion' from other sources not of her own making.

In Casaubon's case there does seem to be something decidedly odd about a member of the established religion trying to rationalize and source 'all Mythologies'. Ironically his life's work can be seen to subvert the Established

Church's espousing of tenets, such as The Resurrection, The Holy Trinity and Original Sin which, like the "Hereafter", cannot be tested against the empiricist methodology of observation and experiment. When Eliot opens up a discussion on myth she also opens up to readers where myths start and finish that might also include the teachings of the very Church that Casaubon belongs to. Eliot tells us that what Casaubon 'aimed' at in his 'Key to all Mythologies was 'that all the mythical systems or erratic mythical fragments in the world were corruptions of a tradition originally revealed' (p.22). This is open to interpretation that what is 'revealed' to Christians in the Bible may be no more than a 'corruption' of previous 'mythical systems'. Eliot's deliberate use of the words 'mythical systems...tradition...revealed' is to link 19th. Century Christian beliefs back to Pagan myth but in terms of it being a 'corruption' of the original. The irony of using the 'great work' of 'a clergyman of some distinction' (p.21) to attack a faith based religion would not be lost on either Eliot's readers or the Church of the day's ruling elite.

Eliot's use of circumlocutory language to describe Casaubon's dislike of music adds to his unsympathetic 'labyrinthine' image. His statement, "I never could look on it in the light of a recreation to have my ears teased with measured noises," (p.60) reflects a psychology not open to different emotions generated by outside sources. Dorothea's perception of Casaubon was to change over time and through marrying him. By way of experience and time she later comes to see his 'mind' in bleak environmental terms, it is closed off; as it occupies 'anterooms and winding passages which seemed to lead nowhither' (p.183). Similarly, her earlier optimism towards her 'marital voyage' eventually becomes nothing better than 'exploring an enclosed basin' (p.184). This is a metaphor describing a lack of change in Dorothea's situation as her trip abroad to Rome becomes no more than a different mode of containment. The change from single girl to marriage and home to abroad still sees Dorothea caught in a kind of existential loop.

Eliot then goes on to criticize Casaubon's use of, and approach to, knowledge. Instead of being stretched by the pursuit of knowledge Dorothea has ended up joining him in his own 'enclosed basin'. Eliot plainly portrays his alienation from others when she states that 'thought and feelings as had ever been stimulated in him by the general life of mankind had long shrunk to a sort of dried preparation, a lifeless embalmment of knowledge'. Alienated from those around him Casaubon's 'knowledge' becomes useless, 'lifeless', and finally embalmed. He does not allow himself, and his theories, to become tested or embroiled in a battle of ideas with others and so his 'thought and feelings' begin to atrophy. Eliot has already undercut Casaubon's egocentric view of women in general, and of Dorothea in particular, and his failure to change over time through the experience of marriage. His world view sees women in terms of "[T]he great charm of your sex is its capability of an ardent self-sacrificing affection, and herein we see its fitness to round and complete the existence of our own" (p.46). Here Eliot is damning the patriarchal ideology from their own mouths. It is an ideology that sees women as no more than an addendum to masculine needs and this further links her view to the work of Mill. Even the language of love is couched in detached circumlocutory terms that subverts the character, his system of beliefs, and in the process, diminishing the reader's sympathy towards him.

In Victorian Britain the tenets of the Established Church were not generally up for discussion, or change, but for men the same applied to their support for patriarchal superiority. Eliot's use of an unchanging "labyrinthine" character shows her readers a man reflecting the belief systems of the day which themselves could be seen as "labyrinthine" and unchanging. Despite all this Eliot then proceeds to place the reader within the character and the world that produced him and this also allows us to see things through his eyes. By means of the character Casaubon Eliot is questioning again just how much anybody can use 'free will' when we are the product of the society and the environment that we inhabit. Eliot supports this argument and makes the case for empathy towards, what appears to be, an unsympathetic character when she states, '[S]uppose we turn from outside estimates of a man, to wonder, with keener interest, what is the report of his own consciousness about his doings or capacity: with what hindrances he is carrying on his daily labours; what fading of hopes, or what deeper fixity of self-delusion the years are marking off within him;' (p.78). Again Eliot is directly taking us into the world of her character and away 'from outside estimates' of this man. Has Casaubon changed down 'the years' through 'hindrances...fading of hopes' and the common human frailty of 'self-delusion'?

Later Eliot develops this idea through the character of Dorothea in what can be seen as an epiphanic moment in her work. Both reader and author are brought together in the statement that although '[W]e are all born in moral stupidity' to which 'Dorothea had early begun to emerge from' she had still failed to see through Casaubon's eyes and 'that he had an equivalent centre of self, whence the lights and shadows must always fall with a certain difference' (p.198). We begin to see that somehow life's effect on an individual can cause 'a certain difference' within that individual and for all Dorothea's supposed saintliness she had failed to even attempt to enter into Casaubon's 'own consciousness'. Eliot is making the point that it is incumbent on us all to move away from fixed positions when judging others. The secular moral within the idea of an 'equivalent centre of self' is a very important theme in *Middlemarch* and is here brought to the surface through Dorothea's shortcomings, which is to be more aware of the needs of others that are quite separate from our own. Also, within these separate passages there is some suggestion that Darwin's theory of evolution can be extended from the effects of the environment on us physically to its effects on us psychology. In short, if we may pass moral judgement on Casaubon we are also placed in the position of having to show some sympathy towards him because he can also be seen as very much a product *determined* by the world he inhabits.

By means of gossip, a local rector's wife Mrs Cadwallader acts as a conduit to transmit the news of Casaubon and Dorothea's forthcoming marriage throughout the community. Her opinion is that "this marriage to Casaubon is as good as going to a nunnery" (p.54). Again we have the use of gossip as a determinist force that can be used to make something happen, or even stop things in their tracks, while also having the effect of threading together different families and classes in Middlemarch. The use of "nunnery" hints at sexual impotence on the part of Casaubon and celibate containment for Dorothea. If we take the human sex drive as an inner force acting on both sexes then Eliot's description, through the technique of free indirect discourse, of Casaubon's view that 'he [had] concluded that the poets had much exaggerated the force of masculine passion' (p.58) only adds to his image of sexual indifference towards women. For Eliot's readers it also has the effect of adding to Mrs Cadwallader's more caustic view of him as a man. In fact Dorothea's new life would be no better than her existing lifestyle in the Brooke home suggesting continuity as before. Again the theme of repetition or of people's lives moving in 'circles'.

In the name of openness and even handedness Eliot also has Mrs Cadwallader criticize Dorothea. To the disappointed suitor Chettam she says "you are well rid of Miss Brooke, a girl who would have been requiring you to see the stars by daylight" (p.54). In her view Dorothea is too prone to allowing her imagination full rein and this can only be seen as a problem in any woman. Here we have Eliot bringing up the issue of women 'policing' women that can also be seen as supporting elements of the status quo but again we have the notion of instability within Dorothea's psychological makeup. But conversely we can also see her character's volatility as a metaphor for a way forward for society. For if society is to change from one steady state to another we must, of necessity, have a period of flux or instability in between these states.

Wilson makes the point that from Coleridge Mill 'had learned to appreciate the role of social and cultural institutions in the historical development of human beings. Mill, like his father, was a determinist with regard to social phenomena but from Comte he had absorbed the idea that social change proceeds in a series of stages: there are "critical periods," in which old institutions are overthrown, and these are followed by "organic periods," in which new forms of social structure emerge and are consolidated.' (Extract p.19). Eliot may be using instability in the character of Dorothea to make the point that some instability is inevitable in society and that this is an essential part of life's cycles. Her outbursts, based on strong feelings, can be seen as a metaphor for periodic outbursts of anger against a conservative society's support for the status quo. Also, we should set this quality in Dorothea against Eliot's unsympathetic portrayal of Casaubon's unwillingness to show his feelings or support change in either himself or others. Throughout the work Eliot's readers are in effect being asked to display openness in their interpretation of the language and events due to ambiguity being built into the narrative.

The critic David Carroll supports this aspect of her work when he makes the point that 'Eliot creates these ambiguous situations in order to show that the final analysis really depends on one's premises - and these are breathed in like air from the social medium in which we live' (*A Critical Reader*, p.319). This suggests that over time our thinking processes as readers are subject to pressure from others, the 'social medium' we exist in, and that they in turn can determine the 'premises' we work to. Also, Eliot herself can be seen to be absorbing ideas belonging to other people that were already in the 'air' in 19th. Century Britain. These same philosophical beliefs are then tested through incorporation into her work making the point that art itself is subject to forces within 'the social medium in which we live'. This can be perceived as supporting a determinist philosophical perspective or, in short, as a form of intellectual Darwinism. That is, Eliot's ideas emerge from 'the social medium' she exists in but also these ideas are already engaged in a struggle to survive against other competing systems of beliefs.

Eliot's use of the words 'microscope' and 'minute causes' (*Middlemarch* p.55) in her study of Mrs Cadwallader's actions and words suggests to us that her role as author is akin to that of the observer scientist. Both Eliot and her character, the medical researcher Lydgate, are conducting experiments but in very different spheres. Eliot's need for individualism within her characters is paralleled in the conversation between Lydgate and Lady Chettam when they both agree 'that all constitutions might be called peculiar' (p.85). Gillian Beer rightly states that '[S]ignificant repetition and variation is an essential principle in the structure of *Middlemarch*' (*A Critical Reader* p.306). Lydgate's belief in, as Brooke saw it, "ideas, quite new, about ventilation and diet" (*Middlemarch* p.85) can also be seen as shifting perspective, much as Eliot does throughout the work, by linking external conditions to the problems of the particular. She is also making a social point that improvement for all would come out of an end to overcrowding allied to a better or more balanced "diet". Earlier Eliot lays out the contrast in living conditions between the country houses of the rentier classes and the tenants on their estates. Dorothea is described as 'taking her usual place in the pretty sitting-room which divided the bedrooms of the sisters,' while simultaneously being 'bent on finishing a plan for some buildings' (p.11). These 'buildings' were to replace what Dorothea saw as the "sties [that] we see around us" (p.29) and this can be seen as a much more political statement that also ties in with Lydgate's concerns for 'ventilation'. The different scenes involving Lydgate and Dorothea also spell out for her readers that the better off in society knew very well the conditions that the worse off were living under. In this particular case both parties can also be seen to be in favour of giving way in the face for the need for change.

Like custom, history, and time, these conditions and other external forces are a theme running through the narrative that suggest people and individuals are subjected to determinist forces that conflict with not only free will but the need for progress that would benefit all. That Lydgate's "ideas" are "quite new" suggests to Eliot's readers that he was implementing changes in "ventilation and diet" that have already been tried elsewhere. In other words it is part of an on-going experiment based on observations by him and others using their senses and experiences that also allow readers to link Lydgate's work to the empiricist school of philosophical thinking. Ambiguously, Lydgate's "ideas" can also be seen to be "performing experiments for the good of all" (p.16) that in effect creates a bridge between empiricist and utilitarian philosophical systems of beliefs. Again Eliot is refusing to be hemmed in by any particular philosophy that might be in the ascendancy at any particular time and this gives her the freedom, as an author, to examine closely what might actually work in practice.

Lydgate's open and experimental view of changes required in medical practice provokes Mr Standish to call these changes "upsetting the old treatment, which made Englishmen what they are" (p.85). Like Brooke worrying about unknown consequences of an action, Standish is making the point that movement in any direction can cause resonances that touch everybody. Again Eliot portrays these ideas through gossip between her characters with Lydgate being placed by this dialogue within what Shuttleworth calls a 'pre-existent web' (*A Critical Reader* p.291) and as an individual component within a 'fixed reality' of forces. Forces within Middlemarch that are already moving against Lydgate's professed desire "to raise the profession" (*Middlemarch* p.85) of medicine. Again we have conservative ideas, or as Shuttleworth calls it, the 'fixed reality', acting as a bulwark in the way of change.

Also, Eliot's use of words "old" and "Englishmen" links times past with the present 'reality' of English character as if history itself is a living component of society. The point can be made that Eliot's fictional time itself is open ended and slippery as she places a future generation of readers in their present observing the thoughts and actions of this previous generation. Bonaparte supports this idea of the work's use of history and time with her extract from an introduction by Eliot's partner Lewes. Namely, that 'Darwin's theory of evolution, emphasizing the genesis of the present in the past, rendered the past a part of the present and of all future time to come' (*Introduction* to *Middlemarch* p.xxviii). In fact the two generations are also linked through having had to endure the stresses brought on by trying to implement two major reform acts. Furthermore, her readers are placed in the position of observing her fictional hypothesis based on the reality of previous changes in society that in this case can also be seen to give them an opportunity to view these events from an empiricist perspective. Here Eliot brings to bear time, experience and observations on the problem of, and the need for, evolutionary change.

Later Eliot encourages a more sceptical view of Lydgate's character by laying out for her readers his inner thoughts on Dorothea that are 'guided by a single conversation'. (*Middlemarch* p.88) Despite her 'undeniable beauty' he found her 'wanting' in the respect that '[S]he did not look at things from the proper feminine angle'. Eliot further erodes our sympathy towards Lydgate when she later states that his 'distinguished mind is a little spotted with commonness' (p.140). As regards to Dorothea the unbiased seeker after scientific truth is shown to have feet of clay in his approach to a woman he hardly knows.

Eliot exposes for us a serious flaw in Lydgate and at the same time she satirizes the male ideal as to what they may find to be 'wanting' in a woman. That her 'beauty' may fit the bill is alright but how does she actually 'look at things' and in any case we are left to wonder what is 'a proper feminine angle'. There is a certain ironic humour, and playing with words by Eliot, in Dorothea's looks being suitable for Lydgate but how she may 'look at things' is not so. Also, at the time of publishing *Middlemarch*, never mind a generation before, she would certainly not be allowed to 'look at things' medical as, unlike Lydgate, Dorothea would be precluded from practising in most of the major professions by their own male dominated professional bodies. Being labelled earlier as 'remarkably clever' (p.7) and that '[H]er mind was theoretic' (p.8) are probably the qualities in Dorothea that are at odds with what Lydgate calls 'the proper feminine angle'. After all if women begin to 'look at things' differently, and investigate the reasons for their own unequal circumstances within a patriarchal society, who knows what the consequences might be. Like Brooke and Standish, Lydgate can also be seen to worry about the unknown consequences that might be brought about through change except in this case it is an avowed modernist that fears women being allowed to think for themselves.

Lydgate's character is again undermined when Eliot portrays him imagining that life with Dorothea would not be 'reclining in paradise with sweet laughs for bird-notes, and blue eyes for a heaven' (p.88). Some of these notions on the role of women could very easily be ascribed to Casaubon suggesting that Eliot sees within the male psyche deep unchanging attitudes towards women. There is a lack of real empathy towards Dorothea by Casaubon, who should know her, but the same applies to Lydgate a man that is 'guided by a single conversation'. Ironically how these two characters 'look at things' is satirized by Eliot all the more because of their respective roles as researchers. Throughout *Middlemarch* she allows the 'faults and virtues' of the characters to unfold gradually before her readers. Our realization of character is in a constant state of flux and this effect on the reader is mirrored when the characters themselves are described as being part of 'a slow preparation of effects from one life on another' (p.88). Not being able to gain an absolute fix on any character is in the words of Bonaparte 'a leap into post-modernism' (p.xxiii) on the part of Eliot.

But in Eliot's work this uncertainty also extends into religion, gender issues, and philosophical belief systems, to name just a few. Incremental change is going on all the time and this takes Darwinian Theory into the realms of the social. The 'slow preparation of effects from one life on another' suggests possibilities for evolutionary change for the better within people that is determined by others and that these changes can then move on and out into society entailing a more general improvement for all. It is a bringing together certain aspects of Darwinian, determinist, and utilitarian philosophy that can subtly change whatever they touch. In other words if, like the flawed character Lydgate, we want change we have to start from within ourselves and people in general rather than attempt to graft it on to them through some sort of societal change. Ironically, Dorothea's earlier idea of changes being needed in society 'for the good of all' is also in this respect found wanting as they appear to be changes that she would impose from above.

Opening with the words that '[O]ld provincial society had its share of this subtle movement' (p.88) Eliot then follows on with a long paragraph containing long sentences to describe a society of 'constantly shifting boundaries of social intercourse, and begetting new consciousness of interdependence'. Eliot's use of 'constantly shifting boundaries' is a sign to her readers that any limit within society will be tested and also any constraints must be flexible enough to allow for necessary change. Her syntax emphasises this as it mimics a society on a journey that is open ended where some people '[S]lipped a little downward, some got a higher footing'. The use of dialect could superficially fix a person's class but Eliot states that 'people denied aspirates, gained wealth' showing her readers that there was movement into the middle-classes, despite a general lack of a classical education for the lower orders. In this case changes were being brought about in society's class structure but it was through a work ethic allied to commerce. This work ethic is an important theme within *Middlemarch* as it allows people to improve their relative position in society. Those who adapted best to a system based on 19th. Century Darwinian economics 'gained wealth' and 'got a higher footing'. It was 'firmness' among 'fluctuation' presenting 'new aspects' of 'personages or families'. Eliot describes the effects on individuals as both a 'double change of self and beholder' with the narrator also moving from a position of addressing her readers directly to a more inclusive 'we' (p.89).

Readers can see that from the perspective of a 'beholder' the person being viewed may change in an outward sense. This can then lead to the 'beholder' in turn undergoing changes in their own psychological makeup because of 'effects from one life on another' (p.88). Here Eliot is suggesting that there is a psychological interconnectedness going on at all times whether we know it or not. If we are affected by others then we in turn bring about changes in them and this leads to a self-perpetuating chain of cause and effect. This also mirrors environmentally driven change in animals and plants that links humans into nature but for Eliot, in our case, these changes can also be extended into the psychological sphere. In other words there are multiple forces, both physical and psychological, that are operating on people that can be described in Darwinian, determinist, utilitarian and economic terms. In such as this case the emphasis, if any, that we give to a particular philosophical perspective is to some extent down to individual reader's interpretations. Also, from a literary perspective, and in a world that can no longer be described in linear terms, we have a more modernist take on 'uncertainty' of outcome that other authors were to reach out for later in the 19th. Century. In fact throughout the work readers can see a sustained attack being mounted on certainty where ever it might appear.

In this sustained 'telling' to her readers Eliot's perspective and role is as fluid as the characters and events she portrays. In other words her narrative technique reflects the fluidity of the world she sees around her. She brings together the 'we' of her and the present readership with 'old England' (p.88) and the times of historian 'older Herodotus' (p.89) to make a point that this 'sort of movement and mixture' (p.88) in societies are repeated over thousands of years. Beer calls such as this 'inclusiveness and extension. Nothing is end-stopped. Multiplicity is developed through the open relation created between the narrator and the reader'. Furthermore we are introduced to 'worlds of others' and 'unlimited worlds of ideas' (*A Critical Reader* p.305). Beer rightly sees Eliot as collapsing the boundaries between 'narrator and reader' and this is aided through her novel use of narrative technique that allows us to see things through the characters' eyes that in turn leads us into the 'worlds of others'. Through our interpretive role, readers also become an intrinsic part of the creative process as we blend with author, characters and, as we saw earlier, the struggle for supremacy between competing philosophical 'ideas'.

We also have Eliot's use of 'subtle movement' (p.88) and this mirrors somewhat her earlier use of 'minute causes' (p.55) with regard to individual actions of Mrs Cadwallader.

Again she can be seen to be linking together the microscopic movements and actions of individuals to the greater movements that go on in a society under the inevitable stress brought on by change. In other words, for good or ill, everything going on within a society contributes to the organic wholeness of that same society. It is another example of Middlemarch society as a metaphorical cobweb where actions resonate across its links or 'threads'. Here Eliot can be seen to be making the point that we all have a moral responsibility for our own actions due to the possible consequences that these actions may have on others. In Eliot's eyes the arguments for or against free will, cause and effect, and a deterministic world, does not preclude us having some moral responsibilities towards others. She effectively makes a case for some kind of balancing point between the forces inherent in a determinist world and our possession of a free will, limited that it may be, that allows us to impose our own moral standards where needed.

Eliot suggests that the contradictions existing within Dorothea are more general than that. It is not only her who possesses 'faults and virtues' (*Middlemarch* p.8) as elsewhere Eliot informs us that Lydgate had 'both virtues and faults capable of both shrinking or expanding' (p.140). This theme of faults and virtues existing side-by-side within people is something that is easily acceptable by readers and gives Eliot's work a 'realist' or mimetic literary tone. Also, as we can see from the earlier discussions surrounding Mill and Darwin, the conflicts within society in general can be seen as contributing to new equilibriums over time. What appears to be a recipe for chaos due to people exercising individual choices can eventually settle into a form of equilibrium and may even improve what went before. Some changes are caused by '[S]ettlers...from distant counties', who in turn set up 'fresh threads of connexion' (p.88). The characters Lydgate, Will Ladislaw and the banker Bulstrode can be seen as part of these 'fresh threads'. The metaphor 'fresh threads' is again a vivid example of the cobweb theme that keeps surfacing throughout the novel.

Repeatedly Eliot presents us with a society where the individual is affected by, or affects, the changing organism that is Middlemarch and at the same time these characters serve the writer's function of moving the plot on. Here she also hints at later turns in the narrative when she speaks of Bulstrode 'as a man not born in the town, and altogether of dimly-known origin' (p.89). In other words she is warning us that all that may be brought in from elsewhere might not be for the good of all. In contrast with opening up to her readers Lydgate's past here Eliot withholds information on Bulstrode's past. This deliberate use of delayed-decoding has the effect of increasing tension by surrounding his character with an air of mystery, and in an aesthetic sense, adding to her reader's curiosity or pleasure. Also, in all this talk of change throughout the work there is no mention of Providence or a Divine plan having a role in any of it. Again she uses language accessible to her readers to present to them philosophical arguments relating to 'cause' and 'effect' that also suggests didactic intent on her part. Eliot can be seen as attempting to change people's perceptions in a world still dominated by patriarchy and religions, these being viewed as possessing 'virtues' rather than 'faults' that then attempt to close down debates on the need for change in other areas. In this respect the author and her art again can be seen as a call for openness, on the part of readers, to new ideas and change. Furthermore, her laying out for her readers of some of the advantages and disadvantages for society through immigration and change are eerily echoed in some of the present day arguments put forward on these issues.

One of the 'limiting' factors on Lydgate is his relationship with Rosamond Vincy who is depicted as 'the flower of Mrs Lemon's school' (p.89). She is trained down to the last detail 'demanded in the accomplished female - even to extras, such as getting in and out of a carriage'. In words heavy with irony and humour Eliot effectively undermines society's view of what is an 'accomplished' woman. Real knowledge, or being perceived as 'clever' (p.8), could only be a handicap in entrapping a passing choice male. Eliot later describes Rosamond's actions in exquisite detail that fills in her character with a certain emptiness of real purpose that can fascinate a reader and at the same time damn women like her. She 'turned her long neck a little, and put up her hand to touch her wondrous hair-plaits – an habitual gesture with her as pretty as any movements of a kitten's paw. Not that Rosamond was in the least like a kitten: she was a sylph caught young and educated at Mrs Lemon's.' (p.p.149/150).

She has sexual attraction in spades but Eliot's descriptive language heaps on the irony. Her 'long neck' is only 'turned... a little' and this exposes her sexual qualities as a pose as if she is no more than a bait to any passing male that catches her eye. Gestures are so ingrained over the years that they are 'habitual'. Her 'wondrous hair-plaits' reminds us of the time spent preparing the bait that also hints at the leisure time available to such women and, critically, what they may find useful to do with their time. Although Rosamond used the 'movements of a kitten's paw' that she was not 'in the least like a kitten' speaks to us of a person tougher than her appearance might allow. For all her accomplishments this sexual commodity, a point rammed home by the use of 'sylph', needed to be 'caught young'. Eliot makes the point that society sends girls to such as Mrs Lemmon's school to be copied from some prototype deemed suitable. Acceptable appearance, 'weak opinions' and an education totally lacking in ambition can be seen as part and parcel of a determinist patriarchal society. As trained, and tough, as Rosamond may be Eliot's descriptive language is damning of her and any woman who may see in her something to imitate.

Furthermore, Rosamond sees marriage to Lydgate as an escape from her class and offering her 'connexions which offered vistas of that middle-class heaven, rank' (p.110). This opening up of a new imagined world could mean visits to 'high-bred relatives' without a thought for 'the money that was to pay' for her 'considered refinements'. Later we are informed that 'the piquant fact about Lydgate was his good birth, which distinguished him from all Middlemarch admirers, and presented marriage as a prospect of rising in rank and getting a little nearer to that celestial condition on earth in which she would have nothing to do with vulgar people' (p.156). For Rosamond the supposed advantages of 'birth' and 'rank' are juxtaposed in her mind with 'vulgar people'. Eliot's use of 'high-bred' and 'celestial condition' to describe the new imagined world of a risen snob is heavy with irony when we note that '[S]he disliked anything which reminded her that her mother's father had been an innkeeper.' (p.p.93/94) Rosamond is seeking to escape from the 'vulgar' trading class in Middlemarch into what she perceives as the 'celestial condition', or 'heaven', that is the rentier classes. In this new secular 'heaven' on earth money does not have to be earned by trade or labour. Here Eliot effectively undermines the authority of religion by her use of religious terms to show us a woman prostituting her sexual attractiveness for gain whether in financial or class terms.

This can be set against Dorothea's perception of her 'marital voyage' within the rentier class as a dead end or 'exploring an enclosed basin' (p.184). Through the character of Rosamond Eliot can again be seen to be making the point that for the condition of women to progress in the latter half of the 19th. Century there would have to be changes in the behaviour of women such as Rosamond and this can also be seen as didactic in intent. Ironically, the way Eliot presented marriage to us lays bare the corrupt motives that different parties may bring to, what was still in the 19th. Century, a mainly religion based ceremony. Also, readers can see all of this as both an attack on women using their physical attributes to progress from one class to another, through the cynical use of the institution of marriage, and an attack on the class system itself that delineates and fractures society. Furthermore, Rosamond's criteria that Lydgate might provide her with 'that middle-class heaven, rank' (p.110) can be seen as another example of Eliot's even handedness towards her characters. After damning male attitudes towards women, through both Casaubon and Lydgate, she now lays bare for her readers some of the defects in the criteria that women have towards the males.

After her marriage to Lydgate Rosamond's ego is again laid bare by Eliot with the words that her 'creditors' were 'disagreeable people who only thought of themselves, and did not mind how annoying they were to her' (p.625). Despite at this stage having got Lydgate into serious financial trouble Rosamond 'had always acted for the best -

the best naturally being what she best liked' (p.626). Here Eliot makes this statement more memorable, and adds to its emphasis, through the use of aesthetics. Her use of the poetic skills of assonance, alliteration and repetition adds to her humorous exposition of Rosamond's sheer selfishness. Her attitude is justified to us as being perfectly reasonable and logical in her eyes. Again we see reason and logic that is inherent in rationalist thinking being taken to extremes that in effect shows us its limitations and warns against it. Also, Dorothea's utilitarian belief in "the good of all" is shown to have its limits in the shape of Rosamond's ego and 'the best naturally being what she best liked '. In fact her greed for materialist things and her satisfying of her senses no matter what the cost to Lydgate's career could also place Rosamond at the extreme end of the utilitarian camp.

If ego is seen as a tool for human survival, and Rosamond is portrayed within the work as a great survivor, then Eliot can be seen to be making the point that it is also a selfish fracturing device that society must contend with. This leads on to a view that she may be suggesting an ironic subversion, or a testing, of Darwinian Theory in that Rosamond's egotistical view of the world means that everything should adapt and change to suit her particular needs rather than her having to adapt to the world she inhabits. Elsewhere Eliot directly informs us that 'Rosamond had a Providence of her own' and that her 'egoism' can be compared to her own 'little sun' (p.248). It is her ego that drives her to see everything as having to adapt to her needs and in this sense Rosamond also looks out on the world, much as Casaubon does, from a particularly self-centred position. Through the characters of Rosamond, Casaubon, and their respective partners, Eliot also departs from the notion of marriage as a happy literary ending thus undermining other authors of her day's more rosy portrayal of this institution.

As an opposite of Dorothea, Eliot's portrait of Rosamond is another thoroughgoing example against ordering society totally along the lines of utilitarian principles. The flaw in Dorothea's support for organizing society for "the good of all" is that it would rapidly run up against such as

Rosamond's lack of, what Brooke earlier calls, "human perfectibility". The multiple meanings that the character Rosamond and her actions bring to the surface again test the efficacy of particular abstract philosophical beliefs and at the same time the way society is actually organized along class lines. Also, by the end of the novel having successfully bent everybody, except Will Ladislaw's affections, to her will maybe we should see her 'egoism' as a success but from a moral point of view this can only be based on what we see as her own selfish needs. Even so as unsympathetic a character as Rosamond may be we are again taken inside her skin and allowed a series of psychological snapshots of her world allowing us the wherewithal to then pass moral judgement on her.

Speaking directly to, and for the benefit of, her readers Eliot takes the forensic approach to Lydgate's character and the support or otherwise for the changes in medicine he is trying to implement. She has work to do 'unravelling certain human lots, and seeing how they were woven and interwoven, that all the light I can command must be concentrated on this particular web' (p.132). As a 'new settler' (p.132) the character Lydgate is 'virtually unknown – known merely as a cluster of signs for his neighbours' false suppositions' (p.133). The use of 'unravelling...woven and interwoven...web' again introduces the cobweb as a metaphor and this has the effect of stressing the importance of both metaphor and repetition to the work in general. Also, Eliot is repeatedly raising the role of opinion in people's lives and their ability to misread any 'signs' that are available. Opposing groups of female patients do battle over the level of 'cleverness' of this medical practitioner but their 'equally strong' views are based on nothing more than 'intuitions'. In fact these women are being deliberately portrayed as being in danger of making 'false suppositions' due to their reliance on what can only be a 'general impression' or 'intuitions'.

As important as public opinion may be as a force for good or ill Eliot is warning her readers that what is said deserves greater substance than an 'impression' or 'intuition'. That Eliot has to 'unravel' what is going on suggests a certain disdain for the intelligence of these warring patients. In fact how much knowledge and education do they bring to bear on their 'intuitions'? In this scene Eliot's linking together of 'false suppositions' and 'lady-patients' immovable conviction' satirizes their ignorance and lack of real knowledge. Ironically, even the educated scientist Lydgate needed only 'a single conversation' to make his judgements on Dorothea showing us how double-edged the sword of 'opinion' can be. A fully rounded individual would be expected to apply his or her knowledge and education at all times, just as the author does, when 'unravelling' for us the 'new settler Lydgate'. Ambiguously, it is also left open to our own judgement which if any of the warring groups of patients might have got the character of Lydgate correct.

The role of author shifts to an investigation of the possibility of a direct link between science and art. Eliot later describes the younger Lydgate, perhaps ironically, that 'his imagination [was] quite unbiased' (p.135). Her exposition of Lydgate's character through interpretation of his 'signs', his 'imagination' and his being 'unbiased' could easily be a description of the author's methodology of constructing her imagined world of *Middlemarch*. Parallels between Lydgate and Eliot are further suggested as the character sees medicine as 'presenting the most perfect interchange between science and art; offering the most direct alliance between intellectual conquest and the social good' (p.136). Throughout *Middlemarch* 'science and art' are continually being brought into use as an authorial tool as is the war of ideas represented here in the form of 'intellectual conquest'. There is a suggestion 'the social good' that most people, of no matter what philosophical stripe, might aspire to may only be attained by open debate leading to solutions based on 'intellectual conquest'. The 'unbiased' Eliot warns us that Lydgate may not manage his ambition to 'alter the world a little' (p.135), which may also allude to her own didactic intent. He like others has to find that he may be subject to a 'process of their gradual change' (p.135) and in his case this came from 'the vibrations of a woman's glance' (p.136). When Rosamond touches his world this causes resonance within the web of his existence and after this things could never be the same again.

Ironically the role of chance as a catalyst for change is given some prominence in the downfall of the religious personage of Bulstrode. This, rather than Providence, had brought Raffles and with it Bulstrode's past as a pawnbroker and dealer in stolen goods into his present world. There was no 'danger of legal punishment' but his past actions would be open 'to the judgement of his neighbours' (p.577). We begin to see that Bulstrode's place in society and his moral world is no more than a careful construct that can be kicked over with just a few words from a rogue out of his past. He wished 'to maintain his recognized supremacy: the loss of high consideration from his wife, as from everyone else who did not clearly hate him out of enmity to the truth, would be as the beginning of death to him' (pp.576/577). Eliot's use of 'recognized supremacy' and 'high consideration' speaks to us of a man who has clawed his way to a more elevated position in his newer surroundings. The hypocrisy of this ostensibly religious person who has lived a lie for decades is laid bare when we see through his eyes that it is others who have an 'enmity to the truth'. He also recognizes that in the process of gaining his position of 'supremacy' he has engendered a very un-Christian 'hate' of himself by others in the community. As a Christian banker and business man Bulstrode would certainly have had to refuse others in their time of need and this begs the question is his 'judgement' based on nothing more than a financial evaluation of those who need his help. His power to hand down from on high his version of 'truth' is based on ill-gotten gains and the concealment of their source. It is not a Biblical 'truth' that Bulstrode fears but a secular 'truth' that is about to seep out from his past.

In this scene Eliot is also opening up to debate the ethics of some people engaged in commerce and how they gain their 'recognized supremacy' in society. Through the character of Bulstrode she can be seen to be questioning or warning about the prevalent acceptance of Darwinian economics as a way up the social ladder. A revelation of the real man would be no better than a form of living 'death' for the new Bulstrode. Wealth, power and religion are no match for the force inherent in public 'opinion' or those nearest to him. Also, Eliot's use of 'judgement' happens to secularize and place the 'Hereafter's' Day of Judgement in, a more immediate tense, the present. He might become 'an object of scorn' (p.577) but more to the point for Bulstrode is the fear of 'opprobrium of the religion with which he had diligently associated himself' with. This pillar of society has wrapped himself 'diligently' in a system of beliefs and the use of 'associated' does hint at an ulterior motive behind his religious beliefs. Eliot's use of fear of public 'opprobrium' of his religion, on Bulstrode's part, also points up the existence of an alternative secular morality, based on the collective 'judgement' of people in general, as a replacement for a code of ethics handed down from on high by any religious body.

This individual's history is a living organism 'not simply a dead history' as it seeps into his present and it is the 'judgement of his neighbours' that will be the feared consequences. Eliot is making the point that a Darwinian world of 'growth and decay' (p.577) exists within history and people and, similarly, within Bulstrode the 'past' now catches up becoming 'a still quivering part of himself' (p.577/8). It co-exists within us not just physically as we grow older but also psychologically. Eliot uses symbolism to portray this with the words 'when we look through a window from a lighted room, the objects we turn our backs on are still before us' (p.578). Psychologically there is no escape for Bulstrode as the 'past' catches up on him despite his use of selective memory to live with it. Quoting from Lewes's theory of the psychological subject Shuttleworth agrees that this duality, his past and present, means that Bulstrode 'lives a double life and has a double world' (*A Critical Reader*, p.300) and this is summed up in the 'lighted room' scene. While passing moral judgement on Bulstrode Eliot also asks her readers to show sympathy towards him. He is 'a man whose desires had been stronger than his theoretic beliefs' (*Middlemarch* p.581) and that this kind of 'hypocrisy' is a 'process which shows itself occasionally in us all'.

As before in the work the authorial voice self-consciously becomes at one with 'us' as we become part of the 'process' but also demands sympathetic openness towards Bulstrode's situation. Again we have perspective sliding first one way and then the other as the we of author and 'us' slips between the outsider's view of Bulstrode to then seeing the world through his eyes. Furthermore, Eliot's use of 'theoretic beliefs' mirrors her earlier description of the frame of mind of Dorothea as being 'theoretic' (p.8). This raises the question are religious convictions no more than 'theoretic' due to a lack of empiricist evidence to support them? Throughout this scene Eliot elevates chance above Providence and the judgement of his peers above the Day of Judgement as she unravels for her readers the character of Bulstrode. If his essential beliefs and his standing in the community are to be undermined Eliot adds the rider that we have to see the world through his eyes if we are to make moral judgements. In fact yet again she is stressing the importance of taking up the position of 'equivalent centre of self' (p.198) before making judgements on people.

In conclusion, throughout the narrative Eliot makes plain that any changes society, or its individual citizens, may wish to implement should be allowed to evolve over time. She also shows us that changes may bring in train forces that we as individuals will find difficult to accept. Although Eliot does seem to come down on the side of a determinist world there is also an acceptance within her work that there is a balancing point between these forces and our ability to exercise 'free will'. Although 'free will' in absolute terms is difficult to sustain as an argument 'cause and effect' is given much more support by Eliot through her theme of interconnectedness within society and the use of the cobweb as a metaphor for actions that resonate out and affect others. The theme of 'freedom and its limits' is portrayed to us through the constraints that are placed on characters and society throughout the work. But we can also see that for Eliot every 'limit' is not just an end-stop for progress in society and towards the end of the work she effectively deals with this problem through her optimistic assertion that '[E]very limit is a beginning as well as an ending' (p.779).

Following on from this we can see that whatever *ism* is laid before her readers it has to be subjected to her rigorous scepticism based on how it might work in practice and the possibilities for unknown, or even nasty, consequences for society in general. Tellingly none of the *isms* within the work manage to rise above the common human frailty of possessing both 'faults and virtues'. In this respect Eliot was ahead of her time when her work is viewed in relation to the disastrous ideological conflicts that came about in the 20th. Century. From a historical point of view Eliot and her generation were well aware of the damaging religious and imperialist conflicts that preceded their period. Consequently, we are made aware throughout the work that if particular philosophical systems are found to be wanting in certain areas, and religion itself does not measure up to society's needs, then there is a role for the introduction of a set of secular ethics.

By questioning the efficacies of religion Eliot opens up the idea of a personal morality as a need in every human being to replace the existing tenets of 19th. Century Christianity. If we don't need religion then we have to recognize that for the good of society in general the moral framework within religion has to be substituted with a new morality that should emanate from within every individual. Eliot gives us a way of seeing the world that might provide this framework for us and this I suggest is her idea of moving towards a position of 'equivalent centre of self' when passing judgements on other's beliefs and actions. This would not only allow us to see the world from another's perspective but it would also modify our views and behaviour because of its effect on us. Having gone through this process we could then be in a better position to pass moral judgement on others but it would be based on a much firmer footing thus benefiting everyone concerned.

Bibliography

Eliot, G. (1998) *Middlemarch*, Oxford University Press, Oxford.

Regan, S. (2001) *The Nineteenth Century Novel; A Critical Reader,* Routledge, London.

Wilson, F. (2006) *Stanford Encyclopaedia of Philosophy,* Extract @ internet address:
http://plato.Stanford.edu//entries/mill/

Further Reading

Da Sousa Correa, Delia. (2001) *The Nineteenth Century Novel; Realisms,* Routledge, London.

Chapter Two

Class & Money issues within the works of Germinal (Zola, E.) and Far from the Madding Crowd (Hardy, T.).

Part One

Zola's documentary literary technique allows him to lay out in great detail the lifestyle of the main protagonists within and without the mining community. Marrying the environment that the miners live and work under to the historical context help give his readers an unsparing glimpse of some of the worst aspects of a, still severely class delineated, late 19th. Century French society. A useful starting point on Zola's naturalist technique is a definition given to us by Nicolette David; '[O]f central importance to naturalism is a belief in scientific determinism, which pervades all aspects of life. It was the task of the naturalist novelist to emphasize the physiological and environmental conditions that determine individual character.' [P.358, Da Sousa Correa, D.(2001), *The Nineteenth-Century Novel*. Routledge, London]. The point David is making is that rather than a religious form of predestination, Zola gives us a secular version that springs from peoples' inherited genetic characteristics and the environment. As the work progresses we find that the problem with this is that where human actions are seen in such determinist terms then where does this leave the exercise of individual free will.

It can also be seen that from the outset of *Germinal* [Zola, E. (1998), Oxford University Press, Oxford. (All references are to this novel unless otherwise stated)] Zola's support for the 'naturalist' literary style suits his obvious didactic intent to criticise the flaws in French society and bring about change. But for it all to work and get his points over he invariably finds he has to incorporate the aesthetic. Despite his obvious sympathy for the miners' situation they still come in for some trenchant criticism, such as, their treatment of women and children within their own families and the community at large. At times throughout the work women and young girls within this community are portrayed as hugely disadvantaged when it comes to ownership, in a sexual sense, of even their own bodies. But it is the bourgeoisie and the capitalist economic system that advantages these people over others that draws his main fire. Their myopic self-indulgent view of the way forward for French society is slated at every hand's turn and can be interpreted as a warning to them that if they refuse change, while at the same time refusing the miners their common humanity, then the future could have a very bleak outcome for everyone concerned.

Throughout *Germinal* Zola argues that despite the treatment handed out to men finding themselves at the lower end of the class system women were also defined as a class within this class. Zola's third-person omniscient narrator informs his readers that the child/woman Catherine's discovery of Etienne's violence towards an ex-boss 'shocked [her] to the depths of her heredity notions of submission and passive obedience' (p.46). Zola's use of 'heredity notions' is a less than scientific take on Darwin's evolutionary theory and to some extent undermines the idea that these 'notions' might be hard-wired genetically into women. At this point in the narrative he juxtaposes what appears to be the norm of passivity within women with Etienne's propensity for violence. The propensity or not, as the case may be, towards violence on the part of both men and women are themes that Zola returns to at regular intervals throughout the work. In the case of women all of this raises the question in the reader's mind of the source of these so called 'heredity notions'. Are they inculcated socially into each generation of women because of their obvious benefits for the males within their community or, more fatalistically, are they a direct result of purely inherited traits placed there by an indifferent natural process?

The dangers to a woman's wellbeing of this 'submission' and 'obedience' are graphically illustrated when Zola introduces us to Catherine's mother. La Maheude had a 'long face, with its striking features, whose ripe beauty had already been undermined at the age of only thirty-nine by a life of poverty and seven children she had borne' (p.20). Zola's insertion of 'long face...striking features ...ripe beauty' deftly introduces the importance of feminine appearance. Also, his use of 'only' adds to the idea of a life handicapped by an inner force of fecundity before it had even got into its stride. Although the reasons for 'poverty' may have less to do with the miners and more to do with the system they all live under, the endless grind of turning out children speaks to Zola's readers of female powerlessness in the face of the more dominant male's sexual needs. Here we begin to see Zola's women as having to submit to, and obey, the male hierarchy within their own class as well as being shaped by, what he sees as, Darwinian 'hereditary' sexual forces. Also, his use of 'a life of poverty' introduces readers to other external determinist conditions that have more or less trapped this woman into a 'poverty' stricken existence. Furthermore, in line with a work titled *Germinal* her inherited 'ripe beauty' also emphasises the earlier point of an inner 'ripe' fecundity within the lower classes, a theme that crops up at regular intervals throughout Zola's narrative.

The miners' women are portrayed as no better than a sexual commodity when they seek credit at the local store owned by Monsieur Maigrat. Zola states that the owner's wife 'vacated the marital bed when the tram girls came shopping' (p.91). A miner would 'send round his wife or his daughter, no matter whether they were pretty or plain, as long as they were compliant'. While neither the owner's wife nor the miners' wives and daughters have much say in these events poverty, and the basic need for food, lead to the women being used by the miners as a sexual commodity in the name of survival. For the women their role becomes little better than a currency to be bartered for with the end result being their use for the sexual gratification of others. La Maheude has to speak 'humbly' (p.90) to Maigrat while begging for credit suggesting a verbal sign of the status of women. Furthermore she is subjected to the 'gleam in his pale, narrow eyes' (p.91) as he 'was mentally stripping her naked'. Zola's use of 'mentally' implies that these women have no recourse against the male imagination and its ability to indulge in what can be described as rape in all but deed. Although 'infuriated', she 'wouldn't have thought it so bad when she was young, before she had had seven children'.

Zola seems to be suggesting that 'young' women accept this misogynist behaviour as ingrained into men and even its link to their eventually having to give way sexually. Here Zola also makes a general point of naivety about the final outcome on the part of any young girl before entering into sexual relations. In La Maheude's case the freedom to satisfy her own sexual needs had led to a maternal straightjacket in the form of 'seven children' a factor that she now obviously regretted. That both La Maheude and the 'tram girls' might be 'compliant' in entering into sexual relations suggests that nature has hard-wired sexual need into women. In other words Zola daringly shows women's own sexual needs as a part of the contract between men and women but with the result for both parties of an endless cycle of sex, birth and 'poverty'. As the work progresses it also adds to the bleak air of entrapment for both men and women due to fecundity and promiscuity within the mining community as a whole.

The cycle of misery blighting these women's lives is portrayed to us with great effect at the miners' bath time. Even within the marriage contract women can be seen as a being used as a sexual commodity. Maheu 'grabbed hold of her again, and this time refused to let go' (p.116). That Maheu 'refused to let go' is an instance of the use of physical force to overcome resistance on the part of a woman who was in his view *his* wife. It was the 'time when his workmates in the village usually started fooling around, only to find themselves fathering more children than they intended'. Zola makes it clear that for the male it is the act of sex rather than the 'fathering of children' that is 'intended' by the miners. No matter what the consequences for the women it is plain that very often the husband's conjugal rights or, to put it bluntly, sex on demand is a male prerogative within the marriage contract.

In this instance La Maheude 'pretended to struggle, all part of the game' and combined with Zola's earlier use of 'again' is a signifier of male persistence and its role in the final outcome. That she 'pretended' can be interpreted as a physical sign of unwillingness where the man wishes to impose on the woman his one sided interpretation of the marriage contract. It could be said that for these women dressing up their resistance as 'all part of the game' is just about the limit they can go to and still have a relationship with the opposite sex. In this small scene we find that miners' wives, no matter what their wishes, lack the power to just say no to their husband's sexual overtures. Zola makes it patently obvious that once into a relationship to all intents and purposes the woman becomes owned by the man. We can also see Darwinian sexual impulses, in the name of procreation, are driving the miners and La Maheude's desperate position is made clear when we are informed, through dialogue, that a child 'three months old' watches her throughout the act.

Zola later shows the extent of the physical force that the miners could resort to in the rape, by the 'big tall Chaval' (p.127), of the child/woman Catherine. Although only fifteen and not yet into puberty '[H]e grabbed hold of her firmly, and thrust her into the shed. And she fell backwards on to the pile of old rope, stopped resisting, and, although her body wasn't ready, she let the male have his way with her, with the hereditary submissiveness that sent all the girls of her race rolling flat on their backs while they were little more than children' (p.130) Again we have the deliberate unscientific linking of women to 'hereditary submissiveness' and what we now see to be their inability to resist male needs in or out of any form of relationship. Zola's use of 'she let the male have his way with her' depersonalizes Chaval's rape of Catherine and puts it on the par of an inevitable event. In fact this is what a 'male', any 'male', could and would do given the opportunity.

In this poverty stricken community women learn that 'while they were little more than children' there was very little point in 'resisting' what cannot be other than described as a violent sexual attack. But Zola's linking of Darwinian theory of inherited determinist characteristics and female 'submissiveness', repeated at different points of the narrative, seems to say that women have no alternative but to give way under the threat of violence that can also be seen to cast doubts on his position in all of this. Or, is he actually saying that this is reality for women and therefore it is a lousy reality for any woman to be born into. In fact readers can make up their own minds as to whether or not he is having his cake and eating it and saying both things at the same time. Also, it is convenient for Zola that Chaval's ability to exercise his free will towards Catherine can only be countered by 'hereditary submissiveness' on her part. A further point is that for Chaval, and in opposition to Catherine's wishes, his free will happily coincides with his inherited sexual needs.

Zola graphically illustrates the conditions the mining community live and love in through food and diet. The whole of the sexual encounter between Maheu and his wife takes place in a 'house [that] wallowed in the rich smell of fried onion, which soon turns rancid, impregnating the bricks of the village with noxious vapours so strong that your nostrils are assailed by the violent odour of this poor man's cuisine from miles away across the country' (p.119). For this community both sex and food 'soon turns rancid' with the 'poor man's' pleasure linked to his 'cuisine' and both women and buildings becoming synonymous with impregnation. Zola heightens the degradation of human relationships within the mining community by his deliberate placing of their life and loves in a degraded environment. Here and elsewhere in *Germinal* we can see that he is prepared to use the aesthetic of metaphor to elevate the naturalist and somewhat brutalist language to a higher level and in the process this can be seen to undermine his own support for a purely 'naturalist' school of literature.

In his *Introduction* to *Germinal* Robert Lethbridge sees Zola's compromise as a necessary 'creative tension between the novel's realistic effects and its symbolic meanings' (p.xiv). Speaking on Zola's embedding of allegories and myth within the work Lethbridge later enlarges with 'the synthesis of the archetypal and the documentary creates a logic which owes as much to narrative imperatives as to the dictates of realities' (p.xvi/xvii). In other words Zola's use of aesthetic in the form of myth, allegory, and we can say his inclusion of metaphor and poetic language, is a necessity both to drive the narrative forward, capture and keep the imagination of his readers, and in so doing serve his didactic purpose.

At certain points throughout *Germinal* Zola brings together the triumvirate of a delineated class, money and work. Although the 'pit engineer, young Negrel...was intelligent and suspicious, and easily became authoritarian and intolerant when dealing with the workmen.' he also 'dressed as they did, and was smeared with coal just like them' (p.52). At a cost to the miners' earnings he demands '[T]wice as many props' (p.53) to be installed in the tunnels but insists it is only for their own safety. The miners' case is '[I]f we were properly paid we'd put up more props'. This illustrates Negrel to be one of them until it comes to the miners being 'properly paid'. Not only do the miners not get paid for installing the props that are required for the safety of the pit as a whole but the injustice of it all is exacerbated when they are 'fined three francs' by Negrel for not installing them earlier. The sheer desperate need to maximise their earnings can be seen as the reason for the miners to put their own safety at risk but conversely why would management put at risk the whole operation just for the short sighted need for profit.

Repeatedly throughout the work Zola places before his readers the shortcomings within the capitalist system for both owners and the workers. He also explains the glue holding it all together with the words '[T]hey were only restrained by the force of hierarchal authority, that military command structure which ran from the lads at the incline right up to the overman, keeping everyone subservient to the person above him.' It is the power of the agents of capitalism and the relative powerlessness of the miners that 'restrained' this obvious need for change. Zola's use of 'military command structure' shows readers a system based on tight control that we later see to in fact point to people far above the 'overman'. From this small but important scene we begin to see that it is others such as the absentee shareholders who control the money that in turn dictates the actions of those below them. In other words money and the pursuit of profit are determinist forces acting on the miners and the agents of this anonymous, unseen, rentier class.

Zola utilizes symbolism and poetic simile to portray both the mechanics of the operation of the mine, the miners who work in it, and the system that drives it all. To Etienne the mine had the 'sinister air of a voracious beast, crouching ready to pounce and gobble you up.' (p.7) Later he sees the miners' travel to the work-face in terms of 'the shaft was swallowing men down in mouthfuls of twenty or thirty at a time, with a swift gulping motion, showing hardly a ripple.' (p.27) It was a man-made animal, 'a nocturnal beast of prey', gorging itself and in fact 'swallowing men' wholesale in its singular pursuit of coal and profits. With the call 'dinner's ready' the cage operator warns those below 'that their next load of human cattle was on its way down'. Not only are the miners treated like animals they also begin to take on the characteristics of animals.

To add to this we later have the vision of Catherine at work who 'seemed to be trotting on all fours, like some small circus animal' (p.43). The use of child labour is graphically described in the same terms through Lydie. The 'little girl, she went back to pushing her tub, covered in mud and racked with pain, straining with all the force of her matchstick arms and legs, like a skinny little black ant struggling with too large a burden.' (Pp.55/56) Zola's deliberate use of emotive words such as 'little girl...matchstick arms and legs' and his comparison of the girl's existence with that of a lowly 'struggling' insect can be seen as a damning of this society's priorities. Later still Zola adds 'The mine never slept; night and day these human insects burrowed into the rock, 600 metres below the beetfields.' (p.65) Again the miners are portrayed as no more than 'another meal for the mine', an offering up of a sacrifice to the beast that 'never slept'.

From the very beginning of *Germinal* the workers are portrayed as buckling under a rapacious profit driven capitalist system with an impersonal man-made environment and all of this enforced by a 'military command structure'. (p.53) Human beings from childhood right up to and including old men and women are conscripted by means of poverty into a system based on returns on capital for its local and absentee shareholders. A system elevated to a new secular religion, a 'greedy, squatting god, who fed off the flesh of 10,000 hungry people who didn't even know him' (p.71). If Zola's language is sometimes colourful it at least serves its didactic purpose of enlightening 19th. Century French readers to what was going on in these somewhat isolated communities. At the same time he effectively undercuts any future defence of ignorance on the part of French society as a whole and in particular its beneficiaries, whether it be the coal they burn or the dividends they receive.

Zola illustrates some mobility existing within the less than fluid French class system. The mine manager Hennebeau had started out as 'a penniless orphan' (pp.200/1) and by dint of education as a mining engineer had worked himself up to a '40.000-franc salary' (p.202) per annum. In contrast to this middle-class professional engineer, Monsieur Gregoire is portrayed through dialogue as being 'a share holder' (p.210) living 'off the labour of others'. Monsieur Gregoire is a local member of the rentier class having inherited his access to shareholder dividends from 'my great-grandfather' who had worked 'hard to make his small investment prosper'. The contrast between a miner's paltry return for his labour, and Gregoire's yearly dividend 'two years ago' of a 'staggering sum of 50,000 francs' (p.79) for his great-grandfather's original investment of '10,000 hard-won francs', shows Zola's readers the ability of capital to grow while the miners' living standards are portrayed as going from bad to worse.

Even in the now difficult economy the Gregoire's could still rely on 'around 40,000 francs a year in investment income' (p.78). Zola compares this economic hiccup for the Gregoires to the Resurrection. 'Their shares would rise again, as indestructible as God himself...It was like a household god, the object of a self-indulgent cult, the patron saint of their hearth and home, cradling them in their big, soft beds and fattening them at their sumptuous table' (p.80). Zola brings together the Christian belief in the Resurrection and Pagan adoration of 'a household god' by a family that has become a 'cult'. The new religion of capital and dividends has now become the 'patron saint' that supports their clichéd 'hearth and home' existence. The ever growing returns, over the generations, on the ironically phrased '10,000 hard-won francs' (p.79), portrays the Gregoires as being worlds apart from the producers of their wealth. Their defence is to contrast themselves positively to the absentee metropolitan based shareholders as they 'try to live soberly on what we have, and even give some to the poor!...For heaven's sake! Our workers would have to be the most arrant scoundrels to want to take as much as a pin that belonged to us' (p.211). Here Zola emphasizes the proudly bourgeoisie Gregoire's bombast and naivety by the use of exclamation marks that in effect further undermines everything he states.

Most of all he is damning the bourgeois rentier class out of their own mouths and also supports this by slipping in documentary information that is very close to the real historical context. Even the professional manager Hennebeau thought that 'years of prosperity had spoiled the workers' (p.207). In earlier times they had earned 'as much as six francs a day in our collieries, twice what they're earning now! And they lived well, and they developed a taste for luxury'. By documenting their income and how the different classes earn it, Zola is laying down for his readers the inherent injustices within the system. Both miners and owners are subject to boom and bust cycles in the economy.

The self-made mine owner Deneulin blames the 'affluence of these last years' for the 'enormous amount of capital that has been tied up, in railways, and ports and canals' which he directly links to the 'the money wasted in absurd speculation' that went with it.

Zola's forensic approach to money, and the uses it may be put to, juxtaposes 'money wasted in absurd speculation' with the luxury of 'six francs a day' that for working miners had now become half of this sum. This discussion between Hennebeau and Deneulin is heavily laced with irony when viewed from the perspective of the 'waste' of those in charge of the money and the perceived luxury of 'six francs a day' for those who have to earn it. It is also apparent that in either boom or bust the capitalist system is a beast that is hard to control. It is ironic that Zola gives these Marxist criticisms of the capitalist system's ability to over invest in the good times, leading to surpluses which in turn lead to a bust, to the more thoughtful Deneulin who sees these outside speculative forces as a danger to everything he has built up. In opposition to this Hennebeau sees the miners' 'taste for luxury' as the root cause of their problems. This again suggests that Zola is arguing that even the apparent winners in the system should open themselves up to the need for change no matter what the advantages might appear to be for them as individuals.

If ever there is hope of a change it lays within the possibilities of the character Deneulin rather than the non-working bourgeoisie Gregoire. Deneulin sees the miners as being as much a victim as himself of the boom and bust. He gives us the savagery of capitalism in action and shows some sympathy for his workers with the words 'we have to make savings by reducing the wages, and the workers are right to say that we are making them pay our bills' (p.208). Deneulin also pinpoints the system's proneness to chaos due to events way beyond the control of France's ruling elite. Speaking 'as if talking to himself' (p.208) he brings together '[T]here's been a famine in India' with '[A]nd when America cancelled her orders for iron and cast iron, she dealt our furnaces a dreadful blow. It's all linked, one tremor is enough to shake the whole world...And our

Empire was so proud of our rate of industrial growth!' Zola makes plain that even an 'Empire' is no defence against arbitrary events taking place at the other ends of the world. The advent of the United States onto the world stage, and the combination of their Civil War in the 1860's which spurred their economic 'growth', was beginning to stunt their need for goods from France. At the same time they need not look to countries like India for new markets if they cannot even feed their own populations. Zola's is a bleak prescient view of an interconnected world that is moving towards a globalized economy. The nasty outcomes of the 1929 Crash in America and the global bank collapses of 2008 effectively put history on his side of the argument, that being, the inherent instability of a rampant capitalist system. A system whereby just 'one tremor is enough to shake the whole world'.

Using metaphor and religious imagery in an ironic sense Zola's anarchist character Souvarine links the mining community's problems to, '[I]t is graven in tablets of bronze that wages should be fixed at the absolute minimum, just the barest sum necessary for the workers to eat a crust of bread and have children' (p.144). In an allusion to the handing down of the Ten Commandments we have the imagery of wages that are 'fixed' like a religious precept and 'graven in tablets of bronze' to elevate what is raw capitalism in action to a new religion. This 'graven' god also needs a future supply of 'children' ready for sacrificing at its alter. Again using the aesthetic of poetic technique, life and death for the miners and their children becomes no more than a 'balanced budget of empty bellies, a life sentence condemning the workers to the prison camp of poverty' (p.144). Supply and demand of the market economy is directly linked to the possible survival rate among the workers. 'If wages fall too low, the workers die, and the demand for new workmen makes them rise again. If they rise too high, the surplus offer makes them drop again'. On a less esoteric front the miners actually have to enter into an 'auction' (p.146) whereby Maheu finds himself in 'savage competition' with his fellow miners for 'a patch of coal fifty metres nearer the shaft'. The end result is that the miners 'took it in turns to drive down the price of a tub-load of coal, centime by centime'.

Here Zola is trenchantly satirising Darwinian economics based on companies competing to survive in the market place. For the miners and their children it is their ability to survive starvation conditions as they compete with each other through wages becoming depressed. In fact the companies lower the wages to compete with each other to try and maintain their dividends as they drive the miners to compete with each other for their own survival. Souvarine's solution is that the world is flawed and that they should 'raze everything to the ground, and when there is nothing left of this whole, vile world, maybe a better one will grow up in its place' (p.142). As if warning France's ruling elite Zola takes them to the extreme edge of political ideologies that are circulating in the ether. To Etienne Souvarine later elucidates on what he sees as a necessary outcome. There should be '[N]o more nations, no more governments, no more property, no more God, and no more religion' (p.242). With a repetitive drumbeat of 'no more' Zola drives home the point that this might be the alternative to offering justice, for the workers and their families, through the more civilized process of managed change. It is left to the ex-radical Rasseneur rather than Etienne to voice a method of managing change. At a later point in the narrative he argues for 'reconciliation' and the 'impossibility of changing the world by sudden decree, and the need to let social change evolve gradually' (pp.285/286). The importance of this statement lies in Zola's juxtaposition of the more authoritarian 'sudden decree' with the more benign 'let' and 'evolve gradually'.

Etienne's answer to Souvarine's nihilist belief in 'this cult of destruction' (p.242) is for the miners to cooperate through 'a provident fund' (p.143) set up to allow them to fight for higher wages through strike action. In the eyes of the miners 'it was the bourgeoisie who had grown fat since 1789' and ironically '[I]n declaring them free, the bourgeoisie had clearly taken them for a ride: yes, they were free to die of hunger, and they made liberal use of this right.' Zola's cynical analysis portrays a society in a simmering state of war with itself. During the French Revolution, and earlier in the 19th. Century, working people had taken to the barricades but Etienne's point is that in a changing industrial society it was necessary to come up with new solutions. In his view the new proletariat had to take things into its own hands by the use of collective action and using their meagre wages to save and so finance the strike actions. Here Zola is making the same point that we can later see in Hardy, namely, that people should cooperate but Hardy sees it in terms of bosses and workers as well. This admission by Etienne of a lack of financial and economic power for the miners is implicitly offset by Zola's concentration throughout the work on the miners' advantage in numbers. For the bourgeoisie the warning is embedded within the work, either 'let social change evolve gradually' (pp. 285/286), through managing it, or face the option of having to deal with a more extremist system of beliefs in the form of men such as Souvarine.

Zola's naturalist documentary literary form effectively uses the environment throughout as a backdrop to his social and economic arguments. The theme of harsh surroundings gives the narrative the feel of being well researched and natural. Zola has the courting couples of the villages meet within a spent coal pit and among 'lifeless machinery, in the shadow of the pit which had grown weary of spewing forth coal, creation was exacting its revenge, in the form of a free love spurred on by wild instinct, which sowed babies in the bellies of these girls who were still hardly women' (p.124). The juxtaposing of 'lifeless' and 'creation' is allied to poetic alliteration in 'form...free...babies...bellies' and this again elevates the language above the 'naturalist' while undermining Zola's apparent commitment to this literary theory. We begin to see that both women and mines will eventually become spent as part of the cycle of life and economic forces. For 'these girls' the productive past of the mine synthesizes with the present of the girls while the present condition of the mine also maps out their future. Metaphorically, the once productive mine is linked to 'the babies' they are fated to produce while in the future they in turn will become no better than the inanimate 'lifeless machinery' surrounding them.

Throughout this scene the watchman 'old Mouque...espied all the young girls of Montsou taking it in turns to raise their lips hungrily towards the heavens' (p.125). The brutalist and the elevated, sexually charged, language bears down on the reader in carefully orchestrated waves as both reader, and watchman, observe the girls satisfying their sexual needs thus giving the text a voyeuristic sense. It was the reality of life in the mining communities, their sexual needs, and people's existence within that Darwinian 'creation' that heaps disadvantages on both the men and the women. The determinist economic and sexual forces only reinforce the powerlessness of this class as the fight for survival in a wasteful economic system, and the handicap of an inner 'wild instinct', conspires to limit their ability to aspire for better things. This is reiterated from Etienne's perspective, it is to 'produce more babies, more flesh fit only for toil and suffering...Yes, all the girls succumbed, it was a force stronger than reason' (p.127).

This time it is Etienne who introduces us to a bleak, timeless, unchanging stasis whereby the present is no better than the past or any hoped for future. Zola's use of alliteration and repeated use of 'more' represents textually a continuous stream of humanity heading towards a world of 'toil and suffering'. Here he deliberately links the sexual activities of the girls to a greater mechanical outer existence. In the eyes of Etienne, for these young girls, by the age of fourteen the game was already up. Earlier we have '[T]he pit girls were precocious; and he remembered the working girls at Lille that he used to meet behind the factories, those gangs of immoral fourteen-year-olds, whom poverty had already corrupted'. (p.122) In social terms it is not surprising that girls cast out to work in the name of economic survival, before their childhood had run its full course, turn out to lack a moral compass and then go on to repeat the mistakes of their mothers before them. After all the main thrust of their education seems to lie in sexual experimentation and the necessity of work in an effort to exist.

A further point in all of this is the emasculation of the males within the middle-classes through the character Hennebeau, for he and his wife 'had slept apart for the last ten years' (p.200). In direct contrast to the miners' perceived sexual control over their wives Hennebeau's wife 'became increasingly irritated, and contemptuous of her husband,' over the years (p.201). After marriage '[S]he soon took a lover' so that eventually 'her husband had not been able to preserve his ignorance, and he resigned himself to the situation after a series of dreadful scenes, rendered powerless by this woman's tranquil impropriety, as she took her pleasure wherever she found it.' Here the middle-class male is 'powerless' while Madame Hennebeau addresses her sexual needs with 'tranquil impropriety'. Zola seems to be saying that a woman locked into a middle-class marriage is less of a sexual commodity and is much more empowered through both her middle-class status and her wealth wherever the wealth had sprung from. Also, Hennebeau's lack of even one heir is in stark contrast to the fecundity of the miners, while the lack of sexual ownership of his wife points to poverty being at the root of the mining community's women and their diminished empowerment in every sense. While there are obvious parallels between the sexual behaviour of the 'pit girls', 'those gangs of immoral fourteen-year-olds' (p.122), and Madame Hennebeau where, like her, each 'took her pleasure wherever she found it', readers can see who might have enough advantages to come out on top.

Zola and, as we can later see, Hardy link the local class structure to anonymous outside sources. Through the perspective of Gregoire readers are informed that it is a metropolitan based 'duke who's our biggest shareholder' in the mine (p.211). For Zola the 'duke' is representative of the hidden face of capitalism and this alludes to the theme running through the novel of 'an unknown god, lying in wait in the depths of his tabernacle' (p.222). Throughout the work Zola moves seamlessly from direct quotation of his characters' words to giving a sense of what is going on in their minds. More like the reporter that he had been in his earlier days, gathering in the various strands for the benefit of his newspaper readers than a purely creative author.

An example of this narrative technique, and a continuation of the theme of the 'unknown god', is portrayed to us through the perspective of Etienne. With the miners now in the middle of a protracted strike action, and distilling the earlier words of old 'Bonnemort', he directly states '[C]omrades, now you've heard what one of our elders has suffered, and what our children will suffer, if we don't put a stop to these thieves and assassins' (p.287) Zola then trips into a summarizing of Etienne's thoughts and words. Readers are informed of 'the fate of the Maheu family from their beginnings, worn out by the mine, devoured by the Company, still starving after a hundred years of hard labour; and he contrasted this with the Board of Directors, sitting there with bloated bellies, positively dripping with money, and the whole crew of shareholders, kept in luxury for a hundred years like fancy women with no need to work, just pampering their bodies'. Zola's use of 'he contrasted this' places himself outside of his character while at the same time employing Etienne's voice in terms akin to free indirect discourse.

Here Zola again depicts a system that despite the march of time is in a state of stasis. On one side we have miners 'still starving after a hundred years' and on the other an anonymous body of 'Directors' and 'shareholders, kept in luxury'. In a long paragraph that somewhat mimics in a textual sense time rolling on, and still through the perspective of Etienne, Zola synthesizes his radicalism with the latent threat of the miners' numbers. '[D]eep down in the mines an army was growing, a future crop of citizens, germinating like seeds that would burst through the earth's crust one day into the bright sunshine' (p.288). Zola adds to the threat of the many towards the few by again using the poetic devices of metaphor, alliteration, assonance and simile. At the moment the bourgeoisie might hold the miners down through force but eventually they will 'burst' out of the mines with unknown consequences for the few. In a novel called *Germinal* it is not surprising that the numbers of miners relative to the middle-classes is important, a term that also applies to fecundity in nature as well as meaning new ideas. Returning to a religious concept of class war Zola gives us '[O]h yes, labour would call capital to account, challenging the anonymous god, who lay hidden in his mysterious tabernacle, somewhere out of sight of the workers, gorged on the blood of the sick and dying that he fed on!' (p.288). Throughout the work Zola time and again elevates raw capitalism to a new religion that for the miners '[D]eep down in the mines' is no better than a secular hell on earth.

Zola graphically illustrates this secular hell on earth in his description of the working conditions for the miners at the Jean Bart colliery. The miners work-face was '708 metres under' and 'three kilometres away from the loading bay' (p.305). They have a reverential regard for Jean Bart as '[W]hen they spoke of this part of the pit, the local miners went pale and lowered their voices, as if they were speaking of hell...The coal-faces here averaged a temperature of forty-five degrees. It was a veritable hell'. The reason for these conditions was that it was adjacent to an abandoned mine that was burning out of control. In line with Dante's myth this burning mine's 'history was lost in the mists of time, and the local miners told the tale of how a bolt from the heavens had fallen on this Sodom in the bowels of the earth, where the tram girls were guilty of the vilest abominations' (p.303) The myth of the labyrinth is synthesised with a biblical 'bolt from the heavens' cast down on the tram girls. But the reader might ask why only the tram girls when their actions are only one half of the equation? Also, for the reader Zola's use of 'Sodom' and 'vilest abominations' actually leaves very little to the imagination as to what might have gone on in 'the bowels of the earth'.

Even in myth it is the males who 'told the tale' giving us an oral history that effectively air-brushes out the male role in all of this. The punishment of this mythical god is to trap only the tram girls 'roasting in their hell down below' (p.304). Zola continues in the vein of a secular hell on earth with '[T]he dark red, scorched rocks were covered in a leprous growth of alum. Sulphur grew like yellow flowers round the lips of the fissures in the rock. At night the foolhardy who risked their eyes to look through these cracks swore they could see flames, and criminal souls crackling on the burning coals deep within.' In this scene Zola harnesses his reader's senses in totality. We visualize the colours 'red' and 'yellow flowers', feel the heat of the 'flames', smell and taste the '[S]ulphur' in the air, and hear the 'souls crackling'. Zola's literary flights are meant to add to what a 'veritable hell' (p.305) on earth might be while again making clear to 19th. Century French readers the real price of the production of coal and the dividends that flow from it.

For Zola dividends and profit are the new secular religion, they have combined to become a new god that rules miners, managers and owners alike. A god that is blamed, complained about, and justified, depending on your point of view or position in society. It sustains the rentier classes, threatens the managerial class, the local owners, and grinds down the miners. But within an earlier stretch of dialogue between Negrel and Gregoire there are clues to fears within the middle classes of a lurking threat to their hold on things. In the ironical words of the mining engineer Negrel '[Y]ou might get looted' out of these 'stolen goods' (p.210). Through Etienne Zola later returns to this and in a sense pins it down while again introducing Marxist theory into his narrative. It was 'Karl Marx's idea that capital had been acquired through theft, that it was the right and duty of labour to win back this stolen wealth' (p.239). The possibility of being 'looted' out of his 'stolen goods' is faced with sheer incomprehension on the part of Gregoire who Zola portrays as living in 'childish tranquillity' (p.210), effectively undermining his physical 'inheritance' in a genetic sense. His use of 'childish tranquillity' also gives his readers a vision of the local rentier class as totally unprepared for whatever the future might throw at them.

The way to hang onto what even Negrel sees as their ill-gotten gains has already been alluded to by Zola. The Gregoires' 'notion of a proper education' (p.92) for their daughter Cecile was aimed at her being, like themselves, 'thinking Samaritans constantly worried that they might make a mistake'. The heavily ironic use of 'a proper education' has Cecile follow the precepts laid down by the generation that had gone before her. They should never give money as this may 'encourage some immoral tendency' in the mining community. Again we have Zola's incorporation of religious precepts but this time the use of 'thinking Samaritans' and an 'immoral tendency' within the lower orders is clearly a get out on the part of the local bourgeoisie to offering any real change, or help, towards the workers and their families. They believe the miners might 'squander' money 'on drink' and so it had always to be 'donations in kind' (p.93). It is ironical that a people incapable of change themselves see only a mining community incapable of improvement.

When confronted with La Maheude's statement 'I've got seven' children Gregoire 'gave a start of indignation'. Their one child is set against La Maheude's seven and this brings directly to the fore the numbers proliferating outside their doors. If their daughter Cecile can be seen as a pleasure to the Gregoire's then this is contrasted with La Maheude's need for children to support the family as the parents age. The numbers for her are both a dire necessity and a disaster but these same 'numbers' can also be seen as Zola's warning of an impending disaster that could engulf this myopic bourgeoisie class. Their myopia is further emphasized by his use of environment as this confrontation, between need and plenty, takes place in a 'room' that 'exuded the moist, heavy, comfortable atmosphere that cradles the bourgeois family in their contented slumbers.' (p.94) Readers have only to cast their minds back to Zola's earlier detailed exposition of the conditions that the miners live, love, and work under, to see just how damning these few words are. In this scene every word is hand-picked to portray the bourgeoisie as being poles apart from the very people whose efforts support this parasitic rentier class. In parts such as here Zola's detailed use of environment moves very close to the naturalist documentary style that also has the effect of emphasizing his didactic intent to undermine capitalism, its class structure and the injustices that flow from it all.

In conclusion, Zola sees a disaster in the making. His belief in scientific determinism portrays a godless world shaped by economic determinism, inherited genetic defects, sexual needs, especially of the males, and the environment. There is some ambiguity in his attitude to female submissiveness where a miner's free will, in the form of Chaval's actions, justifies the extreme of rape of a child/woman. In opposition to this the free will of women is seen to be subsumed by the very need to exist in the face of both violence and hunger. In fact the miners' misogynistic attitudes extend to fathers and husbands prostituting wives and daughters for economic advantage and food. Also, he sees a class system, and the natural needs of people, that are not only oppressing the miners but are threatening the very survival of the local ruling elite that themselves seem incapable of bringing in the changes necessary. In economic terms Zola sees both rulers and ruled as dependent on, and trapped by, the capitalist beast in 'his tabernacle', with lower class women having particular problems. Throughout the work Zola makes the case that dividends and profit are the new secular religion with the end result of degradation of the environment and people that inevitably leads to conflict. His unremittingly bleak view suggests that the sheer weight of numbers among the lower orders will eventually break through bringing about their own solution, for good or ill, like an 'avenging army' (p.524).

Part Two

Throughout *Far from the Madding Crowd* [Hardy, T. (2002), Oxford University Press, Oxford. (All references are to this novel unless otherwise stated)] Hardy depicts a pastoral world that is under stress, a rural existence that is somewhat analogous to 19th.Century urban industrialized Britain. His work is set in a period in which both rural and urban areas of Britain are going through considerable changes with economic hardship for the many. Despite all of this, within rural society, there is still the ability for some to move between the different strata in society making for a more optimistic outlook that in effect colours the narrative throughout. Rather than direct confrontation with societal issues Hardy takes a somewhat tangential approach than can be seen in Zola's less subtle approach to the need for change. But, intentionally or otherwise, in their different ways both parties do raise the important issue of the status of women within the lower orders of society. Hardy also recognizes the role of chance in people's financial affairs and in effect calls for more compromise in what was then a very rigid system of beliefs that supported a red in tooth and claw form of capitalism. He also extends this need for compromise to other areas of Victorian society, such as, cooperation between boss and workers and a more equal status between the sexes.

In the opening chapter of *Far from the Madding Crowd* Hardy's third-person narrator introduces us to the idea of the flawed female as seen through the eyes of a male. This 'unperceived farmer' (p.12), who is already known to us as Gabriel Oak, observes an unnamed girl taking 'a small swing looking glass...in which she proceeded to survey herself attentively. She parted her lips, and smiled' (pp.11/12). Through third-person omniscient perspective this simple act is portrayed in brazen and narcissistic terms. Sliding more to what might be Oak's view, it is a public act that should only be indulged in the privacy of 'the dressing hour in a bedroom' (p.12). Hardy then slips into definite third-person with '[T]he picture was a delicate one. Woman's prescriptive infirmity had stalked into the sunlight, which had clothed it in the freshness of an originality.' From either perspective its 'originality' lies in the public nature of such an innocent act. But Hardy's use of 'unperceived farmer', and later 'point of espial', also paints a detached narrator's image of male furtiveness in what was previously portrayed to us as an upstanding male character.

Hardy does synthesize the narrative perspectives with the words 'A cynical inference was irresistible by Gabriel Oak as he regarded the scene, generous though he fain would have been' (p.12). Already the uncertainty of the narrative perspective is making it quite difficult for the reader to discern what might be the views held by either the narrator or Oak. In either case this can be seen as a misogynistic view of women, a reflection of a general view among the male population, and that this applies to women no matter what their status or class. In fact her status is that she is a woman. This is confirmed by Hardy's use of '[W]oman's prescriptive infirmity' which portrays her actions as an inner flaw presiding in all women. Here the authorial voice seems to support a universal view of what to the reader is still an unknown young girl that we later find to be Bathsheba. What we do learn is that how she looked, her appearance, her image to others, is of major importance no matter which perspective we apply it to. Hardy adds to this misogynistic view of women by not attempting to give her, at this stage, any semblance of an inner voice. We are told what she thinks namely, when looking in the mirror, '[S]he simply observed herself as a fair product of Nature in the feminine kind'. Later we are given in Oak's words exactly what underpins 'her faults' as a woman, becoming in fact 'the greatest of them', is nothing less than "Vanity" (p.13).

This narcissistic take on women in general should be contrasted with our introduction to Oak. The male in this case is much more modest. We are told 'Oak's appearance in his working clothes was most peculiarly his own – the mental picture formed by his neighbours in imagining him being always dressed in that way' (p.9). Here we have a man who ostensibly does not care about his image but who ironically manages to portray an image that is generally acceptable in a man when seen through the eyes of 'his neighbours'. The question could be asked, where is the male's 'prescriptive infirmity' in all of this? Hardy later adds to the notion of Oak's modest male persona with 'his height and breadth would have been sufficient to make his presence imposing had they been exhibited with due consideration. But there is a way some men have, rural and urban alike – for which the mind is more responsible than flesh and sinew: it is a way of curtailing their dimensions by their manner of showing them' (p.10). The problem for the reader becomes, is it irony on the part of Hardy or do we take him seriously in his projection of the modest male persona?

Adding uncertainty to all of this is his use of the verbs 'exhibited' and 'showing' which signifies Oak's part in taking these actions which effectively undercuts his apparent inner modesty. He is further distanced from Bathsheba's imagined narcissism by virtue that his 'presence' relies more on his controlling 'mind' than his outer image of 'flesh and sinew'. But all of this does allow for the idea of this individual's role in the construction of his own male identity. If the surrounding males decide on Bathsheba's inner character it is plain for the reader that men like Oak are more in charge of who they become. But Hardy does add to the uncertainty surrounding this constructed image by the contradiction of Oak the furtive voyeur actively hiding his 'presence' from Bathsheba by spying on her while at other times deliberately projecting a manly 'presence' to 'his neighbours'.

The first sentence of *Far from the Madding Crowd* gives readers Oak's status in society as 'Farmer Oak' (p.9). In fact the title of the opening chapter refers to his meeting with Bathsheba as a 'description of farmer oak: an incident'. Hardy's use in the opening sentence of the upper case in 'Farmer' has the effect of enhancing his status but it also tells us the importance of such status in Victorian rural society. His rural peers had recognized his progress in life by conferring on him the title of "Farmer" Oak' (p.16). Due respect is given to his progress in life from 'shepherd' as a boy to 'bailiff' and then onto "Farmer". But Hardy then places financial insecurity right at the centre of people's existence and progress with the words '[T]his venture, unaided and alone, into the paths of farming as master and not as man, with an advance of sheep not yet paid for, was a critical juncture with Gabriel Oak, and he recognized his position clearly'. In a sentence steeped in Victorian values based on progress in life through the work ethic Hardy also lays out a vision of Oak on a financial precipice.

Also, his use of 'unaided and alone' effectively does away with help in the form of inheritance or marrying into money. Although 'master' and 'man' might be engaged in the same enterprise we are made aware that the subtleties of the class system still exist even at such lower levels.

Furthermore, that Oak's "Farmer" title rests on 'an advance of sheep not yet paid for' reiterates the point of a man living on a financial edge. All of this is confirmed when we are told that this 'was a critical juncture' for Oak 'and he recognized his position clearly'. The fluidity of a person's position in society is a theme that Hardy returns to throughout the work but at this point in the work it also has potential for the aesthetics of suspense, and drama, through delayed-decoding required to hold the attention of his readers.

"Farmer" Oak's downfall comes about mainly through the actions of another. The youngest and less experienced of his two dogs had driven his pregnant ewes 'over the precipice' (p.40). This sudden reversal in his fortunes is compounded by the fact that '[T]he sheep were not insured. – All the savings of a frugal life had been dispersed at a blow: his hopes of being an independent farmer were laid low – possibly for ever' (p.41). This time we have the Victorian ethics of 'savings' and 'a frugal life' but now a life's effort is 'dispersed at a blow'. It is possible to see that the less well-off would not be 'insured' against the chance 'blow' brought about by the actions of a dog. For such as Oak, existing in a Darwinian struggle to survive, money is at the root of his problems to get by as an 'independent farmer'. Along with his ewes he has also fallen over a cliff socially and this is summed up with the words "[T]hank God I am not married: what would *she* have done in the poverty now coming upon me". Darwinian economics of the survival of the fittest in business do not make allowances for a chance 'blow' precipitated by a dog and Hardy's 19th. Century readers would both understand the realism within this and empathise with his character's situation.

Oak's dilemma is then emphasized by Hardy's use of the poetic techniques of alliteration, assonance, repetition, simile, internal rhyme, metaphor and pathetic fallacy. The desolate environment matches Oak's internal misery and this is added to by Hardy's use of the aesthetic of the painter's techniques and the colours employed. Oak 'listlessly surveyed the scene. By the outer margin of the pit was an oval pond, and over it hung the attenuated skeleton of a chrome-yellow moon, which had only a few days to last

– the morning star dogging her on the left hand. The pool glittered like a dead man's eye, and as the world awoke a breeze blew, shaking and elongating the reflection of the moon without breaking it, and turning the image of the star to a phosphoric streak upon the water' (p.41).

It is easy to see that in less desperate conditions Oak would not see the hardness of 'chrome' or the sickliness of the colour 'yellow' in the moon. For him the optimism of a new day ahead in the 'morning star' now becomes no better than a 'phosphoric streak upon the water'. What Oak sees before him is a world that has changed 'possibly for ever' also what could normally be the life giving waters of the 'oval pond' now 'glittered like a dead man's eye'. On any painting this would be a scene of utter desolation even without the inclusion of the dead ewes. An observer's imagination would be drawn to the body language of this single figure as he 'listlessly surveyed the scene'. We would be bound to wonder who he was and what might have happened to him. Purely for the aesthetic of pleasure for pleasure's sake, within this one small scene, Hardy has deftly managed to bring together the aesthetic of the visual arts with the aesthetic of poetry and inculcated all of this into prose.

Later Hardy launches what can be seen as a direct attack on the logic and reason underpinning Darwinian economics. The young dog is 'tragically shot' for its actions, 'another instance of the untoward fate which so often attends dogs and other philosophers who follow out a train of reasoning to its logical conclusion, and attempt perfectly consistent conduct in a world made so largely of compromise' (p.42). It is a direct warning against supporting any system of beliefs without the safety net of 'compromise'. Hardy's use of 'train of reasoning' speaks of an unstoppable force bearing down on people, that in Oak's case can be seen as uncaring economics, but could equally be applied to 'other philosophers' in any field of endeavour. It does suggest that the 'logic' of rural capitalism was not open to 'compromise' leaving Oak, like his ewes, to fall off a 'precipice'. His debts then cause him to liquidate his assets 'leaving himself a free man with the clothes he stood up in, and nothing more' (p.42). For Hardy's Victorian readers it is easy to see that he would be a 'free man' only in the sense that he was not to be confined to a debtors' prison.

While Oak is descending into penury through the chance actions of a dog we are given the contrast of Bathsheba rising up the ranks of the class structure through the chance inheritance of a farm tenancy from a relative. Hardy uses Bathsheba's newly won residence to make telling points about changes going on in rural society at this stage of the 19th. Century. It had been a stand-alone 'building of the early stage of Classic Renaissance' (p.73), that 'had once been the manorial hall upon a small estate around it, now altogether effaced as a distinct property and merged in the vast tract of a non-resident landlord which comprised several such modest demesnes.' This suggests changes happening in the countryside by the merging of minor estates into anonymous larger estates that are, in turn, owned by anonymous landlords. Despite Bathsheba's newly elevated status her future can still be seen to be in the hands of outside impersonal forces that are the main elements driving rural capitalism. Hardy can also be seen to be doubling the rural pastoral world with an urban market based industrial society where family run enterprises were coming under pressure to merge into shareholder owned corporations during the 19th. Century. The anonymous shareholders in these corporations can be directly compared to the absentee landlords of Hardy's fictional pastoral world. In line with this his use of 'non-resident landlord' is a direct reference to this change from an owner occupier to a developing rentier-class form of ownership.

The building itself still had traces of its original manorial intent with its '[F]luted pilasters' and 'some coped gables with finials and like features still retaining traces of their Gothic extraction' (p.73). In a supposed unchanging rural setting Hardy personifies change that is going on through a building's movement from the aesthetic of pleasure to a more utilitarian purpose. '[T]he generally sleepy air of the whole prospect here, together with the animated and contrasting state of the reverse façade, suggested to the imagination that on the adaptation of the building for farming purposes the vital principle of the house had' been contorted to the extent that it was now 'turned round inside its body to face the other way'. He juxtaposes a 'generally sleepy air' with 'animated' and 'turned around inside its body' to emphasize forces that are instigating change.

For Hardy these 'strange deformities, tremendous paralyses, are often seen to be inflicted by trade upon edifices - either individual or in the aggregate as streets and towns - which were originally planned for pleasure alone'. Hardy's use of 'strange deformities' again gives us pleasure associated with the Gothic making the point that he is self-consciously employing the language of Gothic fiction. He is also indicting both rural and urban capitalism and its hunger for change. It is a society discarding a want of pleasure, within a rural or urban setting, for what only works. The descriptive metaphor surrounding the house suggests a society deliberately, and unthinkingly, inflicting on itself 'strange deformities' to suit the anonymous forces of 'trade' and profit. Like the dog, the 'logic' underpinning the market economy is carried to extremes with no account taken of people's need for 'pleasure'. The ambiguity inherent in the passage suggests that people will also have to submit to, and be changed by, these anonymous determinist forces.

Hardy deliberately contrasts the changing nature of the 'manorial hall' with the 'Shearing Barn, which on ground plan resembled a church with transepts' (p.143). This is a place of work that 'not only emulated the form of the neighbouring church of the parish, but vied with it in antiquity'. Here Hardy is giving work the status of a secular religion by giving the context in which it takes place equality with a place of Christian worship. The barn was made up of 'vast porches' and 'arches of stone', a 'dusky, filmed chestnut roof, braced and tied in by huge collars, curves, and diagonals, was far nobler in design because more wealthy in material than nine-tenths of those in our modern churches'. There is continuity as well as change within Hardy's rural setting as 'the old barn embodied practices which had suffered no mutilation at the hands of time'. He also makes a case for longevity and commonality of aesthetic taste with the words '[H]ere at least the spirit of the ancient builders was at one with the spirit of the modern beholder'.

But we also find that despite its age and beauty it was purely functional, '[F]or once Medievalism and Modernism had a common standpoint. The lanceolate windows, the time-eaten arch stones and chamfers, the orientation of the axis, the misty chestnut work of the rafters, referred to no exploded fortifying art or worn out religious creed. The defence and salvation of the body by daily bread is still a study, a religion and a desire'. Here work, wage, and profit come together to outdo the products of a 'worn out religious creed'. The barn's utilitarian purpose 'of the defence and salvation of the body by daily bread' becomes religious in essence.

If religions can co-opt work then so can Hardy thus giving work a more elevated but atheistic meaning. Furthermore, the 'Shearing Barn' is a temple to work and does not need either the superstitions of 'orientation by axis' or a 'worn out religious creed' to support, or justify, its existence. The feeding of the multitudes their 'daily bread' is for Hardy 'a religion'. It is easy to see throughout this scene that he has co-opted the language of religious practitioners to undermine the same religious precepts they support and even their places of worship. Also, unlike the contortions inflicted on the 'manorial hall' over time the 'Shearing Barn' still retains its aesthetic values. It is a place of coming together of owner and workers for the most utilitarian of reasons, namely, 'the defence and salvation of the body by daily bread'. Throughout this scene commonality of purpose, trade, the pleasure inherent in the aesthetic, longevity, and an alternative to the prevailing religious precepts, are all brought together in the 'Shearing Barn' as metaphor.

As well as being an attractive woman Bathsheba's property also makes her a prize in the marriage stakes. But her refusal to marry Boldwood brings to our notice the complexity of her status in society. He is of the right order to marry her in class terms, an established tenant farmer whose 'person was the nearest approach to aristocracy that this remoter quarter of the parish could boast of' (p.121).

Her management of her own tenancy is seen by male outsiders, such as Boldwood, as unwomanly. Marriage to him would mean that she 'shall have no cares – be worried by no household affairs, and live quite at ease' (pp.128/129). Furthermore, '[T]he dairy superintendence shall be done by a man – I can afford it well'. Both 19th. Century women and latter day feminists would see all of this as arrogance on the part of any man by attempting to take a woman out of the world and into the private domain of the household. In fact the Bathsheba we are then presented with is a woman far more complex in character than all of this implies. 'Bathsheba, not being the least in love with him, was eventually able to look calmly at his offer. It was one which many women of her own station in the neighbourhood, and not a few of higher rank, would have been wild to accept and proud to publish' (p.130).

Her need for 'love' within marriage reigns high in her list of requirements but the use of 'eventually' speaks of a woman prepared to take her time. That Bathsheba can afford 'to look calmly at his offer' denotes a more independent spirit through her mixing the emotion of 'love' with the rationale of intellect. She is also different in the sense that she is neither one of the 'many women' nor one of the 'few of higher rank'. Here Hardy is making a direct criticism of the 'many' and the 'few' among women through comparison. Other women would have seen Boldwood as a financial, and class, catch worthy of shouting about from the roof tops. It is no great leap of imagination to see this as a criticism of these 'women' through their willingness to literally prostitute themselves for financial or class advantage.

Specifically on the class front we also learn that she is a woman of 'station' (p.130) but seemingly her tenant status places her below women of 'higher rank'. Furthermore, Bathsheba's 'position as absolute mistress of a farm and house was a novel one'. As much progress in life that Bathsheba makes she still finds herself stuck in a lower 'station', in all probability through the accident of birth. Hardy is also making the point that for the majority in a rural setting marriage is a bargain between men and women. It is a bargain that underpins the position allowing a man to possess a woman and for a woman to be possessed. In fact the man wants possession of the woman while the 'many' and the 'few' among women want marriage and this Hardy calls 'different aims' but 'the method is the same on both sides'. This is an important statement by Hardy again suggesting that the marriage agreement between men and women puts a price on sex turning it into a commodity. But through Bathsheba we can also see that women are free not to go down this road. This particular woman has a choice in the marriage stakes but for some this may not be the case.

To support this point another class comparison can be made between Bathsheba and that of the character Fanny. If Bathsheba can refuse Boldwood we find later in the work that the character Fanny is portrayed as possessing little choice and that this is due to the position both women have within the class system. She is poor and punished, for having *illicit sex* outside marriage, by the poorhouse and death, while Bathsheba survives her eventual entanglements with both Troy and Boldwood. In contrast to Zola, Hardy can be seen to be passing moral judgement on Fanny's behaviour outside the marriage contract thus appearing to go along with the prevailing values of his 19th. Century readers and this could suggest an element of self-censoring on his part.

For Bathsheba it is made plain in the 'shearing-supper' (p.151) scene that she knows her own worth as a woman and this she signifies by placing herself at the head of the table framed 'inside the window'. That she is of a different status to other women is signified to us through the worker's wives 'assisting as waiters'. While waiting on her as a woman we are also presented with the idea of the lower status male workers having a still lower status set of women to wait on them. The reality of 19th. Century Britain is that no matter how far down the pecking order a man may be there is a still lower sub-species for workers' wives to fall into. A further point on this is that Hardy does not mention payment for the work done by these 'waiters' making their position relative to male workers even worse.

Oaks's lower position as a working male is signified to us by her deliberately placing him at 'the bottom of the table' but even then she moves him on to accommodate Boldwood the 'gentleman-farmer'. In relation to both Oak and Boldwood Hardy is exposing Bathsheba's complex view of her status and class. She recognises Oak's inferior status to her in the first case and Boldwood's superior status to Oak in the second but Boldwood's wearing of a 'new coat and white waistcoat' also bestows status from him to her reinforcing her perception of herself. This movement at the table and use of appearance suggests a metaphor for fluidity in status. It is also noteworthy that Bathsheba is artistically framed in 'the window', static, issuing the orders and receiving the deference. As both Oak and Boldwood are interested sexually in Bathsheba this in effect gives her power to issue orders but Hardy undercuts the same power by basing it on her use to this end of sexual attraction.

After Bathsheba's marriage to Troy there is a dawning realization that her situation has changed. Although her 'experiences as a married woman were still new' (p.236) there is a sense of control slipping into another's hands and this is brought to a head in the chapter titled 'wealth in jeopardy: the revel' (p.236). For Bathsheba there is a storm building up in more ways than one. Again Hardy utilizes poetic technique and the visual skills of the artist. With '[T]he night had a sinister aspect' Hardy opens up the coming difficulties with pathetic fallacy within a night scene. It is a scene of conflict and confusion with, 'dashes of buoyant cloud were sailing in a course at right angles to that of another stratum', even conflicting with 'the breeze below'. The clouds are 'films' that give the 'moon...a lurid metallic look'. Readers can see that the opaqueness of viewing the 'moon' through 'films' gives the scene an impressionistic feel that would not be out of skew with the works of such as Turner. Also, the 'fields were sallow with the impure light, and all were tinged in monochrome, as if beheld through stained glass'. There is an unsettling lack of definition in what is presented to either an observer or reader. Even the animal world of sheep, rooks and horses are portrayed as similarly unsettled. It is as if the whole of nature perceives what is about to happen and meanwhile a 'motionless' man observes this.

This backdrop 'was the night which had been selected by Sergeant Troy – ruling now in the room of his wife – for giving the harvest-supper and dance'. The verbs 'selected...ruling...giving' denote a movement of real power from the woman tenant to the male partner in her marriage. But readers can see that either side of the equation's power is puny compared to the forces of nature gathering outside. Meanwhile the 'motionless' Oak stands sentry contrasting with Sergeant Troy's hedonistic indulgences in his 'harvest-supper and dance'. While Oak is seen to understand nature's intent Troy's new status as master is portrayed to us as 'drinking brandy and water' (p.237). While Troy dispenses with the rewards of work 'Oak mentally estimated' (p.240) the crop at risk from the approaching storm to be worth '[S]even hundred and fifty pounds in the divinist form that money can wear - that of necessary food for man and beast'. Throughout this scene Hardy's use of painterly landscape and environment frames the approaching possibility of economic disaster for Bathsheba, her workers, and even her animals.

Oak is in tune with these possibilities by means of his own memory and experiences. Hardy accentuates his portrayal of the natural world through the technique of the personification of nature and incorporation of the Gothic. It was a 'hot breeze, as if breathed from the parted lips of some dragon about to swallow the globe' (p.242) and the clouds have a 'grim misshapen body'. Prior to the coming conflict between man and nature the 'moon vanished not to re-appear. It was the farewell of the ambassador previous to war' (p.243). Later, in the 'darkness so intense' (p.244), the 'lightning now was the colour of silver, and gleamed in the heavens like a mailed army'. The contrasting of light and dark employs the painter's technique of chiaroscuro and is combined with the Gothic to describe the scene he directly relates to war with the forces of nature. Here nature's 'mailed army' is given added strength through language that is directly linked to art and visual design. In all of this contrasting blackness and light Oak 'from his elevated position could see over the landscape at least half-a-dozen miles in front. Every hedge, bush, and tree, was distinct as in a line engraving'. In this case Hardy's use of 'line engraving' does have the effect of definitively linking his artistic prose to the visual works of artists.

In the face of nature's onslaught Oak combines with Bathsheba. The following chapter's title of 'the storm: the two together' helps Hardy's intent of idealising of worker and master cooperating through work. Throughout the whole of this scene readers are drawn into the visceral thrill of being a part of an 'inexpressibly dangerous nature' (p.246). Nowhere is mentioned the power of a Divine Providence ordering unfolding events as 'they could only comprehend the magnificence of its beauty'. The flashes of lightning 'sprang from east, west, north, south, and was a perfect dance of death. The forms of skeletons appeared in the air, shaped with blue fire for bones – dancing, leaping, striding, racing around, and mingling altogether in unparalleled confusion'. Here Hardy's use of short clauses adds to the verb's effect of movement and confusion within 'dancing, leaping, striding, racing around'. Again we have the contrasting chiaroscuro of light and dark, personification of nature, poetic alliteration, assonance and the Gothic inherent in Hardy's use of 'skeleton...dance of death... dangerous nature'. The colour of lightning moves from 'silver' to a more graphic 'blue fire for bones'. Even the thunder was unearthly as 'it was more of the nature of a shout than of anything else earthly'.

For Hardy nobody can explain such forces only 'comprehend the magnificence of its beauty'. The sound of nature's forces can only be described in the opaque terms of 'the nature of a shout'. At the same time as Hardy elevates the scene through the use of poetic language and chiaroscuro he then promptly undercuts everything by self-consciously linking this event to a 'sensation novel' (p.246). Oak 'could feel Bathsheba's warm arm tremble in his hand' as both characters are further enclosed by nature's 'infuriated universe'. Although this is melodramatic in content Hardy's readers could see certain realism in two people coming together for comfort in the face of somewhat detached but awesome forces. Although nature's threats are both economical and life threatening, in the face of these forces, Hardy suggests work, cooperation, and support, for each other suggesting this scene to be didactic in intent.

In conclusion, Hardy elevates the role of chance actions of a dog above that of Providence in the descent into penury of Oak. Despite his own actions being blameless he is forced to contend with a society where people's well-being is largely ruled by Darwinian economics. In Bathsheba's case her ascent into relative security is brought about through a chance inheritance from an uncle but she in turn is nearly brought down by the vagaries of the weather. What could appear to the outside eye as a relatively stable rural environment is depicted by Hardy as a society living on the edge of potential disaster. In fact both elemental and economic forces leave both parties a short step from the Victorian nightmare of the poorhouse. With few exceptions the one group that seems to rise above these forces in Hardy's world are the absentee landlords. As in Zola's case the rentier class is deemed to be impervious to all of this and seem set to go on for ever. In both cases we have anonymous owners, one lot merging estates and the other lot reducing wages and conditions, which they personally do not have to contend with.

By bringing to the surface the frailties and flaws that exists within both society and people, in what some might see as an ideal pastoral setting, Hardy makes universal points on where there is a need for change. Whether dealing with class, or the capitalist system, Hardy shows a need for cooperation and compromise. To some extent changes that are going on within people can be seen in Bathsheba's refusal to conform to rural society's mores on marriage. Her independence goes far beyond being 'absolute mistress of her farm' (p.130), reaching out, for good or ill, to her choices of male partners. But even in Bathsheba's case marriage to a man is shown to lower her status relative to him. While having other options in this field it is her chance choice in marriage of Troy that nearly tips her into disaster. In an often wrongly supposed unchanging pastoral idyll Hardy gives us the reality of radical and somewhat tortuous change that can only be seen through a more forensic approach to their world. His didactic purpose is to open up urban society's view of rural society and in effect gain some sympathy for their more obvious economic and social difficulties.

Bibliography

Zola, E. (1998) *Germinal*, Oxford University Press, Oxford.

Hardy, T. (2002) *Far from the Madding Crowd*, Oxford University Press, Oxford.

Chapter Three

Madam Bovary, (Flaubert, G.) / The Portrait of a Lady, (James, H.) and Narrative Perspective.

Part One

In *Madame Bovary* [Flaubert, G. (1992), Penguin Books, London. (All references are to this novel unless otherwise stated)] the author works mainly on external aspects of his character Emma to give us a perspective of a person who, in nearly every respect, is powerless to have any real effect on the world around her. Time and again throughout the work her expectations are disappointed and, without being an obvious supporter of the feminist cause, Flaubert gives his readers a character that is ring-fenced, and limited, by what he depicts as a smug patriarchal society. The historic and social continuity within this society is mirrored in the repetition that is structured into the narrative. His constant revisiting of the issues raised can be seen to reflect the circularity of his character Emma's existence. From the outset the props supporting all aspects of this provincial bourgeois society, and its inhabitants, are being constantly examined, prodded and, in such a fashion, undermined. Flaubert's use of detail, and the usually distant authorial narrative perspective, helps bring to the fore the circumstances and forces that Emma is up against. In one sense Flaubert can be seen to be attacking these forces by just laying them out for the benefit of his readers but this can be readily interpreted as a more than generous view of his motives. Through his portrayal of Emma we come to see her as used and objectified by a society that is also set out as riddled with banal, second hand, values. In fact Flaubert's heroine is objectified and fetishized throughout the work showing his readers a certain disdain on his part for what had gone before as an acceptable literary heroine. This is not the only aspect of the novel that singles it out from the work of others making it what can be seen as a seminal point in the history of the novel.

In the opening words of *Madame Bovary* Flaubert deliberately destabilises the narrative perspective. At first the reader is confronted with what appears to be a novel in the first-person by use of the opening words '[W]e were at prep' (p.1). This portrays the young Charles Bovary from the perspective of a fellow pupil speaking in a past tense that also has the effect of placing him firmly in the reader's mind as being from a middle-class bourgeois environment. He was 'the new boy' and '[W]e had a custom' of 'throwing our caps on the ground' because 'it was *the thing to do*'. Already Flaubert is insidiously referring to the bourgeois world of 'custom' and its use of second hand phrases in the form of cliché that helps to shape their world. In Flaubert's provincial world 'custom' and clichéd language can be seen as being bred into people from an early age, and as a cultural force that helps to shape this society and condition its people's perceptions. His disdain also extends to the prevailing literary conventions and this is emphasised through his refusal to incorporate quotation marks into his text. In other words from the beginning Flaubert is refusing to allow his work to be circumscribed by existing literary conventions. As we can see later, his movement without explanation from first-person narrative to a detailed background in third-person, of the child's family history, adds to this disdain for fictional convention and what readers of the day might expect from him.

Whether using first or third-person narrative perspective Flaubert can in no way be seen to support the values of this society. We are then told that the child's wastrel father had been cashiered from the army 'in a conscription scandal' (p.3) and he had used 'his personal talents to lay hold of a dowry of sixty thousand francs, in the person of the daughter of a textile merchant, seduced by his good looks.' The nagging doubt is that in order to give us a first-person perspective it is hard to believe that any fellow pupil would be privy to this background information. The father was also 'a big talker' and 'had the prowess of the soldier, with the easy enthusiasm of the commercial traveller.' Flaubert's movement to a more arm's length perspective helps to instil in his readers an image of father and husband as a fake in every sense of the word. His soldierly 'prowess' moves into irony when placed in tandem with the characteristics of being corrupt and the use of the term 'commercial traveller'. We also find that marriage for him was no more than a license for 'chasing after every slut in the village' (p.4) and for his wife a descent into 'swallowing down her rage in a mute stoicism that she kept up until her death.' Here we are given a flint hearted perspective on what is in store for the more romantic among women who may enter into marriage. This is aided by a narrative technique that is often cruelly detached from the story unfolding before the reader. Furthermore, we can see that Flaubert's anti-romanticism and his deliberate use of clichéd language to describe what is essentially a banal background also doubles as an attack on provincial society's values and what he sees as its bleak continuity.

Later he lays out for us more banalities to describe his heroine's background. Emma has also been formed by a culture that in this case had given her 'as they say, *a good education* and that consequently she knew dancing, geography, drawing, embroidery and playing the piano' (p.13). The use of 'as they say' subtly undermines the rest by making '*a good education*' appear to be more of an opinion than a fact. Here, as elsewhere in the work, the use of italics also acts to exaggerate the irony within the question of what constituted '*a good education*' for 19th-Century women. The use of 'consequently' as a link between '*a good education*' and her other activities also makes the whole appear inextricably linked. Through his use of detached irony Flaubert is setting in stone what this society regards as '*a good education*' and the limited horizons available for Emma no matter what her talents may be. In fact she is being measured by others around her against some form of a stereotypical person with not even a nod towards individualism. Even these supposed innocent qualities in any young girl become a packaging of the goods but in the eyes of the reader these innocent attributes have already been darkened by sexual undertones.

At the first meeting between Bovary and Emma her identity moves from 'young woman' (p.10) to 'Mademoiselle Emma' (p.11) as if preparing readers for a change of roles from more innocent youthful pursuits to a new reality. Through the detached third-person voice we see Bovary going through his mundane medical tasks that are deliberately described in detail. Her father's 'fracture was a simple one' and Bovary imitated 'the bedside manner of his professors' while Emma 'set about making some little pads'. The imagery of Emma who, 'kept pricking her fingers and then she put them to her lips to suck them', deliberately conjures up sexual connotations by Flaubert. One also begins to suspect that she is being placed between Bovary and her father in the form of a sexual prize to be given by one and taken by the other. To some extent this can be seen as a repeat of Bovary's own mother being packaged and passed on with 'a dowry of sixty thousand francs' (p.3) to his father. This rhythm of repetition within the novel is both important to its theme of the cyclical nature of provincial life and also to the work's structural form.

Through Bovary the fetishization of Emma eroticises her for the benefit of the reader. Concentrating only on externals we are informed that he 'was surprised at the whiteness of her nails' (p.11). That she might not be what she seems to Bovary, or us, is brought to our attention by her eyes being 'brown' but 'seemed to be black because of the lashes'. The point is that surroundings change our perception of what we see and this in turn unsettles our view of what the author presents to his readers. Flaubert's throwaway line that 'they met your gaze openly, with an artless candour' conjures up an image of accessibility and innocence that further sexually fetishizes Emma. Also, that 'they met your gaze' places the reader, Bovary, and Flaubert, all on the same voyeuristic plane. On occasions throughout the work Flaubert throws off the detached third-person role and not only comes in close to Emma but he also brings his readers in close as well. In this particular case it is hard to see motives other than male sexual voyeurism at work.

Throughout this scene we can also see her portrayed as suspended between the forces of her old identity Emma Rouault and her potential to be the second wife and, taking into account Bovary's mother, even the third Madame Bovary. Emma's identity is to be determined by the male characters surrounding her and this reinforces the nature of the limiting forces that are acting on the character. Flaubert suspends Emma between these two male characters thus mimicking his own detached perspective in his fictional creation. The banality of Emma's existence in her father's home is brought to us by the alliterated and assonated detail of her possessions. The 'big four-poster bed, its cotton canopy printed with pictures of Turks' (p.11) can be seen as an attack on provincial taste. Mademoiselle Rouault's appearance is then described in great detail that is again both voyeuristic for the reader and commodifies her person. She was 'showing some of the fullness of her lips, which she had a habit of nibbling in moments of silence' (p.12). Quite deliberately we are not allowed a view of an inner consciousness of Emma only her 'showing' him her sexual qualities.

This lack of an inner consciousness can have the effect on readers of emphasizing this young girl's role as an unfeeling sexual commodity. Her 'neck' is then contrasted with 'a white collar' and 'black hair' that 'was parted in a delicate central line that traced the curve of the skull'. What the reader and Bovary sees is a purely sexualized object that even on his leaving hands Bovary 'his riding-crop' (p.12) and this subservient act, with the obvious fetishist attachment that people associate with the 'riding-crop', further eroticises Emma in the reader's eyes. Flaubert's metaphor of the 'riding-crop' opens up to us the very nature of the feminine condition in society and how we perceive women but, in all honesty, it does engender doubts we may have on the author's position in all of this. Despite his use of arm's length third-person narration it does not differentiate him from the male in general and their sexualizing of youth and innocence in young girls.

This notion is added to when, in the 'riding-crop' scene, Emma is 'bent over the sacks of wheat' while Bovary 'felt his chest brush against the back of the girl bent beneath him'. Nothing is left to the imagination as Flaubert deliberately eroticizes the scene by his repetition of 'bent' in the actions of both characters and the alliteration in the words 'bent...brush...back...beneath'. Also, readers are given details of what he 'felt' inwardly in contrast to her shy 'red-faced' outer reaction that again adds to the notion of sexual commodification of Emma. Furthermore, in this scene we find the pleasure of the aesthetic is deliberately brought to bear on the events in progress to add to both his reader's, and what we may also see as the author's own, voyeuristic pleasures.

Earlier we saw the shredding of the male as husband through the character of Bovary's father that can also be seen to expose base patriarchal attitudes. Now we have the same treatment dished out to fatherhood through the character of Emma's father. In his eyes 'she was hardly any use to him in the house' and 'too educated for farming' (p.18). Flaubert's ironical description of Emma's *'good education'* becomes far too advanced for her provincial father's purposes. Her 'use' revolves purely around 'him' and 'the house' again bringing to the fore the idea of women as a commodity but this time in terms of work, whether in the house or the fields. We are being told this only through his thoughts and his anxieties thus emphasizing yet again her role as an object. Her actual movement over to her new husband's world is brought to us through the actions and words of Bovary, her father, and her limited role is summed up with his view 'we'd best ask her opinion' (p.19). But for her father one of the most winning aspects of her future husband was that 'most likely he wouldn't make too much fuss over the dowry' (p.18) Even getting rid of her comes down to cost over which she can be bargained and maybe the financial strain to him brought down to a minimum. Who owns, and who can own, who is brought to our attention with the throwaway line '[I]f he asks me for her, he said to himself, he can have her'. Emma may have an 'opinion' but for the men around that is as far as it goes. Flaubert's omniscient internalizing of Pere Rouault through his thinking processes is a pretty damning indictment of a patriarchy and how it goes about supporting its rights over a young girl while noting that her rights hardly comes into the equation.

The signal for the exchange of goods is to be, in the father's words, 'I'll open the window-shutter wide against the wall' (p.19). And through third-person authorial discourse Bovary later sees 'the shutter had jerked open, the catch was still quivering'. The poetic aesthetics of alliteration and assonance are brought to bear on a metaphor that can plainly be seen as sexually 'opening' up Emma, by her father, to an older more sexually experienced Bovary. The use of the ejaculatory metaphor of 'still quivering' can also add to this idea on the part of the reader. Throughout this process not one thought, feeling, or emotion, is ascribed to Emma. In deliberate contrast to this we are later given an insight into the father's inner world by means of his reminiscence on his own wedding to Emma's mother. He 'remembered his own wedding-day, his early life, his wife's first pregnancy; he was proper happy, he was' (p.23). This use of free indirect discourse by Flaubert unsettles the reader as we notice again who owns what, and who, that is further emphasized through the repeated use of the possessive pronoun 'his'.

Like his daughter Rouault's wife is seen in external, subjective, terms and also as decidedly contented with her lot. Rosily he remembers her 'long ribbons...flapping the lace and now and again across her mouth,...her little pink face, smiling quietly, beneath the big gold brooch on her bonnet' (p.24). Bovary's earlier dwelling on Emma's external characteristics is now repeated by her father's reminiscence on his dead wife's external characteristics that gives these events a monotonous continuity. Through repetition the point is rammed home that dead or alive, young or old, the female of the species is there to be objectified. It was the father's 'sweet memories' and these internal feelings can be contrasted with his dwelling only on his wife's external characteristics that humanises him and objectifies her. This romanticizing of the past can also be seen as him stepping into the role of a character in a romantic novel but then Flaubert drops in a previously unknown loss '[T]heir son by now would have been thirty!' He ironizes romance by giving it disturbing undertones and then further punctures it by introducing tragedy. It is the subjective view being juxtaposed with an external reality. This suggests a warning of tragedy that lurks within a bourgeois vision of happiness that is further enclosed within their banal cyclical existence. The narrative slips between past and present showing the reality of an existence that co-exists with tragedy ready to strike or, as in this case, already buried in the character's past.

The wedding itself is used as a great opportunity to lay out for the reader's benefit the existing class system among the lower orders in the provinces. Flaubert tells us that '[P]eople came from thirty miles away' (p.20) to this great event in the couple's lives. Furthermore, and in detail, we are informed '[A]ccording to their different social positions, they wore tailcoats, overcoats, jackets or cutaway coats: - fine tailcoats, revered by an entire family, and taken from the wardrobe only for great occasions'. Some clothes even had 'cylindrical collars, with pockets the size of sacks'. People's 'different social positions' are being signalled to others present through sartorial style. Within this scene Flaubert is making the point that appearance matters as people here are defining each other by the clothes they wear.

In fact they are not only stereotyped but are actively stereotyping each other through their appearance. While feeling above others by parading in 'fine tailcoats' the same people are then immediately undercut by the addition of this inanimate object being 'revered by an entire family'. Others below them might have 'pockets the size of sacks' but those further up the social scale are portrayed in this detached dissection as no better than buffoons. Throughout this scene Flaubert deliberately slips in the existing social mores of the provinces to in effect undermine everything they stand for. Also, writing about seventy years after the French Revolution he is giving us an insight into a caste system among the lower orders that refuses to change and one that in fact mirrors, in some respects, the aristocratic system it wished to blow away. Again we have this bleak notion of repetition extending over the generations and social norms that stubbornly refuse to disappear.

Flaubert also gives readers a flint hearted perspective on the still strong remnants of the French aristocracy. The 'old Duc de Laverdiere' (p.38) is depicted 'with his napkin tied around his neck like a child, an old man sat eating, drops of gravy dribbling from his lips'. His main qualification as 'something wonderfully majestic' in the eyes of Emma was that he 'had lived at court and slept in the bed of a queen!' Using free indirect discourse allows Flaubert to slide at will into the consciousness of his character and in so doing place these thoughts more at the feet of his character Emma rather than himself. While there is a blurring of the boundaries between what the readers might think are Emma's, or Flaubert's, thoughts it is also apparent that in this case he does not wish to come in too close. In fact throughout the work the onus is on readers to interpret for ourselves as, in most cases, Flaubert refuses to either explain or judge what is going on. Also, not only do we get the earlier picture of the lower orders aping their betters but we now have the case of them looking up to them despite the image of 'gravy dribbling from his lips'. Emma is diverted from reality by her need to see romance even in someone who we are told had lived a 'life of debauchery' and 'so they said, had been the lover of Marie Antoinette'. Flaubert's use of 'so they said' again undercuts provincial gossip and their romantic view of an aristocracy that refuses to fade away. We also learn that despite the 'Terror' that followed the French Revolution the aristocracy can surprisingly still hold sway over the imagination of the lower orders.

His forensic dissection of both upper and lower orders of French society can also be taken as a social document on the lack of real change, by the mid-19th. Century, in a country that had endured a root and branch revolution a couple of generations before. Later Flaubert again uses clothing as a uniform to distinguish one class from another. We are told that '[T]heir coats looked better cut, of smoother cloth, and their hair, combed forward to curl at the temple, seemed to glisten with a superior pomade' (p.39). In a telling phrase heavy with irony we are then told that '[T]hey had the complexion that comes with money, the clear complexion that looks well against the whiteness of porcelain, the lustre of satin, the bloom on expensive furniture, and is best preserved by a moderate diet of exquisite foodstuffs' (pp.39/40. Work would be foreign to such an effete, well connected, elite with 'money' being central to every aspect of their being and life style. The repetition of 'their' and the use of 'they' emphasizes the differences with those lower down society's pecking order and this is added to through the surface comparisons of 'complexion' that is repeated for effect. Furthermore, by comparing their 'complexion' to the objects surrounding them Flaubert is also insinuating that in a materialist world people become no better than the objects they consume. His world view gives us a people who may as well be dummies and this is again emphasized by his refusal to give them an inner consciousness. By laying out in great detail the outer world of upper and lower classes Flaubert is being insidiously democratic in his criticism of no matter what class he presents to his readers. In fact the more detail we are given the less everyone becomes and in both cases his arm's length use of third-person narrative also gives him the distance to damn the lot of them.

The gradual dawning on Emma of the reality of her situation is brought to readers in a voice that could equally be that of herself or that of Flaubert. '[B]efore her wedding-day, she had thought she was in love; but since she lacked the happiness that should have come from that love, she must have been mistaken, she fancied.' (p.27) Flaubert's use of 'she fancied' does bring the narrative voice away from what could be third-person closer to a now disillusioned Emma. By way of explanation, and in a distinct third-person perspective, Flaubert then slides from her present reality back to the world of a 'thirteen' year old Emma. As part of her preparation for her future 'her father had put her in the convent' where '[I]nstead of following the mass, she would gaze in her book at the pious vignettes with their azure borders, and she loved the sick lamb, the Sacred Heart pierced by sharp arrows, or poor Jesus, sinking beneath the cross.' Here the actual ritual of 'the mass' is of less concern to the young Emma than death through martyrdom. She is cast as being driven by emotional love as she soaks up clichéd Catholic iconography that can only be meant to undermine this Church's precepts.

To be introduced at such an early age to such unreal beliefs surrounding love and death can also be seen as some kind of preparation for her lack of reality in later life. Sex and the everyday couplings of men and women are also added, through metaphor, to the use of love and death in religious indoctrination. In a perspective that hovers somewhere between third-person and free indirect discourse Flaubert gives us the darkness of the 'confession' where Emma is portrayed as smitten by 'the whispering of the priest'. She is seduced by '[T]he metaphors of the betrothed, the spouse, the celestial lover, the eternal marriage, such as recur in sermons, excited a strange sweetness deep in her soul'. Again we are given the pleasures of poetic aesthetic in the form of alliteration, assonance and the rhyming of 'sweetness' and 'deep' that elevates the mundane of the confessional box to what readers can see to be nearer to the action of lovers. Also, Flaubert's use of short clauses mirrors the panting prose associated with romantic novelists of the day and at the same time moves the perspective closer to the voice of the young girl. The irony is that this supposed contract with God is also being reduced to the institution of marriage that has already been carefully dissected and undermined by Flaubert. Again we have the conditioning of the young heroine but in this case by a religion that is clearly being undermined by the author.

Despite all the efforts of the nuns Emma eventually 'grew bored' (p.30) with 'so many prayers, retreats, novenas and sermons'. Flaubert heaps irony on irony when he adds that celibate nuns had 'given so much good advice concerning the modesty of the body'. Along with the idea of women 'policing' women we have the case of Emma being presumed to not even know the 'body' that she inhabits and so is in need of 'good advice' from such unlikely quarters. Flaubert repeatedly lays out in great detail each and every aspect of her life but in this scene we have the irony of the reality, of the *unreality,* of a convent existence. Throughout the work the author persistently makes plain that whichever way she turns the unreality of the young Emma's expectations are to be dimmed by the constant recurring reality of disappointment. But in the case of convent life we find that the reality is, ironically, the unreal. Even in marriage she later finds herself being 'policed' by 'the elder Madame Bovary' who 'found her *style too grand for her situation*' that ends in 'each woman uttering sweet words in a voice trembling with anger' (p.33). Here we see some hope for change as Emma is refusing to accept the limitations of '*her situation*' with the same 'mute stoicism' (p.4) that the earlier Madame Bovary had accepted '*her situation*'.

Flaubert introduces the Gothic allied to the Romantic genre in a paragraph that opens with the third-person telling of 'convent' life that again appears to drift towards Emma's consciousness but in this case he also introduces the technique of flashback. From what we now see as her present unhappy marital existence Emma moves into her past convent existence as we are told '[W]hen she was thirteen, her father took her to the town, to put her in the convent' (p.27). She then escapes into the realms of Gothic/Romance and the 'cult of Mary Stewart' (p.29), a world of novels about 'love, lovers, loving, martyred maidens swooning in secluded lodges, postilions slain every other mile, horses ridden to death on every page, dark forests, aching hearts, promising, sobbing, kisses and tears, little boats by moonlight, nightingales in the grove, *gentlemen* brave as lions, tender as lambs, virtuous as a dream, always well dressed, and weeping pints.'(p.28).

It is a send up of the totally over the top elements of Romantic writing, accentuated by detail, italics and poetic technique with Emma not only portrayed as attached to literature but more disturbingly as wanting to actually live in a novel. Again Flaubert's use of short clauses, in a meandering sentence, mimics the panting prose and every other trick in the Romantic novels that he obviously despises so much. Nearly every word is carefully chosen to ridicule a genre that in his eyes can be both easily consumed and just as easily produced. Emma the commodity is now portrayed as a consumer wrought by a literature that itself has been reduced to a commodity. Flaubert's attack on the Romantic/Gothic can be seen as an attack on a materialist world that helps to engender materialism within people such as Emma. Also, the use of the term 'cult' speaks of an almost religious worship of a long dead heroine. It is a clichéd banal world of Romantic literature acquired from an 'old maid' as if warning the young Emma what might be, in reality, her final days.

Flaubert makes the point that if people might change; the reality of their existence hardly alters. Through Emma's eyes time is a very slippery context as she moves in and out of the present, later described as 'this calm life of hers' (p.31), and on into her imaginary world of Romantic literature with its use of Gothic environment. These character perspective shifts mirror the fluidity of her feelings. Flaubert 'tells' us that Emma had 'dabbled in the remains of old lending libraries' (p.28) and 'conceived a passion for things historical' and 'would have liked to live in some old manor-house' with 'Gothic arches'. Again he is ironizing feminine literary taste for books based on historical Romance and the 'Gothic'. To escape from the reality of 'this calm life of hers' his heroine is being portrayed as escaping into an invented unreality of thrills and heightened fears of Gothic/Romance. There is a parallel here with Flaubert's readers feeling a slight discomfort at the knowledge that this description could equally apply to them. Also, unlike novelists who had gone before him Flaubert both did not mind alienating his readers or not having a shared moral consciousness with them. Readers are also with his character in her present reliving her past and giving us her vision of a preferred future. This slippery perspective matches a character in, or wanting, change in a world, perceived by Flaubert, as holding out the possibilities of very little or no change.

In a scene where Emma is looking at 'engravings' (p.29) both reader and Flaubert are directly synthesized with her. There are 'nameless portraits of blond English ladies looking out at you, from under round straw hats, with their big bright eyes. You saw them lounging in carriages, gliding along through the park, with a greyhound bounding ahead of the equipage driven at a trot by two little postilions in white breeches. Others, dreaming on couches, an unsealed letter at their side, were gazing up at the moon, through the open window, half draped with a dark curtain.' Through the repeated and inclusive 'you' we are all observers of colour and movement painted for us by the author. By us seeing what she sees, through his literary 'painting', readers are themselves positioned within the scene. In a voice that could be either Flaubert's or Emma's we are then introduced to the fictional world of 'simple virgins... a Gothic cage... sultans with long pipes... dancing-girls... Turkish sabres... tigers...a lion'. The voice of Emma and the author and their respective perspectives seem to blend into one another. Ambiguously it could be Flaubert again being ironic about her sheer lack of taste in literature, eroticising her innocence and the 'convent' circumstances, or a young girl's imagination being taken over by Gothic/Romantic works available to her.

As Emma slips into the past through Romantic and Gothic genres Flaubert is also shifting the narrative perspective from the present of Emma's marriage into her past life in the convent. She is reversing the normal of the perceived nastiness of the Gothic by escaping into it thus allowing Flaubert, by this means, to again take a dig at the excesses of Gothic/Romantic literature. But readers already know that Flaubert really regards this young woman as a sexual object to be gazed at and used and this we sense is the real purpose in her 'calm life' (p.31). She was there to be consumed as Bovary's 'passion' (p.34) that had 'turned into a routine; he embraced at the same time every day. It was a habit like any other, a favourite pudding after the monotony of dinner'. Flaubert's use of 'routine...habit...monotony' speaks to us of male passion that has descended into a rut but his use of 'pudding' places the young Emma in the position of an inanimate object that is there just to be consumed. The question might be asked is Gothic/Romance the only escape from what she, or any woman, might sense is the circular reality of their existence. There is also a link to a more modern feminist aspect of the use of these genres as an opiate to be consumed by women and the ironic point that she can escape all this by retreating back to happier days living in a 'convent'.

Flaubert resorts to simultaneous perspectives on 'the day of the great show' (p.105) but, in this case, he depends on humour as a form of attack on provincial society. His use of hyperbole in the adjective of 'great' sets the scene for what is about to be unleashed. Monsieur Lheureux states, as he ascends 'the little steps up to the platform', thus elevating them above others, that 'they ought to have stuck up a pair of Venetian masts there; with something rather severe and rich for ornament; it would have been a really pretty sight.' (p.113). Homois agrees and replies with '[H]e [the Mayor] hasn't much taste...he's completely devoid of what is known as artistic genius'. The sensibilities and 'taste' of the bourgeoisie professional classes are stripped through the ironic use of deadpan dialogue. The councillor's speech exposes the sheer wind-baggery of this provincial elite and what we begin to see as its supine attitude to their betters in Paris.

He goes on 'to pay tribute to the administrative authorities, to the government, to the monarch, gentlemen, to our sovereign, that beloved king, to whom no branch of prosperity public or private is a matter of indifference' (p.114). Every hackneyed political phrase is brought to bear on a king who 'guides with a hand at once so firm and so wise the chariot of state amid the ceaseless perils of a stormy sea, one who knows, moreover, how to compel respect for peace as well as war, industry, commerce, agriculture and the arts.' In a society where a man's future is in the gift of others it is language reduced to propaganda directed at his listeners that might not do his own ambitions any harm. By laying out in detail the method of conditioning people's beliefs Flaubert undermines support for those very same beliefs he puts before his readers. Here every word and comma is meant to undermine both the local bourgeoisie and those whom they support. Furthermore, the long windedness of this paean of praise is emphasized by it being deliberately contained in a one sentence paragraph that, while showing off, also adds to the author's contempt for these people.

Flaubert uses the background of a councillor's speech as a counter point to Emma's seduction by Rodolphe. The councillor uses clichéd language of rural commerce. He eulogises 'the vine; there, the cider apple-trees; there, the rape-seed, further afield, cheese; and flax; gentlemen, let us not forget flax!' (p.116). In the midst of this long and rambling eulogy to everything and nothing 'Rodolphe had moved in closer to Emma, and he was talking in a low voice, speaking rapidly:' (p.117). Here the intense 'low voice' of her would be seducer is deliberately juxtaposed with the banality of the councillor's words. Rodolphe's pleas are directed at society's morals getting in the way of 'all the purest sympathies [which] are persecuted and maligned, and if ever two poor souls should meet, everything is organized so that they cannot be joined as one.' His play on Emma's 'sympathies' has the obvious intent that he be physically 'joined as one' with her. Amid all these rapid short clauses Emma is being primed for adultery. She notices 'little threads of gold' in Rodolphe's eyes and the 'scent of the pomade in his glossy hair. And then the swooning was upon her' (pp.117/8). Here the third-person perspective has moved in closer to the characters mimicking their actions as Flaubert overlays the panting prose of her would be seducer with the councillor's panting prose describing rural and national priorities. The banal language of both parties is being held up to laughter and irony throughout the scene but it also takes a swipe at both Romantic literature and the materialist society that everyone concerned inhabits.

By the lovers second meeting Flaubert can be much more definitive about Emma's seduction. She now 'stretched back her neck, swelling with a sigh, and, swooning, blind with tears, with a deep shudder as she hid her face, she yielded.' (p.129) Again readers are brought in close at her moments of intense feeling with emphasis being added through the use of alliteration and short clauses. While Emma 'heard in the distance, beyond the wood, on the far hills, a vague and lingering cry, a murmuring voice, and she listened to it in silence, melting like music into the fading last vibrations of her tingling nerves', in contrast we are given only an external observation on her lover. (p.130) The post-coital 'Rodolphe, a cigar between his teeth, was mending one of the two broken reins with his little knife.' By internalizing Emma's thoughts and feelings while at the same time only externalizing her lover Flaubert effectively distances the meaning for the event to both parties.

When the author does internalize his feelings we find that 'Emma was just like any other mistress' (p.154). Her expressions of love he had heard 'from the lips of the licentious or the venal'. Having supposedly moved on in her life we now find that she is now being put on a par with the 'licentious' and the 'venal'. In contrast to Emma he had 'that critical superiority vested in the man who, in every relationship, holds back something of himself, Rodolphe sensed that in this love there lay further pleasures to be exploited. He reckoned all delicacy irksome. He used her brutishly. He made of her a creature docile and corrupt.' While he has a reasoned detached 'critical superiority' she has 'a sort of idiot attachment, full of admiration for him' (pp.154/5). In just one short paragraph Flaubert shreds the Romantic and societal perspectives of the male lover. Emma is no more than a pleasure 'to be exploited' and 'used...brutishly'. She is no longer a human being but 'a creature' and part of his 'pleasures' is that she is now both 'docile and corrupt'. Just to put these two words together opposes the possibility that Emma, or for that matter any woman, might retain any independence and integrity once they enter into a sexual relationship with a man such as Rodolphe. Already we have had the damning of father and daughter relationships, husband and wife, now we have the same treatment meted out to a woman's relationship as 'mistress'. Without readers knowing with any certainty Flaubert's position in all of this he can at least be seen to lay out a classic case for societal dominance and entrapment of women. What we find is that at no point is

Emma allowed to develop as she would wish and then move on.

Even the introduction of adultery into her life only brings things full circle for her, as we are informed elsewhere, that 'by the end of six months, when spring came round, they were, with each other, like a married couple tranquilly nourishing a domestic flame' (p.138). The previous 'calm life' is now an adulterous 'married couple tranquilly nourishing a domestic flame'. In the authorial third-person perspective we are being informed that for Emma there is no escape. Time levels the passions to a 'domestic flame' even in the romanticized context of 'spring'. What Bovary wants is what Rodolphe wants and neither can satisfy the needs of a young woman or her imagination. Emma's 'ennui' (p.86) is fed by the 'domestic mediocrity' of her marriage to Bovary with his 'marital caresses' causing her 'adulterous desires' that in turn become the boredom of 'a domestic flame' with her lover. Through these different perspectives we see a woman incarcerated in a patriarchal world where things may change only to become the same. It is a man-made bourgeoisie asylum dominated by the likes of Emma's father, Bovary, Rodolphe, the councillor and Homois.

Such circularity in people's lives and the world around them can be seen as supporting Flaubert's stated need to figuratively and literally write a novel "about nothing". While in the process of writing *Madame Bovary* he actually 'wrote to his mistress, Louise Colet, describing his ambition to write a book "about nothing, a book dependent on nothing external, which would be held together by the internal strength of its style, just as the earth, suspended in the void, depends on nothing external for its support; a book which would have almost no subject, or at least in which the subject would be almost invisible". (*The Nineteenth-Century Novel, Identities*, Walder. D, p.9) It is easy to see within these aims that no matter which way any character moves in the end all their efforts add up to nothing. The sheer sameness of outcome can also be seen as a seminal moment in the development of the novel as an art form. Besides the parallel of gravity and bodies in space, there is also another parallel that can be drawn with the discovery of zero in mathematics being a pivotal moment in that field. It might be said that Flaubert's pursuit of a novel "about nothing" could be seen as some form of literary equivalent of the discovery of zero in this other, very different, discipline. Or is it just a simple case that over a period of time in any enclosed set of circumstances things inevitably descend into entropy. Readers are free to make their own minds up on just what Flaubert's phrase a novel 'about nothing' actually means.

By the time of Emma's second affaire Flaubert presents his readers with a character undergoing a transformation. Her new lover Leon is motivated by 'a simple desire to please her' (p.226). She becomes the prime mover in the affaire and takes on the male role. In a feminist sense Emma is no longer the woman waiting for something to happen she is now out in the world making things happen. '[H]e didn't question her ideas; he accepted her tastes; he became her mistress rather than she becoming his. She spoke tender words mingled with kisses that carried his soul away. Where could she have learned such corruption, almost intangible, so profoundly had it been dissembled?' She now becomes the Rodolphe to his Emma as she transgresses accepted codes of behaviour laid down by others. The emasculated Leon is there just for the taking as Emma takes on a role exposing a side previously hidden from him. In this scene everything that is the male prerogative becomes in a woman a 'corruption' in his eyes. The repeated use of the possessive pronoun 'her' also places Leon in the role of being acted on by a sexually dominant woman. It is 'her ideas' that are put into action and 'her tastes' that predominate.

Later we are told that '[H]er undressing was brutal, tearing at the delicate laces on her corset, which rustled down over her hips like a slithering snake' and then 'in one motion she shed all her clothes; - pale and silent and serious, she fell upon him, shivering' (p.229/230). The subservient Leon finds all of this 'frightening' further placing him in the supposed role of a woman. It is a disturbing role reversal where he should be the one 'undressing' her in a 'brutal' fashion and 'tearing at the delicate laces on her corset'. Leon becomes the previously subservient Emma as 'she fell upon him' deliberately positioning him both physically as a woman, and emotionally, in the world as seen from a female perspective. Through her affair with Leon we can see a character moving away from an imposed role as the married Madame Bovary and back towards the individual, even if somewhat changed, she had left behind called Emma. By now she has in effect become her own woman not some appendage to a man called Charles Bovary. But here again we find continuity if only of a different kind, the irony being, to get to this position Emma had become what she had learned to despise most in the opposite sex.

In conclusion, Flaubert's use of fluid perspective enables him to sometimes place readers inside the skin of his characters while the majority of the time appearing to be the detached omniscient author. A balance in perspective that despite appearances is well suited to what is an overt attack on a society that has survived revolutions and war with its bourgeoisie and the aristocratic class system still intact. Again and again he returns to the issues raised showing his readers the cyclical nature of the bourgeoisie existence. In Flaubert's world even revolutions can end in a zero-sum situation when applied to the actions of each set of the protagonists. Emma's banal, often powerless, existence is matched by Flaubert's perspective of a society that endlessly repeats itself, literally through its clichéd language, and physically through relationships that inevitably refuse to deliver the change required for the individuals concerned.

The narrative strategy is to attack bourgeoisie values and beliefs through a process of hollowing out of this society. Ironically his ambition to write a novel "about nothing", in the end, leaves nothing alone. To support this Flaubert uses the bourgeoisie's banal language to undermine the language they use in pursuit of love, and also, their active support for religion, the monarchy, materialism, commerce and the existing political order. While they use language to condition people's thinking he uses the very same language to ridicule everything they stand for. By this means Flaubert brings out a surrealist unreality in their version of reality that is exemplified in the forces that his character Emma is up against. This patriarchal society is continually associated with a need for feminine compliance and subservience that can be seen as both highly erotic and as reinforcing the image of male dominance. In Flaubert's world no matter which way Emma may turn for him *her* world stays the same. It is this that can be seen as the root cause of Emma's ennui and, after all, where is the exit in such a circular existence. Despite the work's misogynistic tones for most present day women it can be said to be at least an absolutely honest reflection of what women in the past have been up against and, in some respects, they still are.

Part Two

From the outset of his novel *The Portrait of a Lady,* [James, H. (1998), Oxford University Press, Oxford. (All references are to this novel unless otherwise stated)], James has a much more intimate relationship with his leading character Isabel Archer than Flaubert shows towards Emma. Throughout his work Isabel is portrayed as attempting to both exercise choices and to having a clear understanding of her relationship with others and the world she inhabits. By this means readers can see her as a more empowered woman than Emma in what was still a society dominated by a powerful patriarchy. There are times when James can be seen as distancing himself from an author's freedom to control Isabel's development within the work while his character takes on some of this 'freedom' for herself. In fact a major theme throughout the work is the ability, or otherwise, for people to use their own inner imaginative world to construct an identity in the face of how others may perceive them. In short, to step out of themselves and use their imagination in order to see who they are and who they might become.

As a part of this some characters are also shown to use clothing, property and artefacts as mere props in other's perception of them. In Isabel he also paints a portrait of a highly moral character who, while appearances matter, does not want to be perceived as other than the genuine article. In other words, the point is made within the work that appearances should not be a mask to conceal people's faults or, for that matter, their virtues. In line with this James embeds within his characters an acceptance of 'uncertainty' about what any individual might actually know about another person. To emphasize this there is a strong theme throughout the work that the people have to rely on 'impression' to accrue knowledge about each other. The dangers inherent in all of this 'uncertainty' acts to accentuate the drama that lies within the consciousness of James's heroine making events exterior to her person of a more secondary importance.

In *The Portrait of a Lady* the author's third-person voice is much closer to his heroine than Flaubert's more distanced stance. We are informed, through Isabel Archer's introduction into the world of Mrs Touchett and her relatives in England, that she was now undergoing 'a change in her life' (p.48). The third-person perspective then closes in on Isabel's own world as we are made aware, through her consciousness that 'she felt too wide-eyed and wished to check the sense of seeing too many things at once. Her imagination was by habit ridiculously active; when the door was not open it jumped out of the window'. That 'she felt' makes this a subjective view while 'the sense of seeing' conjures up for the reader a psychological, almost opaque, meaning to what anyone may know as 'seeing'. Here we are being introduced to Isabel's inner sense impressions and her 'ridiculously active' imagination. Already readers can discern that Isabel's 'imagination' may make her an unreliable witness for any events that may unfold.

Also, the notion of an 'imagination' that 'jumped out of the window' makes the reader aware of the important theme of a character's consciousness as action or drama. From early on in the work the use of events external to a character are already being pushed into a secondary role, also James's use of 'habit' brings to his readers a character whose present has a past. In this scene we begin to see Isabel as a work in progress that recognizes her own flaws.

The use of 'too wide-eyed' quickly followed by 'wished to check' her multiple 'sense of seeing' is recognition by James of the need for freedom, on the part of the character, to develop despite, or because of, her admitted perception of her faults. Also, by seeing herself as 'too wide-eyed' Isabel shows an ability to imagine from within an exterior perspective of herself. James can be seen to develop this into an important theme as the work progresses. It also follows that the character Isabel recognizes that she can be other than 'wide-eyed' and that this is, to all intents and purposes, in her own hands. In short, James the author is making his readers aware of the need to allow his creation the wherewithal to develop as the work progresses.

In a voice closer to Isabel than third-person we later learn that Isabel has had 'a very happy life' (p.49) a phrase that hints that she was lacking in some experience. At this point James is using flash-back, not for the only time in the work, to give his main character a hinterland and an historical context. To put it another way, James the artist is colouring in back-ground details to flesh out his 'portrait' for the benefit of his readers. He then goes on that she had never 'known anything particularly unpleasant' and it 'appeared to Isabel that the unpleasant had been even too absent from her knowledge' (p.49). While 'particularly' introduces the notion of gradations in the 'unpleasant' Isabel is in the process of realizing that such a ring-fenced existence from life's realities cannot go on. Furthermore, James's use of the word 'appeared' is allowing himself entry, as author, into Isabel's inner world. That she did not know enough of the 'unpleasant' in her life opens us up to a person who, while appearing confident, is already aware of the limitations of her 'knowledge'.

Later on James reiterates Isabel's lack of experience with the words '[S]he was too young, too impatient to live, too unacquainted with pain.' (p.71). The author's repeated use of the word 'too' emphasizes her inexperience while also allowing the sentence to hover closer to a young woman's more emotional use of language. For Isabel her starting point was to be in 'getting a general impression of life'. Here James is mixing the role of Isabel the passive observer of events with her realization that she is going to have to work for her 'general impression' and this is confirmed through the verb 'getting'. Also, to only manage a 'general impression' is a very abstract term to describe any young person's progress through 'life'. It questions anything we may think we know about life and our observations of events going on around us. He then goes on to state that '[T]his impression was necessary to prevent mistakes'. When added to James's earlier use of 'appeared' it again brings uncertainty to what anyone might actually know for sure. Repeatedly throughout the work we find that what James's characters may see is a more opaque, and in contradictory terms a more real, version of the world. In fact what Isabel knew as 'unpleasant' was 'gathered' second-hand through 'her acquaintance with literature'. Because of this she can only know in a generalized and abstract sense that to experience the 'unpleasant' was 'often a source of interest and even of instruction' (p.49).

At this point James again hovers between a more distant authorial third-person voice and free indirect discourse. What makes this statement more the words of Isabel is that in a work where the author casts some doubt on what we may actually know, there is some irony in the notion of relying on 'literature' for 'instruction'. Even if we accept the link between 'literature' and 'instruction' it has to be said that it is severely limited when put against her need to experience some worldly 'pain'. James is making plain that there is a real need for further development of what, only on the surface, appears to be a finished 'portrait'. With the use of the words 'but it may interest the reader to know that' James moves the perspective away from the character's world to the reader's, and the author's, perspectives allowing him to undermine Isabel's feelings of 'tenderness' towards her dead father. We see what Isabel may not know, as we are directly informed of aspects of her father's character that she is ignorant of or wishes to ignore. We are told that he had 'squandered a substantial fortune' and 'was known to have gambled freely'. Through this we are again warned that Isabel's judgement, and how she sees things, may be unreliable. We can also see that Isabel is beginning to make choices as she attempts to move beyond her more protected middle-class American existence in Albany to a position of wanting to experience the 'unpleasant'.

From the beginning we are made aware of not only the central role of Isabel's consciousness but also James's active intrusions happen to make us aware of his artistic role. Later the reader is again drawn towards a better understanding of Isabel when the authorial voice intrudes with '[T]he poor girl liked to be thought clever, but she hated to be thought bookish' (p.51) and so abstained 'from showy reference'. James then goes on to paint a heavily ironic picture of what can be interpreted as a typical 19th-Century heroine who possesses 'everything a girl could have: kindness, admiration, bonbons, bouquets, the sense of exclusion from none of the privileges of the world she lived in, abundant opportunity for dancing, plenty of new dresses'. As any reader can see there is certainly no unpleasantness in this listing of girlish activities. Like Flaubert, James gives us a heavily ironic view of a woman's role in this society but unlike Flaubert he gives us a world of Isabel seen mainly from the inside out. But again in contrast with Flaubert's Emma we perceive Isabel as having more power at her disposal to take on and assert her own individuality against outside influences.

Even within the family her individuality is emphasized when James tells us that although 'young men' came in droves to see her sisters 'as a general thing they were afraid of her' (p.51). With what we have already learned before, Isabel's cleverness, girlishness and now her ability to emasculate the 'young men' around her helps to build up in the reader's mind layers of complexity within what is a developing character. Generally, Flaubert's Emma can be seen as much more under the control of her author than James's Isabel and it is their different approaches to perspective that helps readers to go along with this idea. By giving his creation much more freedom to develop is James self-consciously moving away from Flaubert's reflection of patriarchal control in society through his much more constrained character? Respectively, both of these characters can be seen as metaphors for what exists in reality for women and what might exist if women were empowered. Another aspect of James's work is, again unlike Flaubert; that by self-consciously intruding into the narrative he raises the profile of *his* artistic consciousness.

Like a painter James adds layer upon layer to his creation. Isabel's impression on Mrs Touchett is made plain through dialogue with her son. She is 'a clever girl - with a strong will and a high temper' (p.59). Her 'strong will' does not just speak of a stubborn stoic attitude to life; her 'high temper', and now emphasized cleverness, are aptitudes that would help to mitigate whatever circumstances and events might throw at her. For her cousin Ralph Isabel's individuality is striking when seen from the outside, '[I]t's her general air of being someone in particular that strikes me'. In her introduction to *The Portrait of a Lady* Nicola Bradbury borrows from Ian Watt who 'linked the philosophy of John Locke with the rise of the novel: for Locke saw that abstraction and generalization must be preceded by the "principle of individuation", which locates the special and particular. Isabel, whose imagination is informed by novel-reading, has a self-conscious protagonist's interest in what sets her apart from others.' (p.ix). Ralph can only know Isabel from the outside and in a very general and abstract way. His use of 'general air' is an opaque sense of this girl's persona but he does realize that she is essentially 'particular' when set against others of her sex.

James can be seen as allowing his creation to partake in the act of forming her own individuality or as Locke sees it her "individuation". Isabel not only knows her place within those who surround her but she also makes it known that she has the measure of her own individuality. In contrast to his creation James informs us, again through Ralph, that '[M]ost women did with themselves nothing at all; they waited, in attitudes more or less gracefully passive, for a man to come that way and furnish them with a destiny. Isabel's originality was that she gave one an impression of having intentions of her own'. (p.82) That 'they waited', were 'gracefully passive' and relied on men to hand 'them a destiny' is a damning indictment of what is essentially middle-class women in 19th. Century Britain. Or, is James really damning the role laid down for women by the society they inhabit, and taking the point further, it could even apply to how women were portrayed by writers in the 19th. Century. Isabel's individuality and her lack of passivity, or 'high temper', in the face of others can also be seen as a road map for feminine activists in the19th. Century. But again there is some doubt in that while '[M]ost women' followed a path laid down for them this one has 'originality' but Ralph can never know this with certainty as he can only base this on 'an impression'. Also, that she had 'intentions of her own' is a further indication that this character is in a position to play an active role in the creation her own individuality.

In support of the idea of Ralph's lack of knowing' (p.81) his cousin's inner world James utilizes a complex architectural metaphor. '[H]e surveyed the edifice from the outside and admired it greatly; he looked in at the windows and received an impression of proportions equally fair. But he felt that he saw it only by glimpses and that he had not yet stood under the roof. The door was fastened, and though he had the keys in his pocket he had a conviction that none of them would fit' (p.81). Like Ralph readers can also admire without actually 'knowing' any character placed before them. Again the use of 'impression' to describe this gradual accruing of knowledge of her character and furthermore he can only see 'by glimpses'. Ralph's vision of what may be going on within Isabel is further restricted by seeing only through 'windows' as he suspects that whatever 'key' he may possess it is unlikely to 'fit' the locked 'door' into her character. There is a parallel between Isabel's wish to only allow so much of her inner-self to be known to others and James's authorial method of drip-feeding what is going on to his readers. If Isabel keeps Ralph in suspense the same can be said of James's use of delayed-decoding for nothing other than the aesthetic of pleasure for pleasure's sake. Continually the author places doubt on how we may know anyone especially a character that is a work in progress particularly when viewed with only a limited amount of information. Also, this shifting between different character's, and James's, perspectives and the differences between them, adds to the effect of unsettling a reader's perception on what *they* themselves can actually know.

James does give his readers a manifesto for a strong moral person. Although he precedes a very prescriptive passage on Isabel's strengths with the authorial intrusion, '[I]t may be affirmed without delay that Isabel was very probably liable to the sin of self-esteem' (p.68). His use of 'affirmed without delay' and 'very probably' can be taken as a warning that 'the sin of self-esteem' could lead her into major difficulties. Moving over to free indirect discourse we find 'she was in no uncertainty about things that were wrong' (pp.68/69). In a very emphatic sense his character 'recognized' that '[I]t was wrong to be mean, to be jealous, to be false, to be cruel; she had seen very little of the evil of the world, but she had seen women who had lied and who tried to hurt each other' (p.69). Through the consciousness of his character and with just one sentence James paints a portrait of a girl with a strong moral outlook, a heart-stopping ignorance of reality, a damning of some members of the sisterhood she had met previously, and due to this, a darkening notion on the part of the readers where any future 'hurt' may come from.

Despite her lack of real knowledge of the 'world' Isabel's confidence is undiminished when she later sees '[H]er life should always be in harmony with the most pleasing impression she should produce; she would be what she appeared, and she would appear what she was' (p.69). That 'she would be what she appeared' recognises her ability to step outside of herself and imagine how others see her. To then 'appear what she was' is to synthesize Isabel's imagined appearance of herself with the actuality of her inner-self. James is recognizing the human facility to construct an identity and the importance of how we imagine ourselves is to all of this. Isabel is also recognizing that she, like everyone else, can only make an 'impression' on others and that this is the limit of how the world may see her. In spite of all of this Isabel would aspire to be the genuine article.

To leaven her views James swings back to a third-person perspective with '[A]ltogether, with her meagre knowledge, her inflated ideals, her confidence at once innocent and dogmatic, her temper at once exacting and indulgent, her mixture of curiosity and fastidiousness, of vivacity and indifference, her desire to look very well and to be if possible even better..'. All of this would in James's view make her 'an easy victim of scientific criticism' but he does add the rider that his fiction is 'intended to awaken on the reader's part an impulse more tender and more purely expectant.' Again we have authorial intrusion that in this case is designed to soften some criticisms of *his* creation something we would have difficulty in finding if we trawled through the whole of *Madame Bovary*. Also, despite her more obvious faults 'her desire to look very well and to be if possible even better' allows James to concur directly with his character's ability to grow, develop, and to play a role in the construction of her own identity.

The Gothic is utilized by both James and Flaubert but in James's case with the purpose of adding atmosphere to a drama that can increasingly be perceived as understated psychological Gothic. On entering Osmond's house for the first time Isabel's perception is that '[T]here was something grave and strong in the place; it looked somehow as if, once you were in, you would need an act of energy to get out.' (p.277) Through third-person perspective readers learn that his home is such that it acts on a visitor's consciousness but its threats to enclose are purely in the abstract. James's repetition of 'you' also has the effect of placing the reader's consciousness within the same drama that is now unfolding around Isabel. Furthermore, his use of 'something' and 'it looked somehow' speaks to us of an indefinable psychological threat to Isabel. To add to this she is then greeted by Osmond 'in the cold ante-chamber – it was cold even in the month of May'. Here James's use of the environment and repetition of 'cold' helps to crank up the psychological tension for his readers. That we know, what Isabel does not know, about Osmond's intention to marry into her new found wealth also adds to this tension on the part of the reader. For anyone entering Osmond's house the impression of incarceration may only be psychological but it is still as Gothic as many a time worn plot that had gone before.

Earlier James had introduced his readers to Osmond's Palazzo Crescentini in terms that can later be seen as a reflection of its owner's character. It had a façade described, in a long self-contained paragraph, as this 'weather-worn, yet imposing front had a somewhat incommunicative character. It was the mask, not the face of the house. It had heavy lids, but no eyes; the house in reality looked another way – looked off behind, into splendid openness and the range of the afternoon light.' (p.249). It is a creditable introduction to what we later find to be a forty year-old collector and dilettante. An introduction that, as we progress through the work, begins to make us aware of the aesthetic image developed by its owner and his psychological makeup. The 'rather blank-looking structure' also had 'windows of the ground-floor, as you saw them from the piazza, were, in their noble proportions, extremely architectural; but their function seemed less to offer communication with the world than to defy the world to look in.' (pp.249/250). On the reader's part James is setting out the ground for a perspective of character seen through taste in architecture.

In a long follow up third-person paragraph readers are introduced to its owner, a 'gentleman who might have been supposed to be entertaining the two nuns was perhaps conscious of the difficulties of his function, it being in its way as arduous to converse with the very meek as with the very mighty.' (p.251) James's use of 'might... supposed... perhaps' again adds to the opaque theme throughout the work of 'impressions' while at the same time suggesting a difficulty on anybody's part to come to grips with this character's outer and inner worlds. Osmond's 'extremely modelled and composed face' (p.251) is a front facing on to the world like any 'blank-looking structure' (p.249) designed by man. Neither would give any viewer much of a clue as to what lay behind. To find it 'arduous to converse' with others is, like his residence, to be unable 'to offer communication with the world' (pp.249/250) whether with the 'meek' or the 'mighty'.

As we have learned through an earlier stretch of dialogue he is more of the same mould of Madame Merle than his future wife. For Madame Merle it is 'I've a great respect for *things*! One's self – for other people – is one's expression of one's self; and one's house, one's furniture, one's garments, the books one reads, the company one keeps – these things are all expressive.' (p.223). By means of separate scenes James inextricably links the identities of both her and Osmond to their surrounding possessions through the use of third-person and dialogue 'telling'. His repetitive use of the possessive 'one's' also has the effect on his readers of adding emphasis to Madame Merle's association with '*things*' that is in itself further emphasised through being italicized and the use of exclamation. Within this scene James is again bringing to the fore the ability of individuals to construct a particular identity. Madame Merle has already stated 'we're each of us made up of some cluster of appurtenances. What shall we call our "self"? Where does it begin? Where does it end? It overflows into everything that belongs to us – and then flows back again.' (p.223). Madame Merle is making the point that identity is so fluid that even the individual involved finds it hard to know for definite whether it begins from within or without. Does identity influence our choice of possessions or do possessions influence our identity. Also, if we may not know ourselves who we are is James making the point that we give the game away unwittingly through '*things*' that are in effect 'one's expression of one's self'. In that case despite Osmond's better efforts his '*things*' will give him away but the difference between him and Madame Merle is that she recognizes the fact making all of this a psychological insight into the human condition.

In direct opposition to this, and a damning indictment of the role of materialist artefacts in the construction of identity, Isabel states 'I know that nothing else expresses me. Nothing that belongs to me is any measure of me; everything's on the contrary a limit, a barrier, and a perfectly arbitrary one. Certainly the clothes which, as you say, I choose to wear, don't express me; and heaven forbid they should!' (p.223) For Isabel her individuality is not a pose to be hidden behind clothes and any other possessions for that matter. In fact they are more likely to be 'a limit' and her use of 'arbitrary' tests the logic of any one person being constrained by artefacts and changing fashions. In contrast to this Madame Merle places her much emphasized oneness at the centre of her possessions while, like his Palazzo Crescentini, Osmond looks back to find beauty through his collection of artefacts from the past. Readers are left in the position of making judgements on the validity of the different arguments laid out by both of these women. On the one side the artefacts maketh the man or woman and on the other side not so. Also, James aesthetic sense places 'a limit' on himself when dealing with Osmond through his framing him in two self-contained paragraphs to describe both his possessions and the character of Osmond. In this case the artist's self-imposed literary constraints can be seen to act as a metaphor for society's willingness to accept constraints created by ownership of artefacts and what would later come to be called the consumer society.

The unknowingness of anything about Osmond is further developed through the perspective of Isabel's aunt Mrs Touchet. She sees the Palazzo Cresentini's owner as 'an obscure American dilettante' possessing an 'uncanny child and an ambiguous income' (p.299). The use of 'uncanny' further adds to the Gothic content of the novel. Also, James's reliance in most cases on external perspectives to accrue knowledge on Osmond can only add to the mystery surrounding him as to internalize him would be to humanize his person. The Gothic element is further reinforced when we view Osmond's daughter Pansy, through Isabel, as 'formed and finished for her tiny place in the world, and yet in imagination, as one could see, so innocent and infantine' (p.303). The use of 'as one could see' suggests movement from Isabel towards James's perspective further cementing this perception of Pansy. Also, unlike his earlier implied criticism of Isabel's overactive 'imagination', we are now presented with the problems associated with a stunted 'imagination' in Pansy. Although we may be taking this argument too far at times James seems to be suggesting that adult humans require 'imagination' to step outside of themselves so as to contextualize their true worth as a person. It could be argued that without this facility Pansy and others like her are less likely to reach their true potential.

Towards the end of a long paragraph we are informed of Isabel's impression of Pansy as being 'like a sheet of blank paper' (p.303). In other words, and disturbingly, adults can make of her what they like. To support this, earlier on James informs us directly that '[S]he was evidently impregnated with the idea of submission, which was due to anyone who took the tone of authority; and she was a passive spectator of the operation of her fate.' (p.258) A further point on this is that 'imagination' allows any woman to work on herself. To move from a 'passive spectator' of the world around her first requires a woman to have her very own internal and active vision of herself that in turn is driven by her 'imagination'. Furthermore, James's use of 'impregnated' effectively means that all of this is put there by others and can be seen to link in with Ralph's earlier comparison between Isabel and other women. While one is 'a passive spectator' the others are 'gracefully passive' (p.82) and while Isabel has 'intentions of her own' compared to her peers Pansy has to allow others 'the operation of her fate'.

Here readers can see the 'sheet of blank paper' as the starting point of a process developing Pansy into a product constructed by Osmond and Madame Merle. Where 'formed and finished' places the young Pansy squarely as no better than any other materialist product, 'innocent and infantine' makes her malleable and useful for what can be seen as more sinister purposes. James's use of key words, such as 'impregnated... submission... passive... innocent and infantine', surrounding the child/woman Pansy, are disturbingly erotic terms for the author to apply to her. It does portray some of the worse elements of male misogyny and their need for female subservience. Ambiguously, in a feminist sense all of this could also be seen as preparation for what lies ahead for any young girl with the father, as in *Madame Bovary*, playing a major role in the process. To add to the air of the 'uncanny', and the powerlessness verging on the erotic surrounding Pansy, readers already know that both Osmond and Madam Merle are involved in villainy and this knowledge is held back from Isabel for reasons of plot and effect. In general it would be a very disturbing portrait of any young girl that is then aggravated by James giving us her own father's role in the creation of this child/woman. This atmosphere, akin to psychological Gothic in the reader's mind, is added through the different perspectives of the characters, their links with their possessions, and in Osmond's particular case, the characteristics of the villa.

Through very fluid perspectives James later emphasizes this unsettling image that is forming around Pansy, a girl that we already have been informed through dialogue will 'soon be sixteen' (p.295). Isabel had consciously 'wondered' at Pansy and as if using her sense of smell 'she had never had so directly presented to her nose the white flower of cultivated sweetness. How well the child had been taught, said our admiring young woman; how prettily she had been directed and fashioned; and yet how simple, how natural, how innocent she had been kept!' (p.341) James's use of 'our admiring young woman' allows both him and the reader to enter into her 'wonderings' while still anchoring these 'wonderings' within Isabel. It is an unsettling perspective of any fifteen year old girl especially when viewed against James's earlier description of her as 'innocent and infantine' (p.303). She has been 'cultivated... taught...directed...fashioned' (p.341) to be no better than any other artefact in her father's possession.

Swinging from verbs to adjectives James then gives us the finished product, namely, 'simple...natural' and most of all 'innocent'. James would know that the combination of both simple and innocence in Pansy, or any girl for that matter, would eroticize her and open her up to the more predatory males. Returning to an earlier point, if she cannot imagine her own self-worth all the better for a future role as an object of male 'imagination'. It can be seen as depicting a prized condition in women that the male patriarchy worked hard to sustain or, more disturbingly, is it a case of an author deliberately using ambiguity to mask erotica in his work? What also masks the darker side of all this is that James deliberately uses his leading female character's thoughts on Pansy to distance himself as author from this element within his work. In other words James the author is refusing to take ownership for disturbing ideas within the work. Whatever its purpose it all adds to uncertainty when interpreting meaning within the novel and even introduces the notion of James deliberately engaging in authorial duplicity. Even his use of environment adds to this dark view of threats to childish innocence by it taking place in 'Mr Osmond's beautiful empty dusky rooms–the windows had been half-darkened, to keep out the heat' (p.341).

At the same time of moving onto safer ground James swings the perspective to a more definite third-person with his intrusion 'I say'. He then goes on to emphasize his earlier statement with the words 'Pansy was really a blank page, a pure white surface, successfully kept so; she had neither art, nor guile, nor temper, nor talent–only two or three small exquisite instincts: for knowing a friend, for avoiding a mistake, for taking care of an old toy or a new frock.' (p.341). Again we have the condition of a child/woman without the blot of experience on her 'pure white surface'. Pansy's hollowness as a preparation for life is exemplified in her 'three small exquisite instincts' and the irony within all of this would not be lost on either the 19th. Century feminists or those women that followed them. Unlike Isabel she could be 'an easy victim of fate. She would have no will, no power to resist, no sense of her own importance; she would easily be mystified, easily crushed: her force would be all in knowing when and where to cling.' In opposition to Isabel for Pansy to 'have no will, no power to resist, no sense of her own importance' is to portray her as having no role in the construction of her own identity. Also, James's use of 'no' in triplicate leaves nothing to the imagination while his repetition of 'she would' places all of this in the future. Like most young girls she has been prepared well to 'easily be mystified', and again using repetition, then 'easily crushed'. This is where it is all leading when the sum total of a convent education, her home life with Osmond, and to some extent Madame Merle, leave her knowing how to look after 'a new frock'.

Even by Pansy's 'sixteenth year' James later directly informs us '[T]hat she would always be a child was the conviction expressed by her father' (p.381). Osmond then takes ownership of any outcome for his daughter, through dialogue with Isabel, when he brags 'I've brought up my child, as I wished, in the old way' (p.381). James's use of the words 'as I wished' and 'the old way' brings together for his readers the power of both males within the family and custom laid down by society with its emphasis on 'I' and 'the old way'. It also makes clear that Isabel, like many a woman's experience before her, is out of the loop on the child's future. That Isabel sees 'the "old way" as 'one of his fine, quiet, sincere notes' undermines her judgement of Osmond. For James's readers maybe Ralph's 'impression' of Isabel's strengths was just that only an impression of substance. Or, does it mean that any relationship with a man holds the danger for a woman that any independence of spirit will eventually be whittled away. In Pansy's case all of this can be seen as a clarion call to women in general, if things are going to change then they have to change very early on in a girl's existence. While the darkened atmosphere of the villa adds to the darkening view that surrounds the character of Pansy it also has the effect of preparing readers for any threats that might be over the horizon for Isabel. By now the reader is beginning to sense that by not seeing through Osmond Isabel is moving into psychological rather than physical danger from a man that can be seen as driven to control others.

Having portrayed the structuring of Pansy's identity to Osmond's taste James later gives us both a construction of his image to the world and a de-structuring of his character. Through Ralph's eyes we come to learn that with Osmond '[E]verything he did was a *pose – pose* so subtly considered that if one were not on the lookout one mistook it for impulse... His tastes, his studies, his accomplishments, his collections, were all for a purpose. His life on his hill-top at Florence had been the conscious attitude of years. His solitude, his ennui, his love for his daughter, his good manners, his bad manners, were so many features of a mental image constantly present to him as a model of impertinence and mystification. His ambition was not to please the world, but to please himself by exciting the world's curiosity and then declining to satisfy it.' (p.424). The repetition and italicising of the word *'pose'* prepares us for what is in effect a savage de-construction of everything that Osmond holds dear about himself. After Madame Merles oneness with her material possessions we are now presented with a man whose 'collections' are no more than one in a list of affectations. The 'image' in both cases is the message but at least with Madame Merle she does attempt to 'satisfy' others through a recognized talent for music. Osmond's control freakiness goes beyond those closer to him by his encapsulating it into the persona he presents to the world.

All of this is much accentuated through James's drumbeat use of the possessive 'his'. It all ties in with the author's theme of psychological Gothic. With Osmond we have a husk, devoid of a soul, fronted with affectations, that gains emphasis by virtue of James again refusing to give his creation any semblance of an inner world. What we are learning about Osmond is what he presents to the world and only through the eyes of others thus deliberately limiting the author's omniscience and at the same time adding to a sense of his character's danger to others. It is almost as if James's character has played a role in penning his own identity conferring on Osmond the same individuation rights that he had given to Isabel Archer since earlier in the work.

Isabel's perception of a deeper relationship than she had suspected between Madame Merle and Osmond is brought to the reader's attention through the use of silence and body language. Coming upon both of them soundlessly 'she had stopped short, the reason for doing so being that she had received an impression. The impression had, in strictness, nothing unprecedented; but she had felt it as something new' (p.438). Isabel had 'to take in the scene' as their conversation 'had for the moment converted itself into a familiar silence' and what 'struck Isabel first was that he was sitting down while Madame Merle stood'. James constructs a drama from her 'impressions' gained through Isabel's sensory perceptions. What she saw and her knowledge and experience of human behaviour add to her perception that they were 'old friends who sometimes exchange ideas without uttering them'. That Isabel 'stopped short' is a bodily manifestation of an inner drama precipitated by an 'impression'. Through 'silence' and body language all three characters are inadvertently giving something away. It could be a scene from a painting, or the stage, with readers now placed in the position of observers looking in on a drama unfolding around a heroine. This revelation of previous form between Osmond and Madame Merle causes the scales to fall from Isabel's eyes. Without incident or action, and relying purely on the aesthetic, James draws the reader into the psychological drama that is gathering pace within Isabel's consciousness.

Later James devotes a full chapter to the internal terrors surrounding the realization by Isabel of her misreading of Osmond's character, the collapse of their relationship and the consequent failure of her marriage. At times James again merges with his heroine's consciousness as Isabel trawls back and forth through her memories to try and understand the failure. Unlike Flaubert's Emma in James's case this realization of a failed relationship was not to be dealt with through the need for escape into adultery. At first we see the action only through the mind of Isabel whose 'soul was haunted with terrors which crowded to the foreground of thought as quickly as a place was made for them' (p.455). The meeting between her husband and Madame Merle had caused a 'strange impression'. Strangeness is an important element of the Gothic but again we find it being precipitated by Isabel's senses and portrayed to us through her thoughts. She is moving towards a perception of Osmond that the reader already feels due to prior knowledge. At this point author, reader and now character are coming together about the true nature of Osmond. What had been an existence in the 'first year of their life together, so admirably intimate' (p.456) for Isabel was now overcast by 'shadows'. Where before and during the early days of her marriage to Osmond Isabel 'had only admired and believed' now there was an air of 'mistrust'. She is not the first woman in literature to find that marriage has taken her from the wider optimistic 'infinite vista of a multiplied life' to 'a dark, narrow alley with a dead wall at the end'. To make matters worse that this has happened to a bright, strong, wealthy, young woman gives readers a taste of the power of the patriarchy, within marriage, to stunt everything that is best. James's juxtaposition of 'infinite vista' with the strongly alliterated and assonated 'dark, narrow alley with a dead wall at the end' takes his readers out of the inner woman, and her hopes and ambitions, into the reality of marriage to, what has turned out to be, a control freak.

Eliot's *Middlemarch* traces an almost identical journey from optimism, and hope, to despair for Dorothea Brooke's marriage to Casaubon. Like Dorothea's husband Osmond 'had discovered that she was so different, that she was not what he had believed she would prove to be' (p.457). Here James is wrestling with the same problems that George Eliot, Kate Chopin and others had tried to deal with, namely, that a woman like Isabel 'was, after all, herself'. His character 'had effaced herself when he first knew her; she had made herself small, pretending there was less of her than there really was.' Stepping out of herself Isabel sees that she had tried to bend herself to Osmond's 'impression' of her. The verb 'effaced' is a deliberate act on her part so that she might blend in with her husband's expectations of what being married to a woman should be. James can be seen to be making the point that all of this is doomed because of innate psychological forces acting on Isabel. She is as much a type as her polar opposite Pansy because 'she was, after all, herself'. James paints a picture that for women like Pansy who are innately, or trained up to be, malleable there might be some chance of living up to male expectations within marriage but for any woman like Isabel it is more likely to lead to despair.

All of this has been precipitated mainly by a 'strange impression' as James places his readers alongside the memories acting on his heroine's consciousness. It was now obvious to Isabel that her judgement had failed her on possibly the most important choice she had ever made and it hurt. In fact she has only herself to blame as 'she had not read him right' (p.458). Isabel had failed to detect Osmond's pathological need to control others around him. It was 'as if Osmond deliberately, almost malignantly, had put the lights out one by one' (p.456) in her world. With the words, 'he had led her into the mansion of his own inhabitation, then, *then* she had seen where she really was', (p.461) At this point James is again using the architectural metaphor. The world Osmond inhabited 'was the house of darkness, the house of dumbness, the house of suffocation. Osmond's beautiful mind gave it neither light nor air'. His mind is metamorphosed into the inners of a building's facade as it 'seemed to peep down from a small high window and mock at her'. James gives emphasis to Isabel's internalized perspective by the use of poetic technique and merging with, and reiterating, her thoughts. He later intrudes directly with '[W]hen she saw this rigid system close about her, draped though it was in pictured tapestries, that sense of darkness and suffocation of which I have spoken took possession of her; she seemed shut up with an odour of mould and decay' (p.463). The 'pictured tapestries' are there only as a distraction for Isabel, similarly 'Osmond's beautiful mind', when in reality she has become enclosed within 'suffocation' and 'darkness'.

This is a Gothic picture of the male ability to imprison a woman from the inside out or what might be called psychological incarceration. For James's heroine marriage to Osmond is a cell to be 'shut up' inside with even the smell of 'mould and decay' that one can imagine in any prison. Through Ralph readers have watched Isabel on a journey from being her own woman to becoming something more questionable. '[W]hat did Isabel represent? Ralph asked himself; and he could only answer by saying that she represented Gilbert Osmond.' (p.423). Speaking for such women down the ages Ralph then adds 'what a function'. In contrast to the way Osmond shuts in all those around him Isabel sees Ralph in terms of '[H]e made her feel the good of the world; he made her feel what might have been' (p.466). The repetition of 'he made her feel' again emphasizes Osmond's ability to drain feeling and optimism from everything and everyone he comes in contact with. The stark differences between both of these characters, one narrow and mean and the other open and generous, is also a warning to any woman where her judgement might her take if she gets it wrong.

As we are told elsewhere Osmond 'regarded his daughter as a precious work of art' (p.567) and this is paralleled by his intentions of using Isabel as an adjunct to his own aesthetic purpose. Again stepping out of herself and seeing herself through the eyes of Osmond, '[H]er mind was to be his – attached to his own like a small garden-plot to a deer-park...It would be a pretty piece of property for a proprietor already far-reaching' (p.463). Her role in marriage was to be complimentary to the rest of his possessions. In Isabel's eyes her 'real offence, as she ultimately perceived, was her having a mind of her own at all' (p.463). James's use of 'ultimately perceived' is a sign of Isabel's delayed-decoding of Osmond's character while 'at all' suggests that she now sees that for a woman the very act of thinking is held up to question. Earlier we had been informed in the bluntest of terms that for Osmond 'she had too many ideas and that she must get rid of them' (pp.459/460). James also brings up the issue of women as a commodity by adding an eerie parallel to Pansy when Isabel sees that 'he would have liked her to have nothing of her own but her pretty appearance' (p.460). Clearly both child and woman are meant only to be an aesthetically pleasing 'work of art'.

James has set up a classic contradiction for any man. It 'was because she was clever that she pleased him' (p.463) but in contradiction to this Osmond had 'expected his wife to feel with him and for him, to enter into his opinions, his ambitions, his preferences;' (p.464). Condensed into less than a sentence James gives us the male need for power and control over women underpinned in this case by an ego that beggars belief. If the end product was not exactly to be a 'blank page' it certainly is not far from it. In the last analysis Isabel is 'expected' to bend her very own subjective inner world to Osmond's will and this again can be paralleled with Pansy's character, somewhat elevating the child/woman above a supporting role in the novel. Despite her cleverness Isabel was to become no better than a simulacrum to Pansy but unlike her Isabel's self-awareness suggests that Osmond had not wholly succeeded in his intent. In fact she had somewhat stunted his best efforts by still 'having a mind of her own' (p.463).

DeLamotte makes the point that in *The Portrait of a Lady* 'James introduces Gothic conventions' that are 'for the most part' belonging 'to the metaphorical rather than the physical level of action' (*The Reader* p.441). I agree with DeLamotte's point about 'the physical level of action' but I would go beyond metaphor to describe the internalisation of Isabel's character. What we see is a Gothic drama conducted within the consciousness of Isabel as she moves from a position of inexperience in life through 'unpleasantness' (James p.49) to a more realistic knowledge of the world surrounding her. Also, as Isabel still possesses 'a mind of her own' (James p.463) at the final outcome this effectively limits 'the insidious encroachment of [Osmond's] personality on her' (*The Reader* p.442). I believe that Isabel is more of her own woman than this allows for. Although at first Osmond may have had 'a rusty key' (*The Reader* p.443) to 'Isabel's intellect' by the use of her sensory perceptions and innate intelligence she eventually moves on to a new level of self-awareness. She in fact escapes from Osmond's attempt to imprison her psychologically when she becomes aware of his 'rigid system' (James p.463) that was in the process of enclosing her. Part of Isabel's escape system is her ability to step out of herself and not only see her own image that she presents to the world but she can also imagine how Osmond perceives her. The Gothic element is enhanced precisely because the world surrounding Isabel is portrayed as acting on her consciousness, a consciousness that had been driven right from the start, and at the end is still driven, by her 'ridiculously active' imagination (James p.48).

In conclusion, James's internalised psychological drama shows us a woman inhabiting a world of conflict between her own core values and forces bent on appropriating her very mind. It is a deeply disturbing portrayal of who has ownership of Isabel's 'mind' after marriage to Osmond. James does give both Isabel and Osmond freedom to develop as the work progresses but in the case of Osmond it is a laying out, layer by layer, of a much darker, and almost evil, persona. Through Madame Merle and Osmond readers are made aware of not trusting absolutely every identity as presented to them. While Isabel's identity flows outwards from an inner-self Osmond's is manufactured like any other artefact belonging to him. Unfortunately for Pansy her identity is wrought by others and can be seen as a warning to women in general of the male control freaks that underpin the patriarchy. James's use of seeing through his heroine's consciousness enhances the intensity of his psychological drama that also raises feminist issues still relevant to modern readers. Conversely, readers are deliberately kept outside looking in on the character of Osmond thus exaggerating his potential for evil. Again, emphasized through external perspective, that Pansy 'would always be a child was the conviction expressed by her father' (p.381) speaks to us of the ability of men to in fact incarcerate character, a condition that he would prefer to force upon his wife. Pansy as a prototype for a grown adult woman is Osmond's endgame for Isabel returning readers to the earlier arguments surrounding male need for infantile women. Making a more general and important feminist point, for women to be other than this is tantamount to insurrection in the eyes of men of the ilk of Osmond.

Bibliography

Flaubert, G. (1992) *Madame Bovary*, Penguin Books, London.

James, H. (1998) *The Portrait of a Lady*, Oxford University Press, Oxford.

Regan, S. (2001) *The Nineteenth Century Novel: A Critical Reader*, Routledge, London

Further Reading

Walder, D. (2002) *Identities*, Routledge, London.

Chapter Four

Race and Gender issues within *The Awakening* (Chopin, K.) and *Heart of Darkness* (Conrad, J.).
Part One

With very few exceptions throughout *The Awakening* [Chopin, K. (2000), Oxford University Press, Oxford. (All references are to this novel unless otherwise stated)] black men and women are portrayed as submitting to the will of mainly white middle-class women who in turn are required to submit to the will of their white men-folk. Chopin's text also takes her readers into the borderline areas that threaten 19th.Century assumptions of gender roles that view white women as modest, sexually submissive to the male, ornamental, and also as economic assets. Male and female blacks are identified by means of a caste system based on colour tone while both these, and the white women, are rarely given first names thus diminishing their individual identity. The black characters have the added problem of recent acquaintance with slavery that places their difficulties in a higher order and a somewhat different historical context. These cultural, economic, racial and gender forces are embedded in a system where "effective political power therefore remained where it had been before the [American civil] war - with an oligarchy, a small ruling clique" that was white, male, and supremacist (Taylor, H *The Nineteenth Century Novel: A Critical Reader* p.478). These gender and racial forces pressing on people can be seen in determinist terms but Chopin can also be seen to be less than keen to ratify the ordering of this society as right and natural. Although the text leans more towards an awareness of gender than racial issues Chopin's exposition of the difference between the character Edna's white female aspirations and the white ordered patriarchal society's controls does allow us, by extension, to also examine the conditions of the black underclass. Although of a different order of circumstances her supposed fixed position in such a society allows room for readers to make their own assessment on the subtle parallels between conditions of semi- slavery based on economic, racial and segregationist forces, and the caging of Southern womanhood in patriarchal conventions.

In the opening scene of *The Awakening* Chopin uses the technique of authorial neutrality and free indirect discourse to both de-personalize and place the main character, Edna Pontellier, in the role of a commodity. Her movements beyond the domestic sphere causes her husband to view her as 'burnt beyond recognition' as he looked on 'his wife as one looks at a valuable piece of personal property which has suffered some damage' (*The Awakening* p.4). Chopin's use of the words 'his wife' shows ownership, a personal possession, and furthermore the use of 'valuable piece of personal property' depersonalizes through the word 'property' what is 'personal' only to him. Already Chopin is not only laying bare patriarchal attitudes but she is also spelling out clearly the distance between these two people within the framework of a marriage, all of which helps double as an attack on this same institution. Her use of aesthetic in the form of alliteration, assonance and wit adds to both the pleasure and the emphasis within the words for her readers. Here Chopin is keeping hold on the attention of her readers but she is also demanding their active interpretation of the text.

At this early point in the work we are already being made aware that ownership of Edna, by anybody other than herself, could be a major factor throughout and should be watched out for. Also, ambiguity is structured into the language of the novel. For instance, is the 'damage' the fact that any movement in skin colour, due in this case to sunburn, in such a racially categorised society would reflect on the husband's status among some of the male supremacists of his day. Or, could it be a general lowering of her status, in the eyes of the middle-classes, to that of a poor white agricultural worker? Whatever the reason the importance of skin colour among the white middle-classes is later emphasized when we are informed that 'Madame Ratignolle, more careful of her complexion, had twined a gauze veil about her head' (p.17). This can also be interpreted as showing that skin pigmentation was of more concern to those around her than to Edna which also makes the point of divisions of approach to this issue among the women. It could also be that some of the women are more susceptible to conditioning by others or maybe they have just given up the fight in what they may perceive to be an unequal struggle with the more powerful patriarchal forces that surround them.

The writer Ammons fails to take into account these subtle ambiguities and differences between the women when she states that *The Awakening* 'is the story of a woman of one race and class' (*A Critical Reader* p.485) even if the author does do as she says by presenting, early on in the work, the black characters as 'nameless, faceless black women carefully categorized as black, mulatto, quadroon, and Griffe' (p.484). Through the characters Edna and Madame Ratignole Chopin suggests in these scenes that white women can also be delineated through the colour of their skin effectively doubling some white women with their worse off servants. At the same time she also makes a feminist point that generally the outward appearance of a woman is an important factor for the male. This also begs the question that if women are no more than a commodity why should any man care what they might think or feel on any issue? Readers can already see an important theme within the novel, namely, for Edna to establish her individuality she must first distance herself from anyone who might wish to place constraints on her.

Later Chopin has both husband and wife play the role of the buyer and the bought when he 'gave his wife half of the money' (*The Awakening* p.9) he had gained through gambling and she 'accepted it with no little satisfaction'. Chopin seems to be suggesting that within the conventional roles Edna is required to show, or even exaggerate, her 'satisfaction' which further imprints the gap between the sexes in her reader's mind. Edna's show of gratitude for a hand out effectively elevates the relative power position of the husband within their relationship. Again there is a suggestion here of 'doubling' Edna, and white women in general, with the more powerless underclass of paid coloured servants. Chopin's use of irony reinforces the image of Southern womanhood's status when Pontellier's present of 'bonbons' to his wife is handed round to 'the ladies' who 'selecting with dainty and discriminating fingers and a little greedily, all declared that Mr Pontellier was the best husband in the world. Mrs Pontellier was forced to admit that she knew of none better'.

Here the narrative's third-person omniscient voice is delivered at arm's length and with a level tone that emphasises the irony but in this case Chopin also suggests that other women play a role in policing Edna's views by her being 'forced to admit'. Furthermore, in this scene Chopin's use of 'a little greedily' shows a certain lack of sympathy for this class of women and suggests that they support their subservient role in a patriarchal society and in fact may even help to sustain it. Her narrative technique again encompasses the poetic through the use of alliteration in the words 'dainty' and 'discriminating' and gives the irony an aesthetic pleasure that adds some humour to a serious, and feminist, subject. It can also be seen elsewhere in the novel that Southern women play a significant role in 'policing' their coloured servants further linking Edna's status, in the reader's mind, to that of the these servants.

Early on in the work Chopin subtly introduces what is sometimes known as *fin-de-siecle* 'uncertainty' by questioning the borderline of Edna's sexuality as a woman. She 'began to loosen a little the mantle of reserve that had always enveloped her' (p.16) and succumbed to the 'excessive physical charm of the Creole', Adele Ratignolle, 'for Edna had a sensuous susceptibility to beauty'. There was a 'subtle bond which we call sympathy, which we might as well call love'. Here the narrative viewpoint reflects the movement within Edna as Chopin moves from her character's perspective to a more fluid and inclusive perspective that brings author and reader together through the repetitive use of 'we'. Elsewhere we find that Adele takes the initiative as she 'clasped' Edna's hand 'firmly and warmly. She even stroked it a little, fondly, with the other hand, murmuring in an undertone, "*Pauvre cherie*" (p.20). The 'action was at first a little confusing to Edna, but she soon lent herself readily to the Creole's gentle caress. She was not accustomed to an outward and spoken expression of affection, either in herself or in others' (p.20). The repeated use of 'a little' speaks to us of both parties having to take care as they move incrementally from what this society expected of them to a real inner, and physical, need. Also, Chopin is suggesting the honest use of the word 'love' to describe the attraction between the two women rather than the euphemistic term of 'sympathy'.

It was an inner determinist force called 'reserve' that had been imprisoning or 'enveloped her' (p.16) and this suggests a need for changes from within as much as from without. Also, Edna's problem was that any movement in this society would only be 'a little' at a time. But, the use of the verbs 'clasped...stroked...caress...spoken' (p.20) also tells us of the preparedness of the women to take action thus undermining the accepted role of the sexually passive female. In this case the aesthetic of poetic alliteration, and assonance, adds to the reader's almost voyeuristic pleasure of peering into the character's discovery of sexual pleasure in the form of another woman. There seems to be a physical and emotional void within the two women that demeans their men-folk and here Chopin also raises questions on the reality and duality of physical attraction. Also, and in a very modernist sense, the polarities of male and female sexuality become more opaque suiting the work to a world becoming less absolutist and more relativist. Edna's inner 'reserve' is being broken down by a Catholic Creole woman's 'outward and spoken expression of affection' and it is actions outside of the character that are transforming Edna from the inside but in this case it is another woman that is acting as the agent of change.

Almost everything Chopin's character does, or thinks, seems to be aimed at questioning and destabilising conventions within the family. This in turn would destabilise the society, and oligarchy, that sets out the rules specifying women's roles. Ammons rightly sees this as 'a woman trying to escape a limiting, caging, assignment of gender that stunts her humanity' (*A Critical Reader* p.484). We can see this as true but in addition if white men may find coloured women sensuously attractive why should a Kentuckian woman not be attracted to a sensuous 'Creole' woman. That Edna can de-gender sexual relations presents a threat to the stability of the patriarchal society of 19th.Century Louisiana because any prop that is knocked away, in such a controlled society, will have effects elsewhere. Also, Chopin's use of uncertainty of interpretation catches the mood of *fin-de-siecle* fiction and is again part of the move away from the more didactic 19th. Century novel based on a more absolute world. Her character transgresses society's norms of behaviour while the author in turn transgresses the period's accepted literary taste and what was in most cases a male dominated canon. By this means the novel also acts as a link to fluidity of character, a subject taken up later in some modernist 20th.Century literature. Furthermore, Chopin's work can be understood as a social document because she is bringing to the surface the prevailing social constraints that work on women, both internally and externally, in late 19th. Century Louisiana society.

Chopin does make what can be seen as a direct a link between the gendered identity of Edna and the coloured people surrounding her. While Edna is making a journey of inner discovery and divesting herself of ownership by others the coloured characters begin to acquire names thus growing in stature. Ammon's 'nameless, faceless' blacks become Celestine (p.88), Ellen and Joe (p.94). This movement towards an individual identity on the part of the black characters is recognized by Ammons but this she sees as 'no more than types' (*A Critical Reader* p.484). Her view of 'stereotypic and demeaning' images of 'black people' is undermined by Chopin when she portrays Edna working up a height because 'Ellen is afraid to mount a ladder' (*The Awakening* p.94). We have co-operation between Chopin's two characters of different races and for its day this can be seen as a surprising concern, on the part of a white middle-class woman, because it takes into account the black hired help's inner fears that also portray her as a character with feelings. Later in the scene she becomes 'the young woman' further humanizing and personalizing the character of Ellen.

Edna's own movement away from her husband is emphasised by Chopin through enhancing her individual identity by less use of the formal Mrs Pontellier. Her husband speaks of this movement away from him as a "notion in her head concerning the eternal rights of women" (p.73) and as they "meet in the morning at the breakfast table", this links her "notion" to a right to withdraw sexual "rights" that he sees as belonging to him. Chopin has already brought to our attention Edna's ownership of her own body by her direct refusal to enter into the marital bed with the words '[A]nother time she would have gone in at his request. She would, through habit, have yielded to his desire; not with any sense of submission or obedience to his compelling wishes, but unthinkingly, as we walk, move, sit, stand, go through the daily treadmill of the life which has been portioned out to us' (p.35). Her own 'desire' for this man is prominent by its absence and in this way the physical relationship with her husband is reduced to the banality of 'habit'.

In this scene Chopin conjures up an air of boredom or, putting it another way, *ennui* about what is on offer within the marriage contract that matches the prevailing spirit of *fin-de-siecle* literature. In fact this man had never totally gained her 'submission or obedience' and this tells us that Edna had always held back something of herself in the relationship. She had only ever 'yielded to his desire... unthinkingly' and furthermore it was no more than a part of 'the daily treadmill of life'. By laying out the difference between male 'desire', their need for 'submission or obedience', and the actuality of what women are prepared to give, Chopin effectively damns male attitudes towards ownership of any woman within marriage. Essentially Edna is no longer to be regarded as a sexual commodity that is on tap 'at his request'. Also, throughout both these scenes the male protagonist is effectively emasculated and this can be seen to further question a need on the part of any woman to submit or obey men in general. Here Chopin and her character are again transgressing the norms of 19th. Century literature and also what was perceived as accepted behaviour of a woman within a marriage at that time. By daring to question what was the accepted literary conventions surrounding women Chopin can also be seen to have moved the novel on at this pivotal moment in literature.

Edna moves away from her identity as a 'mother' early in the novel when Chopin ironically contrasts her with other women. 'Mrs Pontellier was not a mother-woman' where as '[T]hey were women who idolized their children, worshiped their husbands' (p.10). There is some suggestion here that the maternal instinct that we ascribe to women may just be another prescribed rule that is not particularly instinctual either. Again we see these women co-operating with the system as they 'esteemed it a holy privilege to efface themselves as individuals and grow wings as ministering angels' (p.10). The use of 'idolized... worshiped... holy privilege... grow wings as ministering angels' places the women's role in the family on a religious footing. Another religion that places constraints on women that is equal to the marriage ceremony's Christian tenet commanding them to 'Love, Honour and Obey' their male partners. It is easy to see that throughout the work Chopin's character shows scant regard for either the Christian or society's more secular versions of this tenet.

Also, that the women take deliberate action 'to efface themselves as individuals' can be taken as further evidence that the 'old *regime*'(p.66) had conditioned them to act against their own interests. They are portrayed as an unthinking homogenous group and the use of the verb 'efface' can be seen as a harsh view of women actively collaborating in the process. This is a word that implies a deliberate act of removal of any distinction these 'individuals' may have and ties these women in with Ammons description of Chopin's coloureds as 'faceless'. In fact Afro-Americans do not have 'to efface themselves as individuals' as any distinctions the coloured persons have are based on a caste system reliant on their skin pigmentation, the variety of which is itself the result of miscegenation. Also, Chopin's careful laying out of a coloured caste system can be seen as an attack on the hypocrisy of the male, white, ruling elite that of necessity play an important part in miscegenation of the races. This is the same white, ruling elite that conditions their women, other than Edna, into accepting their inferior role in society. To this day feminists still argue women's role in what they see as their oppression showing us just how far Chopin pushed against these turn of the century constraints.

Edna's Presbyterian Kentuckian outsider role is recognised when Madame Ratignolle describes her as 'not one of us; she is not like us' (p.23). This is a phrase that could be applied in either gendered or racial terms as both can be described in terms of the 'Other'. The language used has a certain duality of meaning that allows readers to insert their own interpretations and Ammons should take cognisance of this possible duality of meaning within the text. Chopin does give us clear signs, at times, of a woman who is in the process of transforming herself by asserting her individuality and, as stated earlier, at the same time transgressing conventional, and accepted, modes of behaviour. She adds to the image of these white women as being caged in a social strait-jacket when she describes Madame Lebrun's house as 'from the outside [it] looked like a prison, with iron bars before the door and lower windows' (p.66). Chopin's metaphor signals that changes are due when she tells us more directly '[T]he iron bars were a relic of the old *regime*, and no one had ever thought of dislodging them'. The authorial voice's use of architectural Gothic and 'old *regime*' shows Edna's divergence from patriarchal convention and its caging effect. The metaphor of 'bars... prison... old *regime*' alludes to a caging domestic sphere and the use of 'old *regime*' also suggests the power of a political system that acts to constrain these women down the generations. This 'old *regime*' can also be seen to use both colour and gender to justify their removal of individual identity. Furthermore, Chopin's use of italics suggests a double emphasis of its oppressiveness and the use of 'old' tells of the continuity of the system that both parties can be seen to be up against.

The entrapment of these white middle-class women is portrayed to us in stark terms when Chopin 'tells' her readers that 'Madame Ratignolle had been married seven years. About every two years she had a baby. At that time she had three babies, and was beginning to think of a fourth one. She was always talking about her "condition" (p.11). In fact her personal "condition" can be seen as more a "condition" of any woman of no matter what class or race. That '[H]er "condition" was in no way apparent' insinuates that she realizes something is wrong but she cannot quite articulate where the problem lies. Ambiguously, it is left up to the reader whether her "condition" is a medical one, and therefore an internal one, or more to do with her husband's exercising of his conjugal rights at no matter what cost to his wife's wellbeing. By laying out the truthful reality of these women's lives Chopin opens up to question everything about their existence. In reality Madame Ratignolle can be seen as just another commodity caught in some kind of existential loop turning out the next generation as she herself had been turned out by those women who went before her.

Later Chopin complicates the nature of gender entrapment through Edna's relationship with her second lover Arobin. Through the use of internal monologue we learn Edna wishes to "think", to know herself, "try to determine what character of a woman I am" (p.91). By "codes" set by others she sees herself as, "a devilishly wicked specimen of the sex" (p.91). Outside forces are trying to determine her character while her internal need for individuality is driving her to attain self-knowledge. Whoever sets down the "codes" that constrain her it is made plain it is certainly not her. They are no more than another 'prison' and 'iron bars' (p.66) set in place by 'the old *regime*' but in this case they constrict the sexual freedom of women. Also, what Edna had given up earlier to her husband 'unthinkingly' under the "codes" of the marriage contract was now in the hands of a woman transformed and now prepared to "think" for herself. Again the author can be seen to use her art to transgress the period's acceptable norms by breaching constraints laid down on women by writing in what can be seen as a more seedy, decadent, 19th.Century *fin-de-siecle* context.

In a sexually suggestive passage the character Arobin is used to show us how far the character Edna has moved from granting her husband his conjugal rights and her new role of being satisfied and pleased by males of her own choosing. He 'smoothed her hair with his soft, magnetic hand...He brushed the hair upward from the nape of her neck...His hand had strayed to her beautiful shoulders' (p.102) caressing her 'until she became supple to his gentle, seductive entreaties' (p.103). Edna is portrayed as a woman transformed through choice from her position as her husband's ornamental possession to a woman choosing her sexual partners. For the new Edna celibacy within marriage portrays her husband as a mere cipher while she takes on a role of satisfying her now 'uncertain' sexuality wherever she might. Again we have the emasculation of the husband through Edna's use of sexual partners where she wills. Also, we find the deliberate use of the aesthetic by Chopin, through poetic alliteration, in the words 'smoothed... soft... strayed... supple... seductive' that adds to the reader's pleasure in Edna's hedonistic pursuit of sexual fulfilment. Within this scene, and throughout the work, there is also a clear suggestion of ownership of Edna by an inner force of sexual desire that would upset the prevailing 19th. Century views on femininity and a woman's sexual needs.

From the very beginning of the text Chopin utilizes the sea as an important metaphor for Edna's journey of self-discovery. The authorial voice tells us that 'Mrs Pontellier was beginning to realize her position in the universe as a human being, and to recognize her relations as an individual to the world within and about her' (p.16). Throughout the work the sea is a very important theme. Of necessity it played an important role in evolution, or as Chopin describes it, 'the beginning of things, of a world especially, is necessarily vague, tangled, chaotic, exceedingly disturbing'. The changes going on 'within' Edna are paralleled with a world that is 'vague, tangled, chaotic', a description that places her present existence in a matching chaos, chance and entanglement of different species fighting to survive as they emerge from the sea, onto the land, and up through the evolutionary chain. Edna realises that she is still a part of this 'universe as a human being'. Chopin's use of '[T]he voice of the sea is seductive; never ceasing, whispering, clamouring, murmuring, inviting the soul to wander for a spell in abysses of solitude; to lose itself in mazes of inward contemplation' has the effect of linking the inner Edna and her present to this 'vague' evolutionary past. It is 'seductive', uses the voice of love, appeals to her senses, '[T]he voice of the sea speaks to the soul. The touch of the sea is sensuous, enfolding the body in its soft, close embrace' (p.16). Chopin's use of a series of sense impressions is part of an impressionist theme structured into her novel. It also has the feel about it of later modernist stream of consciousness literature as Chopin delves into the 'inward', the 'soul' and the senses.

All of this is brought together in short clauses that could represent the movement within Edna's own consciousness, the sea, or even act as a metaphor for humanity's need for the sheer physicality of love. Also, throughout the work Chopin mirrors the cyclical patterns we see in nature's rhythms by her constant revisiting subjects covered earlier. Less of the novelistic plot and more the bleak circularity of relationships entered into and then discarded be they husband, lovers, children, father and sister. Or, as tides come and go, night follows day, so go relationships. The duality of meaning within the language in this scene matches Edna's view when younger that 'she had apprehended instinctively the dual life –that outward existence which conforms, the inward life which questions' (p.16). While consciously aligning her character with 'the universe' around her Chopin also simultaneously shows us a woman divided between her 'outward existence' in a predominantly male ordered society and her 'inward life which questions'. Edna may accept herself as being at one with nature but it is clear that she is beginning to question this unnatural 'outward existence' foisted on her through the accident of her gender. The logic of this can equally be extended to a questioning of the 'outward existence' of other races based on the 'accident' of skin tones.

Later in the work Chopin gives us something else that Edna needs to come to terms with other than the more obvious determinist forces working on her. Her kiss with Arobin again throws off this cloak of modesty and submissiveness expected by conventional society. She 'clasped his head, holding his lips to hers' (p.92). Chopin's use of the verbs 'clasped...holding' combined with the alliteration in 'head... holding... hers' adds emphasis to the actions 'she' takes. 'It was the first kiss of her life to which her nature had really responded. It was a flaming torch that kindled desire'. There was within her the 'shock of the unexpected and the unaccustomed'. Repeatedly throughout the novel both Edna the character and Chopin the writer are transgressing their respective gendered boundaries of what was expected. It is new territory, a 'first... unexpected... unaccustomed' as Edna moves through the boundaries put in place by others. Also, there is an existentialist feel of the here and now about the way in which Chopin's protagonist takes her pleasures. Furthermore, Chopin constantly chips away at the male prerogative of sexual selection and this point is rammed home when she has Edna vigorously assert to her other lover Robert that "I am no longer one of Mr Pontellier's possessions to dispose of or not. I give myself where I choose" (p.119). In fact the earlier scene with Arobin is more akin to the accepted role of the male whereby rather than "give" herself sexually she physically takes him and in the process again emasculating the male.

Also, her use of "choose" brings home to the reader the transient nature of her sexual attraction to any man or, as we learned earlier, women in the shape of Adele Ratignolle and 'her excessive physical charm' (p.16). In his essay The Teeth of Desire Bert Bender states that Chopin 'resisted' the notions 'concerning the female's passive and modest role in sexual relations and the male's physical and mental superiority to the female' (*The Reader* p.487). He later follows this up with 'Chopin's women select on the basis of their own sexual desires rather than for reasons Darwin attributed to civilized women, who, as Darwin sees it, "are largely influenced by social position and wealth of the men" (p.487). Chopin does contrast Edna's internal feelings with the determinist forces of her 'husband's reproach looking at her from the external things around her which he had provided for her external existence' (*The Awakening* p.93). Edna's narrative can also be seen as of an internal nature and this is emphasised through juxtaposing this journey with the husband's provision of only an 'external existence' based on possessions. Throughout these scenes involving both men and women Chopin effectively undermines Darwin's theory that women are passive, without lust, modest and choose their partners based on "social position and wealth".

Here Chopin also uses the literary device of a condensed single paragraph chapter (p.92/93) as a mirror to the norms surrounding Edna that also acts as a metaphor for the constraints placed on women in general. Again these same constraints can be easily applied to not only those of another race but to others that we may see, up to this day, as marginalized. As Edna comes to terms with the role of sexual desire in her life she senses the 'reproach' of both her husband and former lover Robert but she now 'felt as if a mist had been lifted from her eyes' (p.93). Something else outside of Darwin's theory of social selection of partners is happening and it was 'that monster made up of beauty and brutality'. The 'conflicting sensations' are 'neither shame nor remorse' as she now realises that 'it was not the kiss of love which had inflamed her, because it was not love which had held this cup of life to her lips'. To say 'it was not love' that was driving her is in itself a sign of a person inching towards some resolution of the question dogging her. What brings on Edna's 'dull pang of regret' is the knowledge that determinist forces exist within women as much as outside of them. What these forces are is an open question but it certainly takes an existentialist hammer to romance as the driving force in all of this.

Following on from this, throughout the work Edna's character is used by Chopin to elucidate the idea that any progress on gender issues will have strong internal as well as external obstacles in the way. If women's inner selves are hard-wired to propagate the species, through sexual desire, then no matter how Edna deals with patriarchal and other determinist forces that are part of her 'external existence' she will still carry within her a determinist force that would, in her case, be almost impossible to resist. Similarly, coloured people inherit characteristics that are outside of their control, that cannot be changed, but in this case they are also restricted on the basis of a codified set of rules placed there by a supremacist oligarchy. Ammons's point about 'Edna's identity as oppressor as well as oppressed' (*The Reader* p.485) is true but in certain respects does not go far enough. She is the 'oppressor' by the mere fact of operating within the economic system that employs black people under conditions of semi-slavery. Although to a lesser extent this same system of beliefs also bears down on her with the added problem, for women of any colour, of being a conveyor belt that can be powered by 'desire' to propagate the species. Edna's 'dull pang of regret' can be seen as the knowledge that evolution has decreed her role in the production of the multitudes. It is a creed that undermines religious, and other powerful, beliefs of the day by replacing them with a bleaker belief that is the 'significance of life' (*The Awakening* p.93). Unfortunately, this inner force of sexual desire can also be viewed as a major obstacle to Edna's absolute right to attaining an individual feminine identity.

In conclusion, throughout the work Chopin satirizes, undermines and questions, male ownership of sexual rights over women. Inside or outside of the marriage contract Edna is portrayed as emasculating the males around her by her determination to take back ownership of every facet of her being. Be it in relation to her body, identity, sexuality or actions Edna gradually detaches herself from the norms put in place by this 19th. Century patriarchal society. Chopin makes the point that in the last resort sexual desire within women cannot be controlled by the surrounding males and in fact Edna's hedonistic pursuit of sexual fulfilment, wherever she wills, could even be a tool for social change and may be even revolutionary. A good example of this is her refusal to be 'caged' by other women and entrapment by the maternal instinct to the extent of walking out on her own children. Also, we can see Chopin's questioning of fixed polarities of sexuality is suited to the *fin-de-siecle* uncertainty of late 19th. Century literature. In line with this vision of a seedy corrupt world both author and character respectively transgress the literary taste of the day and the expected behaviour of a married woman.

Parallels can also be drawn between the dominance by the white oligarchy of their women, through codified behaviour, and the racial dominance as practised within the ideology of white supremacy. The patriarchal notion of the ideal woman as a type is shown throughout the work to be no more valid than Southern society's creation of a whole black underclass. Gender, and racial, roles and identities are being fixed by the same pernicious system of beliefs that tend to ignore rights for others. Throughout the work Chopin's character identifies and resists the social conditioning placed on her by outside forces but in the end she has to contend with the realization that she is also 'conditioned' by nature's internal force of sexual desire. Despite this Chopin's work can be seen as a general warning that the subjugating of people on a racial or gendered basis is a position that will eventually be extremely difficult for any society to sustain.

Part Two

Conrad's novel *Heart of Darkness* [Conrad, J. (2002), Oxford University Press, Oxford. (All references are to this novel unless otherwise stated)] can be seen as a narrative that poses questions to 19th.Century readers living in a society that was largely driven by an ideology supportive of imperialism. Part of the support for this ideology rested on imperialism being dressed up as a mission to civilise and modernize subject peoples around the planet. In opposition to this perception of imperialism, and in a sense widening the discussion into the present day, Edward Said integrates 'imperialism' and 'its history' into the much broader statement that '[D]omination and inequities of power and wealth are perennial facts of human society' (*The Nineteenth-Century Novel: A Critical Reader* p.508). Within the work Conrad structures ambiguity into a multi-vocal narrative that allows his readers a multiplicity of interpretations ranging from sceptical to conservative beliefs in the imperial mission. He also brings to our attention that this is a society that to a large extent supports gendered specificity put in place by a patriarchal ruling elite. At the same time we are shown 'inequities' existing at home in 'power and wealth' terms and also between the settlers abroad and those they rule over. Whereas Chopin tends to draw parallels between gender and racial 'inequities' by bringing to the fore the constraints placed on white women, Conrad can be seen to use the underlying philosophy of the imperial mission to bring to our attention a more universal idea of 'inequities'.

In the opening scene of Conrad's *Heart of Darkness* he is already mapping out the ideological underpinning of the 'inequities of power' within an advanced 19th.Century industrial power. Marlow's narrative is filtered to us through another narrator who remains anonymous with both being part of a group of male professionals at leisure. It is more than 'the bond of the sea' (p.103) that brings this all male group together. Their titles are 'Director of Companies', 'Lawyer', 'Accountant' and Marlow, who the narrator tells us 'still "followed the sea" (p.105). By this listing of titles Conrad brings to the reader's attention those who effectively run the show in this industrialized economy. But we are also made aware of this society's propensity to reduce individualism to the occupations "followed" by these men. Furthermore, it is a scene of male bonding that shows his readers women being totally excluded from both their professional and leisure activities. Through his narrator Conrad drifts back and forth historically. He then introduces us to more males, this time adventurers 'knights all, titled and untitled' (p.104) who in the past have set out from the Thames 'bearing the sword, and often the torch'.

Again we have the introduction of titles but in this case it is more directly related to the 'sword' and 'torch' aspect of the imperialist mission. In an ambiguous sense Conrad could also be questioning the use of titles as a gloss to legitimize the actions of people or society in general. Whether for company or country these men carry out the duties laid down for them. By this means the individual becomes at least one step removed from having to answer for his actions. The end product of these adventures is portrayed to us in the form of the *'Golden Hind returning with* her round flanks full of treasure' (p.104). Here the Polish born Conrad's implied criticism of his adopted society's actions abroad, through the use of 'sword' and 'torch', is now feminised and carefully softened by his use of 'Hind...round flanks'. But the very opaqueness of the language does allow us an interpretation that ranges from a boy's own adventure story to a group of 'knights' and others bent on rape and pillage abroad. Despite all this Conrad can be seen to be making the point of little actual change in attitudes having been affected at home or abroad through imperial adventures of no matter what stripe. Said calls such as these actions a 'fracturing [of] societies, separating peoples, promoting greed, bloody conflict, and uninteresting assertions of minor ethnic or group particularity' (*The Reader* p.509).

The Thames links Marlow's band of brothers to their rapacious predecessors and these 'adventurers and the settlers' (*Heart of Darkness* p.104) are in turn quite deliberately linked by Conrad to "Romans" (p.105) who had found a "darkness" (p.106) in Britain that was only "here yesterday". Here Marlow's voice has directly taken over the narrative from the anonymous narrator. Also, the use of him as a surrogate author within the text conveniently distances Conrad both from Marlow's views and his implied criticisms of an ideology that was well supported by his turn of the century readers. This displays a suggestion of nervousness on Conrad's part of the censorious power of the 19th. Century's ruling elite or, more generously, it could be a bid to get out of the straitjacket of self-censorship accepted by some authors of the period. From the start Conrad's supposedly romantic travellers/adventurers tale is already being laced with a healthy dose of late 19th.Century scepticism. The tale within a tale encompasses a history within a history that also has the effect of compressing time and gives us a sense of circularity within these events and history. It is a circularity that would not be lost on any 'group particularity' of that period, or since

Still being quoted to us directly Marlow then goes on to inform us that the Romans on their mission to civilise a Britain, of "marshes, forests, savages" (p.106) were also "a wonderful lot of handy men". His use of the obviously sceptical "if we may believe what we read" suggests that any conqueror's record should be hedged in by uncertainties and this is emphasized by his deliberate insertion of the words "if" and "may". The implication can be drawn that a Britain that was itself once a land of "utter savagery", now sends its "wonderful lot of handy men" to face "disease, exile, and death" abroad. Later in the narrative Marlow confirms this point when he quotes the station manager in the Congo saying that his men are "[A]ll sick. They die so quick, too, that I haven't the time to send them out of the country – it's incredible!" (p.136). All of this encloses Marlow's entirely male mission into a historically repetitious cycle that can raise questions in the reader's mind of the validity of any imperial mission whether the Roman, Elizabethan or Victorian versions. There is also a suggestion here of very little difference between a bad Europe of old and, what later in the novel can be seen as, a bad Africa with both having an air of menace about them. It is as if an adversarial nature is questioning the right of the imperialists to be where they have no right to be.

The sheer scale of European ambition is brought home to Conrad's readers when Marlow states that "[T]he conquest of the earth, which mostly means the taking it away from those who have a different complexion or slightly flatter noses than ourselves, is not a pretty thing when you look into it too much" (p.107). His use of "mostly means" allows room for a different and much harsher interpretation to the prevailing notion of civilizing through "conquest". But Conrad's use of "ourselves" also includes Marlow's companions, and effectively the British state, in this much darker view of imperialist ambitions. Ambiguously, he can be seen to be encouraging his readers to "look into it too much" rather than to accept uncritically any propaganda that might support the land-grabs going on in Africa and elsewhere. The scale of the land-grab in Africa is brought home to readers when Marlow later remarks on the "vast amount of red...a deuce of a lot of blue, a little green, smears of orange...a purple patch" and "the yellow" (p.110) on the company map.

There is an element of irony in Conrad's pedantic use of the colour coding used to designate who owned what among the European powers. The importance of the subject Africans can be seen to lie in their absence of any right to ownership to the land they were born to. To strip them of what is rightly theirs Conrad shows us that it is a necessary part of the process to first turn them into non-persons or even a sub-species while taking what belongs to them. There is a parallel within all of this in that what separates the British subjected by the Romans from the newly subjected peoples is that they have "a different complexion or slightly flatter noses" (p.107). As the Romans "were no colonists" just "conquerors" the implication is that the British project is both long term and more humane. With a heavy hint of irony, and again including his immediate companions, Marlow makes the excuse "[W]hat saves us is efficiency – the devotion to efficiency". Each set of colonists are separated by history but for Conrad's readers parallels can easily be drawn between modern 19th.Century colonists "taking it away" from others of a different colour and the "robbery with violence" used by the Romans against such as the British. These newer colonists may have an almost religious "devotion to efficiency" (p.107) but Marlow's multi-layered and ambiguous narrative allows the thought to come to the surface that this is no more than just camouflage for their real intent.

He then portrays the Roman basis for imperial expansion as an "idea – something you can set up, and bow down before, and offer a sacrifice to..." (p.107). It is left to readers whether a Victorian, almost religious, "devotion to efficiency" would be any more of a benefit to a subject people than a pagan Roman "sacrifice" to an "idea". It is notable that Marlow then runs out of words on the essence of the "idea" and the outer narrator leaves this in suspense thus adding to the opaqueness of 'Marlow's inconclusive experiences' (p.107). In this sense Conrad's novel inculcates uncertainties in his reader that raises more questions than he answers and this in turn catches the mood of *fin-de-siecle* fiction as one century moves into another. Also, the wait for change that is implicit in the approach of a new century mirrors Marlow and his band as *they* await 'the turn of the tide' (p.103) that will take them on a journey whose destination is left open ended. As a metaphor the ebb tide, like the change of century, tells us that something will happen but we may have little or no control over events other than this fact.

These 'uncertainties' are carried over when Conrad blurs gender boundaries by portraying Marlow as feeling emasculated through using his aunt "to get a job" (p.109). The words "I, Charlie Marlow, set the women to work" (p.109) hints at Marlow demeaning his status as a man by needing to use a woman to further his ambitions. That she in turn was using "the wife of a very high personage in the Administration, and also a man who has lots of influence" (p.109) to further these ends suggests that the power of this "wife" ultimately rests on a sexual connection with this holder of "influence". Again we are shown who are the possessors of real power and at the same time the limits of a woman's "work". Marlow then patronises her further, and women in general, by seeing her as "out of touch with truth" (p.113) and although she is an "excellent woman" she was susceptible to the "humbug" that was being "let loose in print". That is, the propaganda in the press and elsewhere that underpins imperial adventures abroad.

This scene also suggests that Marlow is regaining his manhood at the expense of his aunt by lowering her status but he also depicts the male characteristic of being concerned with the views that other males may take in about him. He does show signs of scepticism towards her view of the colonial mission and his being "an emissary of light, something like a lower sort of apostle". Despite the use of uplifting language Conrad's insertion of "apostle" seems to tar Marlow with the same brush as the "pilgrims" (p.168) we meet later in the narrative. A group of men whose actions Marlow comes to see as epitomising the cruelty and greed inherent in the colonialism of the 19th. Century. Ironically as he looks down on his aunt because of her gender classification she in turn looks down on people because of their colour and culture by seeing Marlow's role as "weaning those ignorant millions from their horrid ways" (p.113).

Both Marlow and his aunt can be seen to be conditioned one way or another by the forces surrounding them. But the aunt's illusions could equally be the illusions of "those ignorant millions" who swallowed the propaganda supporting the imperial mission. The multiple meanings within the language employed by Conrad could easily allow readers to place the "ignorant millions" and "their horrid ways" among those at home as much as those abroad. Again he chips away at the supposed enlightened ideology underpinning imperial expansion when Marlow "ventured to hint that the Company was run for a profit" but there are also elements of the misogynistic in his attitudes towards women. Furthermore, there is a sense that within the narrative technique Conrad is engaged at times in a process of deliberately alienating and upsetting his readers who may believe in the imperial mission. By forcing them back from the text this could give them the required distance to prepare *them* for a 'modernizing' of *their* beliefs. In Said's view Conrad maintains that 'we are in a world being made and unmade more or less all the time' (*The Reader* p.516). The instability that Said sees is reflected in the language, and its uncertainty of meaning, throughout Marlow's tale. Whether dealing with the system of beliefs supporting imperialism or the patriarchal conventions surrounding gender, Conrad leaves the reader to fill in the gaps with their own interpretations that in effect gives *them* an active role in the whole process.

Again through the perspective of Marlow Conrad later suggests that Kurtz's native mistress is representative of Africa and its condition. His words, "[H]er face had a tragic and fierce aspect of wild sorrow and of dumb pain mingled with the fear of some struggling, half-shaped resolve" (p.168), are analogous to the pain and grief being inflicted by imperialist policies in Africa. Conrad reinforces this idea in his readers by the use of simile when he likens her to the "the wilderness itself, with an air of brooding over an inscrutable purpose", in effect, synthesizing her with the land she inhabits. In contrast to her oneness with her surroundings he portrays the invading white males as alienated and fearful. Marlow states that "[T]he pilgrims murmured at my back" (p.168) and one of the whites threatened "to shoot her". She is a woman, unarmed, unpredictable and yet engenders fear as her feminine primitiveness is beyond their experience. Said states that '[E]ven if you prevail over them, they [the subjugated] are not going to concede to you your essential superiority or your right to rule them despite your evident wealth and power' (*The Reader* p.508). Kurtz's native woman certainly does not 'concede' to the invader's 'essential superiority' giving Conrad's metaphor a relevance to the later struggles between the colonized and the colonizer in the 20th.Century. Also, and in a more universal sense, readers can see that elements within society, up to the present day, who see themselves as marginalized through ethnicity, lack of wealth, gender, would themselves show a tendency not to 'concede' to the 'essential superiority' of others.

Neither the "pilgrims" nor the native woman speaks the other's language and this also points up a theme, repeated throughout the novel, of the difficulty of communication. Marlow frequently allows his words to trail off, the invader cannot talk to the invaded peoples and this "superb" (*The Heart of Darkness* p.168) and "magnificent", although "ominous", woman fails to communicate across both the gender and racial divides. Here there is a suggestion of a psychological fear of this woman who is standing up to the male "pilgrims" and others of the invading parties. Within all this Marlow is joining in the gendering of feminine appearance "savage" or otherwise. Also, the narrative synthesises the woman with the "immense wilderness". The personified environment is a "colossal body of the fecund and mysterious life [that] seemed to look at her, pensive".

The "fecund' forest and the "wild and gorgeous apparition of a woman" (p.167) are both portrayed as "mysterious" and here he joins the "pilgrims" when he also finds "something ominous" (p.168) about her. For Marlow there is a mystery of life in both and he is depicted as reaching for a meaning beyond words. Even the wilderness sees the "image" in her "of its own tenebrous and passionate soul". Throughout the work Marlow consistently finds it impossible to describe events, surroundings, and characters with any certainty. Said rightly points out that for Conrad things are 'neither unconditionally true nor unqualifiedly certain' (*The Reader* p.514). He refuses to clear up doubts surrounding this "mysterious life" that in the last analysis leaves it up to the reader exactly what he may mean. For the reader it raises large difficulties in trying to decipher a text with so much ambiguity structured into it but this also has the effect of opening it up to each generation's interpretation.

In this confrontation Conrad seems to be suggesting a process of emasculation that does not fit the boy's own genre of adventure tales. His use of "inscrutable purpose", fusing her into "the immense wilderness" and "fecund and mysterious life" blends her sexual identity with nature, a mysterious past and an unknown "purpose". In this case Africa's dark "wilderness" mirrors for Marlow a 'darkness' in the very nature of this woman's femininity while at the same time the very maleness of the "pilgrims", and maybe even himself, is being emasculated. Also, by elevating the native woman at the expense of the invading whites there is implicit in all of this a questioning of the ideology of racial superiority underpinning imperial expansion. Here the story within a story that is also part of a continuum of histories manages to question at the same time the encompassing patriarchal and imperial ideologies and the system of beliefs that lie within. The invader's arms are portrayed as "the thunderbolts of that pitiful Jupiter" (p.167) and such as this technology is ironically pitted against a "savage" unarmed woman at one with her surroundings and representing continuity in the world she inhabits.

Here Conrad also seems to be questioning the worth of European technology and specifically their reliance on arms in any final subjugation of colonized peoples. The "pilgrims" reliance on technology implies a repetition of the folly and effectiveness of the actions of the French "man-of-war...shelling the bush" (p.114/115) and its guns firing "a tiny projectile" one at a time aimlessly into "a continent" (p.115). The boy's own version of conquering "a continent" is held up to ridicule as the effort to subjugate a land mass and its inhabitants now becomes surreal due to the fact that "there wasn't even a shed there" (p.114). In contrast to all of this, and in a direct criticism of European actions, we are informed that the indigenous natives "wanted no excuse for being there". No matter how pointless it is still all part of what Marlow calls "the merry dance of death and trade" (p.115). Again the imperial mission to civilize and modernize is undermined but this time it is through directly linking arms and killing to the "trade" of empire. Repeatedly throughout the narrative Conrad undermines the lie of the 'efficiency' (p.107) of the European version of the imperial mission and its fig leaf to civilize and modernize so called primitive peoples around the planet.

The Belgian version is later depicted by Conrad as "sordid buccaneers... there was not an atom of foresight or of serious intention in the whole batch of them, and they did not seem aware that these things are wanted for the work of the world. To tear treasure out of the bowels of the land was their desire, with no more moral purpose at the back of it than there is in burglars" (p.133) He lays bare the sheer short-sightedness and ignorance of the imperialist mission. They are nothing but "sordid buccaneers" and "burglars" as they go about their business to "tear treasure out of the bowels of the land". This is a very strong statement by Conrad aimed at the morality, and economics, driving European ambitions in Africa. Taking on board the above carefully chosen words by Conrad it is hard to agree totally with Said's statement that '[A]s a creature of his time, Conrad could not grant the natives their freedom, despite his severe critique of the imperialism that enslaved them' (*The Reader* p.516). It is more than a 'severe critique' to brand the colonizers as illegal "burglars" as it more than questions their right to be there to enslave the natives in the first place.

Following up this point, by naming this group "the Eldorado Exploring Expedition" Conrad effectively links what is actually going on in Africa to the Spanish *conquistadores* (see Explanatory Notes p.211) who had themselves looted their way round the Americas in the 16th. Century. The obvious question can be asked, namely, is the British version any different to that being pursued by the Belgians or those who preceded them. Furthermore, throughout the narrative the rights of the indigenous peoples are conspicuous by their absence whether African or otherwise. In what can be seen as a warning to every generation he has Marlow say that the strength of "conquerors...is just an accident arising from the weakness of others" (p.107). Where the British were weak under the Romans it is now the turn of others to take up that role, as his readers could themselves judge, through the example of a Spanish Empire that was in severe decline by the 19th. Century. The logic at the heart of Conrad's existentialist version of history's circularity allows us to ask ourselves the question whose turn will it be next as a subject people. The subject Africans can easily be seen a mirror to a future for the people of the competing European empires. Although carefully distanced through the device of two narrators Conrad is giving an emphatic warning of the instability inherent in all of the imperial missions down the centuries and any other form of overbearing ideology that might follow.

Later on, and again through the perspective of Marlow, Conrad seems to be satirising Kurtz's 'Intended' (p.181) by concentrating on her appearance. In addition to this neither the 'Intended', the 'aunt', the native mistress or the secretaries 'one fat and the other slim' (p.110) are given individual identities at any stage of the novel. Also, his use of 'Intended' places her in the role of a possession of Kurtz who is by now a dead man suggesting a reaching out from the grave and giving the scene a surreal slant on the position of women in general. She is put in the objectified position of being "in mourning" (p.183) for her loss of Kurtz on his mission abroad. She "was not very young - I mean not girlish. She had a mature capacity for fidelity, for belief, for suffering". It is as if she is playing a role with all the trappings of widowhood in a scene that can be seen as ironic. She is the faithful non-wife deprived of her emissary sent out on his imperial mission for the company. The readers already know the reality of Kurtz and the "wild and gorgeous apparition of a woman" (p.167) who had been his mistress. In contrast to the "Intended" this one "walked with measured steps... treading the earth proudly" (p.167).

Kurtz's relationship is a sign that he has transgressed the 19th.Century restraints based on racial differences. That Kurtz is lost to this "woman" touches on the Victorian concern for the de-civilising effects, on white adventurers, of "the wilderness" (p.168) and even the dilution of the white race through miscegenation. But in an ambiguous sense, in his contrasting of these two women from different cultures, Conrad could be suggesting that something has been lost in the 19th.Century society's progression to a more rigidly gendered but 'civilised' society. He also links the importance of feminine appearances across the cultures as the mistress wore "brass leggings...glass beads...bizarre things...that hung about her...She must have had the value of several elephant tusks upon her" (p.168). The native woman's appearance is valued as a commodity and put in terms of the rate of exchange for ivory. This idea of the 'value' of the women's appearance would also strike a chord with Chopin's character Mr Pontellier. Ambiguously, did only her fellow natives exchange ivory to enhance her appearance among them or did Kurtz gift her trinkets to impress the natives. Either way appearance matters across the racial divide whether the 'Intended' or the "savage and superb, wild-eyed and magnificent;" (p.168) woman.

Conrad's use of regular tone throughout the work underpins the irony of the savagery perpetrated on the natives by the 'civilizing' whites. Ironically "[A]ll Europe contributed to the making of Kurtz and...the International Society for the Suppression of Savage Customs had entrusted him with the making of a report, for its future guidance" (pp.154/5). Even in this statement there is no way Britain can be excluded from what is going on. It is "[A]ll Europe" in the man's genes and the policies being pursued are emphatically "International". Historically this codifying of the behaviour of other peoples is a fig leaf that can be wheeled out to suppress anyone who opposes the norms set out by any European ruling clique. First of all the indigenous peoples have to become a sub-species by portraying their culture in terms of "Savage Customs", this then allows the *superior* Europeans to indulge in totally unacceptable practices. Conrad gives us the bitter irony of Europeans shadowing "Savage Customs" while formulating bureaucratic policies that are in themselves evil, these are then camouflaged in wordy propagandist banality for general consumption in their home countries. Earlier Marlow had brought to our attention this point when he sees some captive Africans and states "[T]hey were called criminals, and the outraged law, like the bursting shells, had come to them, an insoluble mystery from over the sea" (p.117). The direct link with the actions of the French "man-of-war", (p.114) through the use of the simile, "like bursting shells" is a very strong sign to Conrad's readers that the legitimacy of this "outraged law" comes from the barrel of a gun.

Furthermore, these patently unjust actions by the Europeans are brought within the remit of an "outraged law" that was an imported "mystery" to them. It is left to the reader's imagination as to what kind of due process, lacking in proper transparency, would have these men "called criminals". In all of this business where is the independent judiciary, a proper defence, a jury of their peers to find them guilty, which is the front line in any so called civilized society. That Kurtz's report was "vibrating with eloquence" (p.155) only adds to the banality while undermining, through satire, the imperial mission to civilise. By stating Kurtz's manifesto Conrad also eloquently undermines it. To the natives Kurtz and the Europeans have to be "in the nature of supernatural beings...a deity" and "[B]y the simple exercise of our will we can exert a power for good practically unbounded". This damning satire on European behaviour again differs, somewhat, with Said's view that 'Conrad could not grant natives their freedom, despite his severe critique of the imperialism that enslaved them' (*The Reader* p.516). We may only have the words of the twice removed and sometimes unreliable Marlow to go on but none of this reads as support by Conrad for the notion that what was going on in Africa should be in anyway acceptable.

Like the imperialist propaganda Kurtz dresses things up by the use of "power for good" (p.155) but he has already undermined the effect by prefixing these words with "our will". Conrad consistently undermines the effectiveness of European "will" throughout the work whether it is, such as, the actions of the French "man-of-war" (p.114) or the armed "pilgrims" and their "thunderbolts of that pitiful Jupiter" (p.167). Earlier Conrad had laid out a warning to his readers that other empires had exercised their "will" over other peoples only for these empires to fade away to virtually nothing. Also the deity's exercise of "will" and "power" would easily transfer to a European context and be applied to marginalized groups back home. Abroad these "supernatural beings" (p.155) need not consult those they reign over making the point that the lack of communication in this case is based on arrogance. That underneath Kurtz has slipped out of control is emphasised when he moves from his "appeal to every altruistic sentiment" with his final call to "[E]xterminate all the brutes" even if it is unclear who "the brutes" are. This declaration is also given emphasis through Conrad's use of delayed-decoding by deliberately placing it at the end of Kurtz's "eloquent" manifesto. Ironically, this personified 'heart of darkness' is a product of European civilisation. Although ambiguous, Conrad's use of Kurtz to portray the prevailing view that some people can be categorised as a sub-species, whether these be men, women or even whole nations, does anticipate some of the horrors that this view led to in the 20th.Century.

The 'Suppression of Savage Customs' should also be set against the scene where Marlow, on coming to Kurtz's outpost, perceives what he first thought were "half-a-dozen slim posts remained in a row, and with their upper ends ornamented with round carved balls" (p.157). Through a series of sense impressions and the technique of delayed-decoding Conrad is making us aware that Kurtz had tipped over the edge and moved beyond the experience of his inner narrator. We are later informed that on closer look "I saw my mistake. These round knobs were not ornamental but symbolic" (p.164), they then turn out to be "heads on the stakes". Ironically this "blow" to Marlow is explained in an almost casual sense as a "mistake" in his perception. Here Conrad lays out for his 19th. Century readers real "Suppression" in action while at the same time giving a clue as to who might be the "brutes" mentioned elsewhere.

In the end Marlow realizes his "mistake" but what about the "mistake" by Europeans of the day that swallow the propaganda that the actions of their fellows in Africa were a "power for good" or, even more laughably, that they were engaged purely in the "Suppression of Savage Customs". Furthermore, "one knob of wood" had become " black, dried, sunken, with closed eyelids, - a head that seemed to sleep at the top of that pole, and, with shrunken dry lips showing a narrow white line of the teeth, was smiling too, smiling continuously at some endless and jocose dream of that eternal slumber". Here savage actions are deliberately contained within the everyday normalcy of "sleep...smiling...dream" and "slumber". Conrad's language is stripped and paired down giving this unfamiliar scene the effect of the familiar that helps to add to the horror on the part of the reader. What is later described as Kurtz's "unsound method" (p.169) that worried the manager is laid bare for the readers through similes and euphemisms that force home the so called "subtle horrors" (p.165) of the imperialist enterprise.

Conrad then juxtaposes reality with the unreal when the "manager" states "that there was nothing exactly profitable in these heads being there. They only showed that Mr Kurtz lacked restraint in the gratification of his various lusts" (p.164). Having already undermined the "efficiency" of the imperialist enterprise Conrad now makes plain that some of the actions of the colonists need not even be "profitable". The system of beliefs supporting imperialism is gradually unfolded throughout the work as "hollow at the core" (p.165) just as Kurtz himself is described. Conrad seems to be suggesting that there is a thin veneer overlaying civilised behaviour that had been pierced in Kurtz's case and, as a warning to others, that the 'wilderness had found him out early... I think it had whispered to him things about himself which he did not know' (p.164). Underneath we are no better than the worst savage as Marlow's part in the civilising mission that is now a "fantastic invasion" becomes a probing into the human consciousness.

When speaking about the journey earlier in the work Marlow states that "[I]t seemed somehow to throw a kind of light on everything about me - and into my thoughts" to which he adds, using repetition as emphasis, "not very clear either. No, not very clear" (p.107). It is also a journey into his inner-self but as always with Marlow what he sees is opaque or "not very clear". What we know about ourselves is held up to question and also that the world about us may not be as we think. Conrad repeatedly questions what we think we actually see which is emphasised when Marlow tells his audience that 'the head that appeared near enough to be spoken to seemed at once to have leaped away from me into inaccessible distance' (p.165). The image of the leaping head is brought to us again by the narrative technique of delayed-decoding adding to the reader's horror of Kurtz's actions.

In conclusion, Conrad questions the right of any one nation to subjugate and occupy another with the concomitant cruelty it entails. He also exposes the use of press propaganda to sustain morally corrupt colonial missions of no matter what stripe. That any man might use the mask of a duty to country or company to excuse responsibilities for his actions is also persistently undermined. In making the point of the circularity of history he draws a distinct link between the actions and behaviour of previous defunct empires and their 19th. Century equivalents. In Conrad's world there is no get out clause for the colonizing powers in the form of a civilizing role or the mask of bringing 'efficiency' in the scramble for Africa. He also warns his readers that power over these subjugated peoples abroad rests on "an accident arising from the weakness of others" (p.107). To make a more general point, history shows us that this relative "weakness of others" can be seen as a very unstable base to underpin any society at home or abroad, especially within the context of the approach of a brand new century and the expectations that were inherent in this. If Conrad questions what we think we see around us, and even our own inner 'thoughts', then surely much about 19th. Century beliefs, and the society that spawned them, are open to question as well. Despite his use throughout of opaque language and ellipses it is hard to believe that Conrad was not aware of the parallels between his attack on imperialist ideology and the inequities of power that existed at a more domestic level

He also pinpoints the notion that a woman might rely on a man but Marlow feels emasculated by his reliance on an 'aunt'. Also, the colonizers are depicted as in fear of a woman from a different culture despite their armed advantages over the natives. Through these examples we can see that at home and abroad Conrad takes up the gender issue of emasculation of the male. Elsewhere we find examples such as women's identity, appearances and their general lack of power. The ambiguity that is structured into both novels allows a wide range of interpretation that also encourages the reader to extend beyond the particular in each case. Both Conrad and Chopin blur the gender boundaries while Conrad can be seen to attack imperialism in such a way as to include other issues mentioned. Likewise, I'm sure that Chopin would be aware of the racial implications in Edna's pursuit of an individual identity in a segregated society.

Bibliography

Chopin, K. (2000) *The Awakening*, Oxford University Press, Oxford.

Conrad, J. (2002) *Heart of Darkness*, Oxford, University Press, Oxford.

Regan, S. (2001) *The Nineteenth Century Novel: A Critical Reader*, Routledge, London.

Further Reading

Walder, D. (2002) *Identities*, Routledge, London.

Chapter Five

Dissonance: Societal, Sexual and Generational within Dangerous Acquaintances. (De Laclose, C.),

A Vindication of the Rights of Woman. (Wollstonecraft, M.), Fathers and Sons. (Turgenev, I.), Selected Stories. (Mansfield, K.).

Part One

The epistolary form of the novel *Dangerous Acquaintances* while appearing to Laclos's readers to be authenticated truth also lends itself to the art of duplicity between the main protagonists [de Laclos, C. (1989), Ark Paperbacks, London. (All references are to this novel unless otherwise stated)]. The latter in this case being an art that is honed and utilized for what can be seen as an attack, conducted on military terms, against the character and being of both the young convent educated Cecile and the married woman Madame de Tourvel. The task of the libertine Valmont, and his co-conspirator Madame de Merteuil is made all the more easier by the previously cloistered existence of their intended victims. Laclos not only tackles the general lack of both education and preparedness for life of such as these women but also, in the words of the translator Richard Aldington, 'Laclos intended [the] work as an attack on the upper classes of the *ancien regime*' (*Introduction*, p.4).

There is also a thread throughout the work attacking what are in effect a male dominated Church, its teachings, and its role in subjugating women in general. As well as all of this part of Laclos's didactic intent is to show us a society whereby men such as Valmont, for no other reason than that he is a male member of this ruling elite, can feel free to put the two women mentioned under a sustained attack both in a moral and physical sense. From a feminine perspective, this is the power of the patriarchy at its worst and Laclos shows this as leading directly to the extensive use of duplicity on the part of women placed in such a position. In fact we find throughout the work that duplicitous behaviour is one of the very few means of defence at the disposal of the two targets in question. At various points Laclos manages to bring to the surface feminist issues that would not be out of place right up to the present day and such as this can be seen as quite a departure from the accepted norm on the part of a male author writing in the latter half of the 18th. Century.

Right from the opening letter Laclos lays out for his readers the unpreparedness for the real world of the young Cecile. In words that can be seen to be heavy with irony he opens her letter to her friend Sophie with, '[Y]ou will see, my dear, that I have kept my word and that bonnets and pompoms do not take up all my time – there will always be some left over for you' (p.65). Laclos's use of 'bonnets and pompoms' helps readers enter into Cecile's childlike world and effectively spells out an existence that verges on the useless. Heaping on the irony, Cecile sees all of this as an improvement on her previous convent existence as 'Mamma' now 'asks my opinion in everything and treats me much less like a school-girl than she used to'. The irony is further enhanced when this is followed by her mother's dictum that she has 'to see her every day when she gets up; that I need not arrange my hair until dinner time because we shall always be alone, and that she will tell me every day when I am to join her in the afternoon'. It is easy to see that the prescriptive existence of the convent has been replaced by a no less prescriptive domestic routine. Instead of the nuns 'policing' her every movement it is now the mother's turn to take on this role.

It is a change from a girl who has been previously institutionalized through a convent education to a girl who's life now revolves around 'bonnets and pom-poms', her appearance, and where she may be at any designated time of the day. The irony is lost on Cecile that she has graduated from the institutionalized 'school-girl' to, what for her, is now an institutionalized domestic ornament. Her expectation is that she will now be married off as 'Mamma has told me so often that a young lady should remain at the convent until she is married' (p.66). The point that Laclos is making is how much all of this prepares any 'young lady' for their future dealings with the opposite sex. It is almost as if the system employed is bent on preparing young girls for what their mothers hope may never happen to them.

By the second letter readers are introduced to the forces that are gathering around Cecile. That the conspiracy to subvert Cecile's honour is kick-started by another woman only adds to the corrupt image of late 18th. Century French society, a point embellished as the work progresses. On the one hand we have the innocent who has been contained in a convent to prepare her for whatever the future holds in store for her, and on the other, we have those who will take advantage of the norms that they helped to set up and work to keep in place. In line with these norms Madame de Merteuil sums up Cecile with the words, she 'is really pretty, she is only fifteen; a rosebud; ignorant to a degree and entirely unaffected' (p 68). Her looks, age, virginal status, lack of education and her other worldliness, are all brought together as qualities to attract the libertine Valmont. Along with these virtues possessed by Cecile Merteuil also stresses 'the income of sixty thousand *livres* which goes with the Volanges girl'. This combination of money, innocence, beauty and obedience to others may be attractive to a future husband but Laclos is making the ironic point that these virtues in a young girl are also attractive to the likes of sexual predators such as Valmont, while at the same time making her more easily exploitable. In fact it is the very lack of experience and knowledge of the outside world in a girl with a cloistered education that can leave this 'rosebud' susceptible to being *deflowered* by the more experienced Valmont.

Laclos portrays Cecile to us as a child-woman available as a financial and sexual commodity to any passing male with the right social connections. Also, as the novel is written in the contemplative form of a series of letters, giving it the feel of the private thoughts and truthfulness between the individuals involved, Laclos can harnesses these qualities within the work to stunt the actions of a censorious elite. The epistolary form also allows him to utilize the imagination of the reader to give his work an erotic content while at the same time giving the lower orders in French society an insight into the real world of their ruling elite. What their betters are up to, and the erotic content of the work, can also be seen as part of the design to keep the attention of readers. By harnessing the imagination of his readers in this way Laclos can then further his didactic intent to undermine the *ancien regime* and at the same time lay out the more obvious disadvantages that a young girl can labour under. That Cecile was born into wealth is seen as no defence against the forces that are gathering around and ready to destroy her, a point that would not be lost on women lower down the pecking order in 18th. Century France.

In Letter III Cecile's lack of control over her future is portrayed to us as almost total. On the important question of whom she might marry she states 'I am still kept in ignorance, my dear' (p.68). She also complains of being subjected to the male gaze with the words 'for it must be very difficult not to blush when a man looks steadily at you' (p.69). Cecile is on display for others to inspect as if some less than rare commodity. Laclos then emphasizes this idea with 'I think I heard two or three times the word "Pretty" followed by "Awkward" and later, as if she is not even present "[W]e must let her ripen". Cecile recognizes that her purpose in life is the marriage stakes and all she can wonder is 'I wish I knew what is to be'. What Laclos is pedantically laying out for his readers is that she has been carefully conditioned over her still young life to accept this lack of control over her future by the nuns, her family, and also the prevailing customs and mores of the society surrounding her. Cecile knows, and so do the adults around her, that she is very nearly powerless to resist whatever they might inflict on her.

Writing to Merteuil Valmont recognizes her lack of sophistication and naivety with the comment '[T]o seduce a girl who has seen and knows nothing, who (so to speak) would be handed over to me defenceless' (Letter IV p.70) is to him a prize so easily attained that she is not worth the effort. In just a few words a libertine sums up Cecile's unpreparedness for life. In opposition to those nearest to her this outsider sees Cecile's lack of an all-encompassing education and her innocence as making her 'defenceless' against any passing sexual predator. For Valmont what is worth the effort is 'Madame de Tourvel, her religious devotion, her conjugal love, her austere principles. That is what I am attacking; that is the enemy worthy of me; that is the end I mean to reach;' (p.70). In military terms he is 'attacking' what are in fact the abstracts that define a married woman's qualities in this society. A society that demands these 'principles' be in place only to then allow her to be destroyed for having them. Valmont also sees women as part of women's problems '[I]t is fortunate for us that women are so weak in their own defence' (p.71). This being a point about the feminine condition many of those later feminists who followed would agree with wholeheartedly. Through Valmont's own words the lower orders in 18th. Century France can now begin to see an aristocracy that once fought for their country as reduced to seeing a woman's virtue as the 'enemy'. The ambiguity in all of this allows others to see this militaristic campaign against a virtuous woman as a metaphor attacking the moral bankruptcy of the *ancien regime*.

Throughout the work Laclos portrays Merteuil in a very different light to Cecile, a girl driven by her feelings and emotions, similarly Madame de Tourvel with the added problem of being a woman endangered by her own 'principles'. Merteuil attacks religion, a set of beliefs that she perceives as stupefying women in general. To Valmont she states, 'your prude is religious with the sort of religion which condemns a woman to perpetual childishness' (Letter V p.73). By women adhering to 'religious' precepts she sees them as being condemned to 'perpetual childishness' a condition that would open them up to control by others, something that is obviously alien to Merteuil. Although 'twenty-two and has been married nearly two years' de Tourvel can still be seen by another woman as nearer Cecile's immature fifteen-years. Laclos has now added religion to the other handicaps of innocence and a lack of a substantial and balanced education that opens up such as these two women to damage by others. At the same time he can be seen as putting into place a platform from which to mount an attack on the notion of romantic love, especially through the characters of Valmont and Merteuil.

For Merteuil seduction equals duplicity. She sees that for women in general 'some sort of pretext is necessary; and what could be more convenient for us than a pretext which makes us appear to yield to force' (Letter X p.81). In fact her preference is for 'a sharp and well conducted attack, where everything is carried out with order but with rapidity'. A military person would recognize 'force...attack...rapidity' as the language of military manoeuvres but in this case it is a sexually experienced woman's perspective on the male art of seduction. Any linking of romance and seduction are not a consideration for Merteuil, for her it is more a woman pretending to be the victim of near rape for what can only be deduced as for appearances sake. Furthermore, all of this 'preserves an air of violence even in those things we grant, and cunningly flatters our two favourite passions – the glory of defence and the pleasure of defeat'. Even an 'air of violence' can only be interpreted as near physical coercion while mock 'defence' is a veil put up for the dubious reality that the woman is in control throughout her seduction. Here Laclos raises the question, what kind of society demands of a woman that she has to only appear to be giving in to what in fact she wants to happen? Also, is the 'air of violence' just a sham, contributed to by the woman, to give the male a feeling of physical strength and sexual potency? If so it can be seen to be a situation that could very quickly spin out of control for any woman. All of these points have to be set against Merteuil's willingness to place Cecile in the hands of Valmont knowing the limitations of this fifteen-year-old child's well trumpeted lack of experience. Despite her ability to work the system in a man's world it is hard to see Merteuil as an early prototype for any feminists that followed.

Throughout the work Madame de Tourvel is depicted as being of utmost concern that any written evidence of communications between herself and Valmont do not fall into the wrong hands. This also happens to give Laclos's epistolary form an air of artistic authenticity, or even a primary source of evidence, whereby the letters have been dredged up through either research or discovered by accident. Adding to the work's supposed authenticity Merteuil demands evidence of a successful seduction of Madame de Tourvel in the form of written communications. In Letter XX to Valmont she states, '[A]s soon as you have had your fair devotee, and can furnish me with proof, come, and I am yours. But you know that in important matters only written proofs are accepted' (pp. 96/97). In this context the euphemism of 'had' is a fairly obvious reference to sexual intercourse that also drains the act of any romantic connotations. Furthermore , what is essentially a private act between two people has to be dragged into the public arena as she demands, '[C]ome, come as soon as you can and bring me the proof of your triumph – like our noble knights of old who laid at their ladies' feet the brilliant fruits of their victory' (p.97). Again we have the need for written 'proof' and the misuse of militaristic language that ironically undercuts, by elevating, the boudoir antics of the *brave* Valmont.

On his part he sees letters of communication as an important element in the process of encircling de Tourvel in a web of blackmail in order to seduce her. 'I should be certain that from the moment my fair one consents to write to me I shall have nothing more to fear from her husband, since she will already be compelled to deceive him' (Letter XL p.139). In this case a woman's fear of loss of virtue in the face of the public puts her in the position of having to succumb to the loss of that very virtue. Ironically de Tourvel recognizes all of this in a letter to Valmont with the words 'what woman could admit she was in correspondence with you! And what virtuous woman can make up her mind to do what she feels she will compelled to hide?' (Letter XLIII p.141) It is no accident that both Valmont and de Tourvel use the term 'compelled' in relation to women and duplicitous behaviour. As part of wearing her down to entrap her he is always placing de Tourvel on the back foot, a condition that most women in her class would recognize. Throughout the work Laclos is laying out for us a society whose values are so one sided, and hypocritical, that is very hard to see any redeeming features in it even if the woman has the supposed protection of wealth.

Earlier Merteuil touches on sexual ambiguity within herself and Cecile. '[S]he is naturally very caressing, and I sometimes amuse myself with her; she grows excited with incredible facility; and she is all the more amusing because she knows nothing, absolutely, nothing, of what she so much wishes to know.' (Letter XXXVIII p.131) Cecile's innocence, and a lack of a substantial education, have left her a blank page for both Merteuil and Valmont to work on. She is tactile, easily 'excited', and completely ignorant of sexual matters, what better combination could these two predators wish for. Furthermore, Cecile's lack of 'character nor principles' adds to this image of being a blank page, or a void, ready to be filled in but then Merteuil also states that '[S]he is really delicious!' Again Merteuil is giving us an insight to her character that can be seen to add to uncertainty surrounding her own sexuality. In a letter to her friend Sophie Cecile gives us her perspective of her developing relationship with Merteuil. '[A]t least I can love her as much as I like without there being anything wrong in it, and it gives me a great deal of pleasure. However, we have agreed that I am to appear to not love her so much in front of other people, especially in front of Mamma' (Letter XXXIX p.133). Cecile's efforts to conceal her feelings for Merteuil are a sign of corruption beginning to take root. Also, through her duplicitous behaviour we again have women living out a sham existence just to suit the customs and mores put in place by this society.

Cecile's confused sexual identity is later elaborated on in Letter LV to her friend Sophie. Love and friendship are becoming intermingled as she leaves behind her convent friendship with Sophie. She states 'but the friendship I am speaking about I feel for Madame de Merteuil. It seems to me that I love her more like Danceny than like you, and sometimes I wish she were he...the truth is that between them they make me happy' (p.165). Here Laclos gives us a young girl whose sexuality is in a state of flux that in effect opens her up to the charms of Merteuil. In an opaque way she is seen to be attracted sexually to both the male and females in her life but this attraction is seen by her to be clearly different to her convent 'friendship' with Sophie. A further point is that, from the perspective of a censorious society, any form of a sexual attraction between two women would be seen as transgressing the boundaries of both societal and literary taste but at the same time it would be seen by some women as nearer their own reality. Furthermore, taking into account the 18th. Century context within which the book was written, Merteuil's willingness to prostitute herself by offering herself as a sexual reward for the downfall of another woman, and then go on to sexually seduce a fifteen-year-old girl, would in fact do very little for the cause of the *ancien regime.*

While Merteuil is shown to have both reason and control over her life Laclos's character displays nothing but contempt for those 'unbalanced women who rave of their "sentiment" (Letter LXXXI p. 222). For her the war between the sexes is both physical and, specifically, dangerous for women. In contrast to her position, Merteuil tells Valmont '[Y]ou fought without risk and necessarily acted without wariness. For you men defeats are simply so many victories the less. In this unequal struggle our fortune is not to lose and your misfortune not to win' (p.221). In short, society's rules surrounding sexual seduction are rigged against women and in favour of men. For Merteuil these 'unbalanced women' are engaged in a high risk 'unequal struggle' that they are totally unprepared for. Unlike her their intellectual processes are suspect because they are driven by "sentiment", suffer from an 'excited imagination' and have 'never reflected' (p.222).

In contrast to these foolish women who are slaves to their emotions, Merteuil has her 'principles' (p 223) to guide her and these are the result of her own 'profound meditations'. Not only has she created her own principles, she further states 'I am my own work'. This can be seen as a reflection on the ability of an individual to step outside of themselves, in the first instance imagine who they are, their potential, and then to become that person. Through this extraordinary character, Laclos is also subverting the view of God as her maker by giving her God like qualities in her own creation. She also understands the danger in any communications with a man being turned against women at a later date. They are 'those sweet letters which are so dangerous to write' (p.223). Furthermore, she deliberately sets herself apart from these other 'women who are not afraid to confide these proofs of their weakness to the person who causes them, imprudent women, who cannot see their future enemy in their present lover'. Again we have the vision of weak women willingly giving themselves over on a platter to a 'future enemy' through the propensity of men to utilize their communications in the form of blackmail. While men are portrayed as blackmailing control freaks most women are seen as driven by emotion rather than reason and even if true in some respects it is a very bleak view, especially in respect of the male of the species.

Merteuil sees herself as the polar opposite to these women, from earlier on in her life she had taken the time to 'observe and reflect' (p.223) and as regards to 'love and its pleasure' she had no 'desire to enjoy, I wanted to know' (p 224). This is a woman who would agree to some extent with, what we see later, Wollstonecraft's vision of a self-educated woman with the ability to reason and who was guided by her own principles, not the opinion or views of others. Her lack of feeling would be one area where Wollstonecraft would differ with a character such as this in real life. Merteuil sees herself as an original, a prototype, 'since I was born to avenge my sex and to dominate yours, I must have created methods unknown to anybody but myself' (p.222). Her reason and lack of feeling are her defence against becoming the victim of men and suffering, what she sees as, the curse of degradation that so many women have experienced. Even if men can be said to have asked for this, without considered change it is still only a recipe for perpetual dissonance between the sexes.

For Valmont, without the well-honed skills of Merteuil, women are nothing more than performing animals to be pushed and prodded where he wills. Writing to Merteuil he states 'I like to see, to watch this prudent woman impelled, without her perceiving it, upon a path which allows no return, and whose steep and dangerous incline carries her on in spite of herself, and forces her to follow me. There, terrified by the peril she runs, she would like to halt and cannot check herself' (Letter XCVI p. 260). For this otherwise 'prudent woman' any form of love for such as Valmont outside of marriage leaves her exposed and 'terrified by the peril she runs'. Adding to this internal determinist force within de Tourvel we have the 'steep and dangerous incline' of external determinist forces set up by men such as Valmont that 'forces her' to act against her own self-interest. He then makes it plain that she is there purely to be used: '[T]he time will come only too soon when, degraded by her fall, she will be nothing but an ordinary woman to me' (p.261). Her ordinariness in this case is the loss of her 'prudent woman' status, in other words his satisfaction requires that her virtue has to be 'degraded' in the eyes of society. Valmont also needs 'to see, to watch' (p.260) to satisfy his voyeuristic instincts but that is not all, he has to then see her break on the wheel that he has carefully set in place.

He later elaborates in Letter CX on his philosophy towards women in general through the character of Cecile. Here he cynically corrupts to then destroy what is still only a child/woman. By now Valmont sees himself to be in a position to 'accelerate her education' (p.305). Further commodifying Cecile he refuses to give her a Christian name, she is 'the scholar [that] has become almost as learned as the master. Yes, truly, I have taught her everything, including the complaisances' (p.306). She has now been trained to acquiesce, to please, and it is notable that Valmont states her new skills in the plural. His leisure hours are divided between attempting to seduce de Tourvel, whom he also tends not to give a name to, and 'in composing a kind of catechism of sensuality for the use of my scholar. I amuse myself by naming everything by the technical word; and I laugh in advance at the interesting conversation this will furnish between her and Gercourt on the first night of their marriage...She does not imagine that anyone can speak otherwise.' A listing of religious principles by use of the word 'catechism' becomes a summary of sex based 'sensuality' but more than that he goes on to corrupt the very language of love that the girl might otherwise have used.

Laclos's use of 'naming everything by the technical word' leaves very little to his reader's imagination, transgresses prevailing literary taste, and sails close to what one would think any 18th. Century censor might allow. For Valmont Cecile has now become no better than an unpaid prostitute as we can see reiterated in Letter CXV. He can now 'make use of her...absolutely as my own property, and without any more difficulty to obtain from her what one does not even dare to exact from all the women who make their living by it' (p.316). Over time Cecile has been so conditioned sexually by Valmont that she now services him with what even a paid prostitute might baulk at. Merteuil takes up this theme in an earlier letter. Speaking in relation to Cecile she sees her future as a 'facile woman' with a 'facility of stupidity which yields without knowing how or why, solely because it is attached and does not know how to resist. These sorts of women are absolutely nothing but pleasure machines' (Letter CVI p.295) Feminists down the years would agree with Merteuil on the need to 'know how to resist' on the part of women but it is a bit rich knowing how these co-conspirators have conditioned this fifteen-year-old girl to suit their respective purposes. This societal situation of 'women as pleasure machines' can only come about by this ruling elite's insistence on a cloistered existence for their young girls that inevitably leads to an ignorant unpreparedness for the real world awaiting them.

In the character of Valmont, Laclos shows us an aristocracy who instead of fighting the external enemy are now only intent on using their talents in the art of seduction. By Letter CXXV he can now boast to Merteuil of his successful seduction of Madame de Tourvel, '[S]he is conquered, that proud woman who dared to think she could resist me! (p.335) For Valmont her carefully constructed 'virtue' is no defence to a sustained attack in fact it only 'increases a woman's value even in her moment of weakness'. Here Laclos is making the point that over her still young life this society has inculcated Madame de Tourvel with certain standards that are now, ironically, highly prized by a libertine. Buttressed only with their pride and 'virtue' Valmont sees women, in general, as being psychologically incapable of resisting his advances and only able to put up 'a more or less well-feigned resistance to the first triumph'. For him they are hard-wired to give way and even in that moment they are duplicitous to both themselves and their lovers. Valmont elaborates this point later when he describes as "prudes" the women he has conquered before as putting up a 'provocative defence [which] never covers but imperfectly the first advances they have made'. For him their 'provocative defence' is only a case of playing to the gallery for the sake of their image and furthermore their 'first advances' betray their own sexual needs. But any woman could say that he would say that wouldn't he as long as it suits his own ulterior motives. Readers already know that this man is a control freak who uses blackmail to entrap a woman and then blames her for then cracking under the pressures applied. The question raised is that if women are hypocrites what does all of this say about male hypocrisy?

The actuality of Valmont's seduction of de Tourvel is again brought to readers using militaristic language. It was no ordinary 'capitulation…it was a complete victory, achieved by a hard campaign and decided by expert manoeuvres' (p.336). But his 'feeling of glory' is needed to stave off the gnawing doubt that he 'might depend in any way upon the very slave I have enslaved myself'. This is a chilling portrayal of a man refusing to give into, or show, any emotions towards this woman and in a sense his fear of becoming the mirror image of what he sees as a weak and emotional woman. As well as seeing women as conditioned by this society it is no great leap to see men such as Valmont as being equally conditioned not to show an emotional side to their own nature. Whether intentional or otherwise, through the character Valmont, Laclos's work gives us a perspective of the male of the species as an incomplete human being. In fact his 'victory' is purely physical; he gives nothing and takes at will. Later we get comparisons with 'Frederic' of Prussia when he says 'I forced the enemy to fight when she wished only to refuse battle', and then patting himself on the back like the narcissist that he is, 'by clever manoeuvres' (p.341). All of this, he believes to have been conducted according to the 'true principles of this war, which we have often remarked is so like the other'. Through the character of Valmont, Laclos is showing his readers the extent to which the French aristocracy had corrupted the 'principles of war' for their own immoral purposes. The seduction of Madame de Tourvel becomes a 'complete victory' (p.336) for Valmont. He does show some feeling towards her and later goes on to say 'I had to make an effort to distract myself' (p.342). He is, in effect, conditioned to give up nothing or is it that his male take on the militaristic rules of engagement do not allow for him to show feeling and emotion in any relationship with a woman?

In conclusion, Laclos's use of the epistolary form serves to show that art itself is duplicitous but it also epitomises the duplicitous nature of the main protagonists that in itself is a reflection of the society they inhabit. By attempting to persuade his readers that these documents are real like most writers he is also trying to persuade people that the events, and the characters, are in themselves real. Through the aesthetics of form, metaphor, ambiguity and irony Laclos is also painting a society that is almost fatally flawed. It is a society that is skewed in favour of, such as, the co-conspirators Valmont and de Merteuil who will abuse whatever powers they possess, including the faculty of reason, to bring down what are essentially two decent women. In fact it is their 'virtues' that makes these women such a prize for any libertine encroaching on their world.

Even de Merteuil recognizes that a lack of experience and a balanced education, a surfeit of emotions, opens up such as Cecile and Madame de Tourvel to circling sexual predators of the like of Valmont. His actions are also an example of the *ancien regime's* warlike skills being allowed to atrophy to the point that they are now directed at women, especially 'virtuous' women. A more telling point on the uselessness of this particular ruling elite is harder to imagine when we take into account the context of a nation that, at this point in its history, was in fact heading into a revolution. As well as a patriarchal society skewing the tactics of war in the direction of these women Laclos also gives us a Church whose religious precepts seem bent on stupefying women in particular. What he makes clear throughout is that what the Church and family don't want to come about is made all the more easier by a cloistered existence that the Church facilitates and the very 'virtues', much prized by libertines, that is foisted onto them from an early age.

Part Two

While Laclos engages with elements of the female condition with some subtlety this is manifestly not the case with Wollstonecraft's sustained rhetorical attack on the disparate values underpinning patriarchal societies. Throughout the work she openly attacks the notion that in some way or other the character and being of a woman is peculiar when set against that of the male. In her own introduction to *A Vindication of the Rights of Woman* [Wollstonecraft, M. (2001), The Modern Library, New York. (All references are to this work unless stated otherwise)] she takes a well-aimed unambiguous kick at what she sees as the root cause of these inequalities existing between men and women. Wollstonecraft states 'I have turned over various books written on the subject of education, and patiently observed the conduct of parents and the management of schools; but what has been the result? – a profound conviction that the neglected education of my fellow-creatures is the grand source of the misery I deplore, and that women, in particular, are rendered weak and wretched by a variety of concurring causes, originating from one hasty conclusion'(p.xxi). For Wollstonecraft women are subjected 'to a false system of education' and this she has 'gathered from books written on this subject by men who, considering females rather as women than as human creatures, have been more anxious to make them alluring mistresses than affectionate wives and rational mothers'. Right from her opening paragraph Wollstonecraft is anxious for her readers to see women as part of a common humanity rather than as some species that is separate from, and different to, the male. It is the whole system, from authors and publications to the 'conduct of parents and the management of schools', which conspires against educational opportunities for women.

She also draws direct comparisons between the wrongs of the aristocracy's hereditary right to rule and the same accident of birth giving the common man rights over women. Another of the props supporting male subjugation of women that comes under attack from Wollstonecraft is religion and its use to this end of biblical interpretation all the way back to Adam and Eve. In the case of male rights over women, for Wollstonecraft it is the end product of 'alluring mistresses' that this male dominated society requires and for this purpose they must first be 'rendered weak and wretched'. A standard education, the equal of one available from the start for men, would give society 'rational mothers' equipped to make choices that would benefit the next generation and at the same time introduce husbands to intellectually equal and 'affectionate wives'. Wollstonecraft's stance on education for women can be seen as introducing changes that would seep into every aspect of society. Her phrase 'human creatures' means what it says, with what she argues later as the exception of physical strength, it is the requirement of absolute equality in other areas between the sexes, not only in the bedroom but out on into society and starting with a girl's rights from birth followed by her education from childhood.

On the question of relative physical strength Wollstonecraft states '[A] degree of physical superiority cannot, therefore, be denied, and it is a noble prerogative! But not content with this natural pre-eminence, men endeavour to sink us still lower, merely to render us alluring objects for a moment; and women, intoxicated by the adoration which men, under the influence of their senses, pay them, do not seek to obtain a durable interest in their hearts, or to become the friends of the fellow-creatures who find amusement in their society' (p.xxii). On the issue of relative physical strength she is giving credit where credit is due but then we have the barbed comment that 'men endeavour to sink us lower'. Right from the outset Wollstonecraft's rhetoric is also aimed as much towards the women who see their power in sexual attraction as to the men who have conspired to turn them into nothing better than a sexual commodity.

Here women come in for open criticism, they are 'intoxicated by the adoration of men' and if men are driven by 'their senses' what does a woman's 'intoxicated' state say about them? Within this framework both sexes are in it for the ephemeral 'moment' when we question how long these women will be 'alluring objects'. Wollstonecraft is also making the point that women could move from being 'objects' to 'friends' of the opposite sex, a more than subtle change that would give women greater equality within the generality of relationships. Also, any notion of equality between the sexes would question the religious precept that women should love, honour, and obey, within marriage, a cornerstone in what was a Christian, legal, ceremony. Furthermore, Wollstonecraft would know that, in a social sense, the idea of equality between the sexes, within or without marriage, was bound to frighten the horses in the patriarchal societies existing in Britain and right across Europe at the end of the 18th. Century.

She does see both men and women as being conditioned differently towards marriage. In her chapter titled 'The State of Degradation to which Woman is Reduced', she states 'men, in their youth, are prepared for professions, and marriage is not considered as a grand feature in their lives; whilst women, on the contrary, have no other scheme to sharpen their faculties.'(p.54) The 'contrary' for women is '[T]o rise in the world, and have the liberty of running from pleasure to pleasure, they must marry advantageously, and to this object their time is sacrificed, and their persons often legally prostituted.' (Pp.54/55) While men have duties that may 'sharpen their faculties' and open them up to wider horizons women are often reduced to the narrow pursuit of 'pleasure'. Furthermore, Wollstonecraft's deliberate linking of marrying 'advantageously', 'their persons' and 'prostituted' seems to be warning women that the state of marriage under these circumstances is nothing better than a form of legal prostitution. There is also an element of sarcastic irony attached to her use of 'liberty' when it is couched in terms only associated with 'pleasure'.

Later Wollstonecraft touches on the possibilities for gradual descent into prostitution on the part of a single girl. Speaking of mistresses she makes the case that having 'personal fidelity' still requires that '[T]he woman who is faithful to the father of her children demands respect, and should not be treated like a prostitute' (p.67). Although she goes on to say that this is not an attack on the institution of marriage it is also certain that in an 18th. Century context this very reasonable stance would not wash with the powers that be. Whether it is the man himself, or society, or both, that would treat her 'like a prostitute' is left open to question. One thing we can say is that a woman in this position would depend far too much on the goodwill of the man in question and, due to the moral strictures of the time, how much help could she expect from anyone else? Wollstonecraft then deals with young girls drawn into vice, a major industry in Britain's large cities during 18th. and 19th. Century. These girls are *'ruined* before they know the difference between virtue and vice, and thus prepared by their education for infamy, they become infamous. Asylums and Magdalens are not the proper remedies for these abuses. It is justice, not charity, that is wanting in the world!'

There is a theme within *Vindication* that women are educated to utilize their bodies in or out of marriage and this is summed up in the term 'education for infamy', so the logic of Wollstonecraft's case is no wonder they then 'become infamous'. With them 'having no other means of support, prostitution becomes her only refuge' which neatly makes the point that the ill-educated woman is prone to living on the edge of disaster. Society's answer is to contain such '*ruined*' women in 'Asylums', as if they were mad, or 'Magdalens' (see notes p.206), institutions that were built for the sole purpose of holding what must have been a large number of prostitutes. Either way it gets these women out of sight and into a 'charity' that in effect could then open them up to further abuses, a solution that late 18th. Century women readers could well imagine. In a statement that would raise eyebrows, even in the 21st. Century, Wollstonecraft brings together the sexual status of women in or out of the marriage contract with this all 'arises in a great degree from the state of idleness in which women are educated, who are always taught to look up to a man for a maintenance, and to consider their persons as a proper return for his exertions to support them.' (p.67). To use the words 'consider their persons as a proper return' is to equate a woman's body to a 'return' on investments made. It then beggars the imagination as how this might have gone down among women in society who saw themselves as above all of this. But it is fair to say that Wollstonecraft forces ostensibly respectable women to face up to the notion that some of them may be prepared to become a bought sexual commodity.

In opposition to possible female descent into 'infamy' she later attacks the deliberate use of 'ridiculous falsities' (p.126) to keep children in ignorance of the human reproductive cycle. This Wollstonecraft believes is done for 'mistaken notions of modesty' when in fact '[C]hildren very early see cats with their kittens, birds with their young ones, etc. Why then are they not to be told that their mothers carry and nourish them in the same way?' A more daring point buried in this is that it would almost certainly raise the very act of procreation in their young minds. In general Wollstonecraft believes that 'it is best to tell them the truth' as they would only find out eventually through 'improper company' such as 'ignorant servants'. The main thrust of her argument seems to be that a form of sex education at an early age, especially for young girls, might save them from a great deal of heartache on reaching sexual maturity.

Like Laclos, Wollstonecraft sees the existing feminine character as a construct of society but, due to the rhetorical nature of her work, she can be much clearer that it is a construct of character that is sexual in nature. Under the chapter title of 'The Prevailing Opinion of a Sexual Character Discussed' she states '[W]omen are told from their infancy, and taught by the example of their mothers, that a little knowledge of human weakness, justly termed cunning, softness of temper, *outward* obedience, and a scrupulous attention to a puerile kind of propriety, will obtain for them the protection of a man; and should they be beautiful, everything else is needless, for at least twenty years of their lives' (p.11). She manages to condense into a single sentence arguments surrounding the female condition that go back through the millennia and some that in fact still exist to this day. The verbs 'told' and 'taught' brings to the surface the 'policing' of women by their mothers. That it is all done 'from their infancy' shows the seriousness of intent, on the mother's part, that also manages to include mothers in the blame game for the condition of women in general within this society. Girls are 'taught from infancy' that the traits required, to 'obtain the protection of a man', as if nothing else is needed, is 'cunning', a willingness to give way in the face of a man that is exemplified by a 'softness of temper' and, using the double emphasis inherent in italics, a duplicitous appearance of '*outward* obedience'. In defence of mothers maybe they see that if they inculcate other than these qualities into their daughters then they would be up against forces that could in fact destroy them. But then it all also hinges on whether their daughters are 'beautiful' or otherwise.

Taken in the context of a late 18th. Century reading there is a certain sarcasm in any woman relying on the 'protection of man' when Wollstonecraft gives so much space in her work to the need for well-educated independent women. That men are not to be relied upon is made clear in that he requires looks and that these may offer a woman his 'protection' for 'at least twenty years'. It is not only the '*outward*' appearance of looks and 'obedience' that matters for a woman's well-being but she must also pay 'scrupulous attention to a puerile propriety'. For Wollstonecraft any straying on a woman's part from society's customs and mores could have consequences on how her character might be perceived by those around her.

Later she attacks the lack of reason underpinning male attitudes towards what they consider 'propriety' on the part of a woman. She states '[M]en, indeed, appear to me to act in a very unphilosophical manner, when they try to secure the good conduct of women by attempting to keep them always in a state of childhood' (p.12). Wollstonecraft later reiterates the notion of women being kept in a permanent 'state of childhood' when she states that 'one-half of the human race should be encouraged to remain with listless inactivity and stupid acquiescence' rendering them, '[T]o remain, it may be said, innocent; they mean in a state of childhood' (p.56). In Wollstonecraft's eyes the 'Sexual Character' of woman now becomes 'stupid acquiescence' and 'a state of childhood', a 'state' that would render them powerless over their own person and, more seriously for women, sexually malleable to male intent.

In her attack on this conditioning of women suitable for male intent Wollstonecraft states that 'great men [are] often lead by their senses' (p.12) and that this leads them into 'inconsistencies'. She places Milton in this category and sees 'inconsistencies' mirrored in his great work *Paradise Lost*. To make her point on the foibles of 'great men' Wollstonecraft leads her attack with a quote of his description of 'Eve with *perfect beauty* adorn'd' whose position in relation to Adam is defined as '*Unargued* I obey; so God ordains; /God is *thy law, thou mine*: to know no more/Is Woman's *happiest* knowledge and her *praise*,' (p.12). For Milton the ignorance inherent in 'to know no more' is all that is required of a woman by 'God' or man, and we can deduce from all of this also the Church of his day. After all if God bestows looks on a woman all she has to do is 'obey' silently and be happy about it. Also, '*thou mine*' effectively hands ownership of her person over to the man. In other words a permanent 'state of childhood' allied to subservience is the order of the day for this particular 'great' man.

All of this is set against an Adam who is later shown to be not entirely satisfied with these subservient qualities in Eve. Furthermore, Wollstonecraft's double indenting through italics only adds to the obvious sarcasm in the quotes used. Through selective quoting there is a definite intent on the part of Wollstonecraft to not only undermine Milton's philosophical stance but also the role of the Established Church that supports female inequality in just about all matters. Here we see the arguments supporting the male patriarchal edifice, justifying women's position as a sub-species, goes all the way back to biblical interpretation of God's word. Although the contradictory version still portrays Eve as unequal when seen through Adam's eyes there are some substantial riders added with,

> 'Hast Thou not made me here Thy substitute,
> And these inferior far beneath me set?
> Among *unequals* what society Can sort, what harmony or true delight?
> Which must be mutual, in proportion due
> Given and received; but in *disparity*
> The one intense, the other still remiss
> Cannot well suit with either, but soon prove
> Tedious alike; of *fellowship* I speak
> Such as I seek, fit to participate
> All rational delight' (p.13).

Having argued the case for inequality between men and women by virtue of God's will Milton now seems to believe that in reality God has made a hash of it. He still labours the point that God has made man his 'substitute' on earth 'And these inferior far beneath me set' suggests that women, in the form of Eve, are still to be regarded as 'inferior' to a biblical Adam. Milton then portrays a dawning realization on the part of the first man on earth that all of this inequality has the effect of diminishing 'harmony or true delight'. Here he also recognises the principle of mutuality in relationships with, the pleasures of 'true delight' have to be 'mutual, in proportion due /Given and received'. Wollstonecraft's use of double indentation in this extract juxtaposes the reality of *'unequals'* and *'disparity'* that favours men with the necessity of *'fellowship'* between the sexes, something not a million miles from the case already argued earlier by the author.

Her use of apparent contradiction in a leading literary figure like Milton has several effects on her audience. In the first place she is attributing the supposed feminine defect of contradiction to men, while at the same time undermining, or attempting to dent, male reason. In contrast to this, throughout the work Wollstonecraft is using the language of polysyllabic words, and long and sometimes convoluted sentences, to underpin her own austere 'reason'. While attacking the prejudices which are designed to 'secure the good conduct of women' (p.12) and the male 'reason' which supports them, she is also subtly transplanting the supposed gender qualities and defects between the sexes. By closing the gender gap between the sexes Wollstonecraft also happens to emasculate the 'great' Milton. But in defence of Milton he does place us in the skin of an Adam who sees all of this as a 'tedious' basis for a relationship with what the Bible tells us is the only woman on the planet.

Wollstonecraft then continues knocking out further props supporting what was, by any judgement, a society based on partiality. Using the words of the renowned 18th Century economist Adam Smith Wollstonecraft launches an attack on males who see themselves as born to rule over others, including their fellow men. There are obvious parallels between the accident of birth that advantages his target, the aristocracy, over others and the accident of birth that gives man a God given dominion over woman. Smith rightly questions "the great" and "the easy price at which they may acquire the public admiration" (p.53). In this case Wollstonecraft's quoting of Smith can be seen, by extension, to undermine any person's dominion over another, sexual or otherwise. In Smith's words "[B]y what important accomplishments is the young nobleman instructed to support the dignity of his rank, and to render himself worthy of that superiority over his fellow-citizens, to which the virtue of his ancestors had raised them?" Here Wollstonecraft is allying her cause for equality between the sexes to Smith's laying out a case for equality of opportunity in a society that to all intents and purposes would become a meritocracy for all.

He goes on to question the "important accomplishments" that these men actually possess by virtue of birth by listing the talents he deems necessary for a man to rise in society. These are "[I]s it by knowledge, by industry, by patience, by self-denial, or by virtue of any kind". Readers can begin to see that, once people begin to question the unequal status of women, to make any progress in this matter it may be necessary to re-order society in general. In the context of the 1790s this demand for equality, in her case sexual and in Smith's case male and class based, would be political dynamite and we can be sure that Wollstonecraft would know this. Even the title she has chosen for her book lines her up with Thomas Paine and his work *The Rights of Man*, a radical much hated by the establishment of the day. But within the title of Wollstonecraft's work there is also the sub-text that Paine does not go far enough in relation to women's rights, something that she wishes to rectify.

In support of the absolute need in women to utilize their reason the next paid up member of the 'great men' society that she takes on is Rousseau. Wollstonecraft's preamble to her attack on Rousseau effectively prepares her readers for a demolition job on the 'great' man that entails using the weight of his own words against him, a tactic that she rather favours throughout the work. On the condition of woman and its causes she states, '[I]t would be an endless task to trace the variety of meannesses, cares, and sorrows, into which women are plunged by the prevailing opinion, that they were created rather to feel than reason, and that all the power they obtain must be obtained by their charms and weakness' (pp. 56/57). To show Rousseau's difference with Wollstonecraft's views on the importance of education for women to relieve all of this she directly quotes him with, "[E]ducate women like men and the more they resemble our sex the less power they will have over us" (p.57). They both see 'power' as important but Wollstonecraft easily demolishes Rousseau with '[T]his is the very point I aim at. I do not wish them to have power over men; but over themselves'. For women to have power over their present and future actions, and choices, would make them central to their own being. But her quoting of Rousseau still makes the point, hammered at throughout the work, that men wish to deprive women of a proper education to make them dependent on them.

The motive behind Rousseau's point is that it opens women up to male sexual intent. For Wollstonecraft this state of dependency on men has conditioned them into 'neglecting the duties that reason alone points out, and shrinking from trials calculated to strengthen their minds, they only exert themselves to give their defects a graceful covering'. She then clinches her point that these 'defects' only 'serve to heighten their charms in the eye of the voluptuary' (p.57) Again women are seen to be collaborating in perpetuating their role as decorative and peripheral to their own being. But by drawing 'great' men, such as Rousseau and Milton, into what she sees as the wrong side of the argument is Wollstonecraft also placing her targets in the role of 'the voluptuary'? They can both be clearly seen to be attempting to neuter any progress towards equality of 'power' between the sexes that educating women might bring about. While Wollstonecraft's position is based more on reason than feeling Rousseau's position is shown to be based more on feeling than reason, a neat reversal of supposed gender roles that deftly undermines his case.

The question also arises, what is the 'power' over men that he means, is it as Wollstonecraft sees it to 'feel' rather than 'reason' or is it just that a woman should only rely on her 'charms and weakness'? It does not take much of a leap of imagination to see that, especially for Rousseau, a woman can only really rely on 'power' over men by sexual compliance or as Wollstonecraft makes clear their combination of 'charms and weakness'. In her *Introduction to A Vindication of the Rights of Woman* Katha Pollitt also takes on Rousseau's misogynistic views on women in general. Speaking of *'Emile*, his novel of education, he designs for young Sophie an upbringing calculated to turn her into a docile featherhead' (p.xvi), the precise root point about male power over women that Wollstonecraft labours with throughout her work.

In the chapter titled Writers Who Have Rendered Women Objects of Pity, Bordering on Contempt, Wollstonecraft returns to her attack on Rousseau by again using the weight of his own words against him. He states "women have, or ought to have, but little liberty; they are apt to indulge themselves excessively in what is allowed them. Addicted to everything to extremes, they are even more transported to their diversions than boys" (p.79). For the 'great' French philosopher the obvious question arises, where is the evidence to support what can only be seen as opinions or even bilge. He follows the certainty of "women have" with an opinion "or ought to have" that by any theory of philosophy is rendered useless. To describe the character of women with the deliberate use of the words "excessively...addicted" and "extremes" is just another case of leading his readers by the nose rather than logic.

Rousseau then buries any hope for progress for women's rights when he refers to their lack of "liberty" in the anodyne terms of "habitual restraint" (p.80) and sees this condition as extending over "their whole lives". Knowing the actuality of women's lives he then advises them "[T]he first and most important qualification in a woman is good nature or sweetness of temper: formed to obey a being so imperfect as man, often full of vices, and always full of faults, she ought to learn betimes even to suffer injustice, and bear the insults of a husband without complaint; it is not for his sake, but her own, that she should be of a mild disposition." For Rousseau all of the saintliness has to be on the part of the woman and that no matter what the defects within the male persona they have to bend to them and "obey". Also, it is easy to see that the sub-text to, 'it is not for his sake, but her own, that she should be of mild disposition', is the actuality of a physical threat to any woman who might be otherwise towards a man. For a woman reading these very extensive extracts from Rousseau's writings it is obvious that, for Wollstonecraft, he is an easy target in her aim to undermine through ridicule male misogynistic beliefs.

Wollstonecraft also takes the view that misogynistic attitudes and a general lack of preparedness for life that is epitomised through an unequal education for girls also extends into the death of their parents. 'Girls who have been thus weakly educated are often cruelly left by their parents without any provision, and, of course, are dependent on not only the reason, but the bounty of their brothers'(p.60). Without the support of her parents 'when the brother marries' this necessarily 'docile female' then becomes 'an unnecessary burden on the benevolence of the master of the house and his new partner'. A single girl becomes trapped into a state of dependency for no other reason than being born a woman with, in all probability, no support from the sisterhood in the form of 'his new partner'. Wollstonecraft deliberately employs the language of charity, a charity that totally depends on the 'bounty' or 'benevolence' of a male sibling. As with the Christian God in heaven He giveth and He is also in the position to taketh away. This she aptly describes as 'eating the bitter bread of dependence' (p.61). For Wollstonecraft the status of a bereaved daughter is just another sign of a singular lack of rights for 18th. Century women that extends all the way from birth, childhood, marital choice, and on through their lives.

In her chapter on 'Modesty' she states '[T]o render chastity the virtue from which unsophisticated modesty will naturally flow, the attention should be called away from employments which only exercise the sensibility, and the heart made to beat time to humanity rather than throb with love' (p.122). Here Wollstonecraft effectively disconnects 'chastity' as a virtue from 'modesty' by labelling it 'unsophisticated'. Rightly she does not see these as necessarily linked as in the actuality of life a modest person need not necessarily be chaste or vice versa. Also, the reality of society as it existed in the 18th. Century is that 'chastity' and 'modesty' are mainly to be applied to feminine behaviour making this just another inequality that women have to bear. Here Wollstonecraft is not arguing for an abandonment of 'sensibility' but for the 'heart made to beat time to humanity' rather than the link to the more romantic version of 'love'. It is a much more elevated view of 'sensibility' that brings in all of 'humanity' rather than the 'sensibility' of 'ignorant beings whose time and thoughts have been occupied by gay pleasures, or schemes to conquer hearts'. To emphasise her point she then juxtaposed these 'ignorant beings' with the more elevated view of a 'woman who has dedicated a considerable portion of her time to pursuits purely intellectual' (p.122).

For Wollstonecraft there has to be more to life than feminine feeling and 'schemes to conquer hearts'. To some extent she accepts that women may be trapped by determinist 'sensibilities' buried within their psyche but for her this is no excuse for not balancing all of this with other 'pursuits purely intellectual'. Later she notes that whatever the woman's inherent intellectual talents that 'many men stare insultingly at every female they meet' (p.124). For Wollstonecraft the immodesty inherent in the male gaze is just another aspect of 'habitual depravity' lurking within their psyche. She then raises the use of verbal 'brutality' on the part of men who 'bring forward, without blush, indecent allusions, or obscene witticisms, in the presence of a fellow-creature'. All of this can be seen as a deliberate process to de-sensitize women in preparation for what can only be seen as male sexual intent. The actions of these men Wollstonecraft sees as a 'want of modesty ...as subversive of morality, arises from a state of warfare so strenuously supported by voluptuous men' (p 125). Rather than this state of conflict there is an alternative offered and that is for a 'man of delicacy' who 'looks for affection' but then that would emasculate the male by bringing forward his 'sensibilities'. Also, her use of military metaphors, whether it be women setting out to 'conquer hearts' or men operating 'a state of warfare' against them, encapsulates the unequal terms of the confrontation between the sexes and the tactics employed.

Still employing military metaphors she then warns women that once these men take their prize they will inevitably boast of their 'triumphs over women'. Wollstonecraft recognises the 'state of warfare' that exists between the sexes, which in turn has to lead to a victory or a defeat. In her view there is only one loser and this 'dreadful reckoning falls heavily on her own weak head, when reason awakes'. In the context of the late 18th. Century Wollstonecraft daringly raises a woman's sexual needs that in a sense places them on a par with men. For her '[W]omen as well as men ought to have the common appetites and passions of their nature, they are only brutal when unchecked by reason: but the obligation to check them is the duty of mankind, not a sexual duty' (p 130). For her the notion of a 'sexual duty' to control these determinist forces within women is also a requirement of the other half of the equation as underlined by the use of the more general 'mankind'. But, by women and men having 'common appetites and passions' Wollstonecraft effectively places women in the role of a being rather than that of some kind of sub-species to the male.

In conclusion, throughout the work Wollstonecraft emphasises that a woman's lack of rights and a proper education creates an unhealthy state of dependency on men. In her eyes all of this has not only been forced onto women by a very powerful patriarchy but it has also been colluded with by what she sees as a large body of women. For most males, of no matter what stripe, a combination of ignorance, innocence, beauty and obedience, in a woman make her both an attractive proposition and easier to exploit. Time and again Wollstonecraft undermines the notion of male supremacy, often through ridicule, that was to elicit a severe reaction from the ruling elite's leading lights. Typical of this was Horace Walpole who was later to label her "a hyena in petticoats" (p.vi). This is not surprising when Wollstonecraft gives the world a perspective of this late 18th. Century patriarchy as an occupying enemy force that holds women down for the very purpose of hanging on to every advantage they have over them.

Throughout the work Wollstonecraft keeps returning to the point that male exploitation of women does no good for society in general as it has only led men into 'a state of warfare' (p.125) with what should be fellow beings rather than the actuality of woman as the enemy. She rightly portrays this society as owned by men of no matter what class that in effect allows them to run it as a benefit match for themselves. No matter what the perceived progress of women in general the point can still be made that even in the 21st. Century some feminists see them as desperately hanging on to their last vestiges of power. That over two hundred years later some of her arguments surrounding the condition of women in society are still to be dealt with shows the power of the forces Wollstonecraft was up against and the courage of her stand in such a day and age.

Part Three

In his *Introduction* to *Fathers and Sons,* [Turgenev, I. (1998), Oxford, Oxford University Press. (All references are from this novel unless otherwise stated)], Richard Freeborn touches on the state of flux existing in Russia prior to 1859. After Imperial Russia's defeat in the Crimean War (1854-5) he states 'it became clear that internal reforms were essential' (p.x). In this period Turgenev was 'regarded as the champion of the oppressed peasantry and to that extent "progressive". Politically speaking, though, Turgenev was a "liberal" one who believed in gradual reform' rather than 'revolution' which 'held no great appeal for him'. (p.x.) In this sense the author himself was 'representative of the fathers' and opposed by young Russians who believed that 'if only society were changed on rational, socialist lines, human beings could be changed also and a "new man" could be created' (p.xi.). The younger generation was also being called upon 'to repudiate the liberal, aesthetically based values of the older generation of the intelligentsia'. As the work progresses Turgenev questions the ability of anyone to abandon aesthetic completely in the name of a more utilitarian existence. In short, what becomes apparent to his late 19th. Century readers is that these two generations of 'fathers and sons' are locked in combat over not only socialist egalitarian principles but also an individual's aesthetic needs. As well as this Turgenev portrays a society that is divided on class lines but also individuals prone to fragment psychologically as the pressures build on them.

Right from the opening paragraphs of *Fathers and Sons* readers gain a sense of a society that is riven by class divisions. Although the 'landowner' Kirsanov is brought nearer the lower orders with his 'dusty overcoat and checked trousers' his 'servant' is portrayed unsympathetically as having 'small, lacklustre eyes' and displaying 'unctuous body movements' (p.3). While Kirsanov is portrayed as a less than grand member of the Russian aristocracy there is a feeling that the servant is resentful of his position in life by his use of duplicitous 'unctuous body movements' to mask real feelings. At this level within the aristocracy, although possessing 'an estate of some five thousand acres', these owners are still presented to us, through sustained 'telling', as quite a naive set of people. Even '[H]is father, a general who had seen active service in 1812, a Russian gentleman, semi-literate, course-grained, but without malice' has to be seen as a mixture of certain qualities that are then deliberately undercut with his being portrayed as 'semi-literate' and 'course-grained'.

On a wider scale, Turgenev's deliberate setting of the novel in 1859 adds resonance to the characters he is presenting to the reader. This period in Russian history follows the European revolutions of 1848 and Russia's defeat in the Crimean War. The country is perceived by its own intelligentsia to be at a critical point of balance between its reactionary feudal system and the need to modernise and go forward. While Turgenev may be seen to be in favour of change his portrayal of the servant does not signal a desire to move power over to this class in anything like wholesale terms. In other words from the opening page readers get a sense that he sees the way forward in somewhat opaque terms.

Later in the work Turgenev alludes to the changes that of necessity are in train and the difficulties that follow on. Although the 'Emancipation of the serfs' did not become law until the '14th. February 1861' (p.xxvii) Turgenev 'shows' through dialogue between father and son the changes that are already affecting rural areas of Russia. Kirsanov states 'I've had a lot of trouble with the peasants this year... They're not paying their rent. What can you do about it?' (p.10) Again we detect a less than generous view on the part of Turgenev towards the majority peasant population. While the 'son' Arkady sees the movement from serf to 'hired labourers' as sufficient in itself the 'father' sees the new peasant as slipshod and uncaring with the words '[T]hey don't know how to treat the equipment'. Throughout this scene there is a sense of a society whereby things are slipping out of control with new more liberal ideas being foisted on an older generation that does not know quite how to cope with the changes beginning to bear down on them.

In fact throughout the work Turgenev sees social change as a slippery slope full of uncertainties. Later in a long convoluted paragraph reflecting on the new order brought in train by changes at Marino he depicts Kirsanov as out of his depth. 'Worries about the farm increased day by day and they were unhappy, senseless worries. The fuss and bother with the hired workers had become intolerable. Some demanded a settling of accounts or bonuses while others left after having received payment in advance' (pp.138/9). While this may appear as the workers being out of control Turgenev does add the flip side to all of this. 'The threshing-machine ordered from Moscow turned out to be useless due to its weight. Another was put out of commission the first time it was used' (p.139). This is a combination of technically inept management ordering the wrong equipment while placing demands on ill trained workers that are manifestly not up to the job. Even the 'farm's own women workers had put up their charges to an unheard-of degree and the crops meanwhile were running to seed' (pp.139/140). In the face of this mayhem all his brother Pavel can offer him is the inane advice *'Du calme, du calme'* (p.140).

On the approach to his family's house and lands, the narrator focalises through Arkady by 'telling' us of a countryside that was very little changed from 'the old maps of the time of Catherine the Great' (p.12). This hints that the last attempt to try and modernize this sprawling country had occurred at the hands of a German queen during the period of the 18th. Century Enlightenment. Russia's rural backwardness is depicted in its 'tiniest mill-ponds with frail dams, and little villages with low peasant huts under dark roofs, often with half their thatch gone, and small threshing barns all tilted to one side with walls made out of woven brushwood and gaping openings beside dilapidated haybarns'. Turgenev's use of environment is a metaphor for a society incapable of renewing itself, that in practical terms cannot even give shelter to neither man nor beast, or protect the product of the land from the depredations of the weather. Furthermore, the Russian Orthodox Church, as one of the main props of what is drawn as a still feudal society, is also portrayed as incapable of keeping its church buildings in good order. The 'stucco had fallen in places' and the crosses were 'all higgledy-piggledy'. Turgenev is presenting us with a society fallen into decay that lacks respect for its past and one that had even allowed the 'graveyards', containing the remains of previous generations, to go 'to rack and ruin'.

All of this is the inheritance of the 'sons' from their 'fathers' that the author articulates, through Arkady, as a major theme of the novel with the thoughts 'it can't, just can't stay like this. Reforms are essential'. The question is how these changes can be implemented successfully. Pathetic fallacies abound with the words '[T]he roadside willows were like beggars in tatters with torn bark and broken branches' (p.12). He later contrasts this harsh view of the natural world by swinging the perspective over to the 'romantic' element within Arkady's psyche with, '[E]verything around glinted green and gold, everything softly and expansively waived and shone under the quiet breath of a warm breeze' (p.13). Turgenev's use of poetic technique is being applied to both the romantic, and the harsher, view of the Russian countryside. What is also emerging is that the utilitarian view of the way forward is not going to suffice. Arkady's internal fragmented views reflect the divisions within Russia at large and between the generations. Also his thoughts define his dislike of the present state of his country with allusions to a more 'romantic' view that suggests a greater love for Russia and even a reason for caring. In fact the dilapidated works of man are unfavourably compared to the beauty inherent in the works of nature. But even nature itself seems to be suffering with the 'torn bark and broken branches' of the willow tree. The sum total is a fragmented world inhabited by characters that in this case reflect this fragmentation from within.

The problems facing those charged with running the estate are listed by Bazarov through dialogue with Arkady. He states '[T]he cattle are in a poor state and the horses are decrepit. The buildings are also needing repair and the workers look like a crowd of inveterate loafers, while the bailiff's either a fool or a rogue, I can't make out which' (p.44). Bazarov's nihilist beliefs become a philosophy of despair as from the Czar down to the lowest peasant nobody seems to have the capacity to turn things round. In their different ways the answer for both sides is to import foreign ways and cultures. As well as the mention of Catherine the Great in the past there are Bazarov's allusions to English efficiency, through the practicalities of his room's furniture, with the words, 'English washbasins, that's progress' (p.18). While at the other end of the class spectrum the dandy, Arkady's aristocratic Uncle Pavel Petrovich Kirsonov, 'sat down at the table. He was wearing a stylish morning suit in the English fashion, his head crowned with a small fez' (p.22). Here we have Bazarov's utilitarian beliefs contrasted with the Pavel's aesthetic needs in the shape of 'English fashion' all be it with a touch of the Russian 'ways of life in the country' through the addition of 'a small fez'.

This inferiority on the part of the Russians towards the English is then extended to the German scientific community. In dialogue between Pavel Kirsanov and Bazarov on 'physics' and the 'natural sciences' Bazarov states 'the Germans are our teachers' (p.25). Pavel has already conceded the point that the 'the Teutons have been very successful recently in that sort of thing'. While allowing for the qualities of 'Schiller' and '*Goethe*' he then attacks the Germans with, '[B]ut now they only seem to have a lot of chemists and materialists' (p.26). This doubles as distrust of science and an attack on importing materialist beliefs that of necessity underpin Bazarov's utilitarian theories. While other European powers are modernizing Russia is portrayed in this scene as gripped in a state of inertia. Furthermore, his use of irony in the term 'Teutons' does not hide the fact that the game is up for the ruling elite but there is also huge distrust at handing over the process, and direction of change, to either ignorant peasants or well educated nihilists. A further barrier between the peasant and their ruling elite is their ability to trip in and out of the French language to conceal intent and what is going on from the peasants around them (p.11). Also, to willingly substitute your own language with a foreign import has to open up the ruling elite to the charge of succumbing to a 19th. Century version of cultural cringe.

Turgenev's use of dialogue in chapter 10 'shows' us just how wide the gulf is between the 'fathers' and the 'sons'. While others are present the main verbal 'battle' (p.48) is again between the nihilist Bazarov and the aesthete Pavel. To the utilitarian Bazarov, even philosophy is 'romanticism' (p.50). He condemns everything, 'we've got to clear the ground' (p.50). Bazarov's attack on contemporary Russian society takes in 'art and unconscious creativity and parliamentarianism and a legal profession...when the real business of life was about one's daily bread, when the grossest superstition was stifling us' (p.52). We know that a parliamentary system of rule did not exist but Turgenev's use of 'a legal profession' casts doubt on whatever it is that calls itself a legal profession in 1850s Russia. Again Bazarov's contempt for the peasantry becomes obvious when he states that they would be 'glad to steal from each other simply in order to drink themselves silly'. To Pavel Petrovich the tone of this ideology is destructive lunacy. The nihilists are out to 'smash things' (p.53) simply because they are there and 'without even knowing why you're doing it'. In his view this 'banal maxim' pits 'civilisation' against 'brute Mongol force'.

Here Turgenev has drawn a clear line between the utilitarian nihilist and the aesthetic needs of the older aristocrat. While both would see themselves as part of an elite imposing their standards on the lower orders there is also the idea inherent in their beliefs that Bazarov reflects an ugly more brutal world, and Pavel, the need in everyone for romance and beauty. In this scene Turgenev is putting his finger on a still unresolved problem in the arts: the reflection in, such as, modern art and architecture of ugliness and functionality, and humanity's need for aesthetic beauty just for its own sake. In this 'showing' Turgenev is making clear the dangers inherent in managing change. It would not be lost on his educated Francophile Russian readers how quickly apparently more reasonable ideologies than Bazarov's nihilism could descend into the "terror" that followed the French Revolution. We can also see divisions within the nation state between European Russia that was in danger from her other Asiatic self and its "Mongol" hordes. As valid as some of Bazarov's criticisms might be of contemporary Russia Turgenev articulates, through Pavel Petrovich, his fears that things could get out of control.

His treatment of the female character in *Fathers and Sons* reaches maturity in his presentation of Odintsova. She immediately 'stunned' Arkady 'by the dignity of her bearing...Her bright eyes shone calmly and intelligently' (p.73). She was a woman in control of herself who 'chatted just as freely with her partner as she had with the grandee, calmly making a play of turning her head and eyes and once or twice calmly laughing' (p.74). Turgenev's repetition of 'calmly' in effect distances her from his earlier portrayal of the more agitated, even histrionic, feminist Kukshina who 'was always in a state' (p.67). While calmness is an outward display of control Odintsova's 'play of turning her head' is to deliberately utilize all of her qualities, especially her looks, to gain effect. The central core of her character is presented to us as a woman of the lower aristocracy who has known hard times but has overcome them. Odintsova is mature, sexually attractive, widowed, and lives without a male partner.

Also, her country estate exudes order and taste. 'Behind the church a long village stretched out in two rows of houses with chimneys visible here and there among the straw roofs. The manor house was built in the same style as the church, a style known among us as belonging to the age of Alexander I. The house was painted yellow and had a green roof, white pillars and a pediment bearing a coat of arms' (p.81). It is a portrait of a well-kept estate that also manages to encompass what is best from the past. She is a free agent whose estate is well run and well built, and it is these qualities that are juxtaposed, by Turgenev, to the Kirsonov's inefficient running of Marino. Furthermore, unlike others of her sex or class she makes no pretence for the need to speak French to elevate her status in the eyes of others as, '[S]he had read several good books and was used to expressing herself in good Russian' (p.79). Braced with these qualities this woman has the confidence to take Bazarov's utilitarian views head on.

Odintsova starts out from the position that we need the arts '[I]f only to know how to understand people and study them' (p.84). While he attacks individualism by comparing people to being no different to 'trees in a forest. No botanist is going to be concerned with each individual birch tree' (p.84). To which he elicits her mocking stinging reply '[S]o, according to you, there's no difference between a silly man and a sensible one, between a good one and a bad one'. Odintsova is making the point that there is a lack of common sense in Bazarov's ideological position.

This is reinforced by Turgenev when he has him state '[W]e know approximately what causes physical ailments, while moral diseases derive from poor education, from all the rubbish with which people's heads are filled from birth onwards – in short, from the shocking state of society. Reform society and there'll be no more disease.' To place 'moral diseases' at the feet of a 'poor education' and reform as the holy grail to 'no more disease' can be seen to be naïve to say the least. Furthermore, Bazarov refuses to define in detail these 'moral diseases' or the reforms that might eradicate them making him susceptible to the charge of self-indulgence and empty rhetoric. Odintsova easily refutes all of this with 'when society is reformed there'll be no more stupid or bad people'. In contrast to the 'fathers' Kirsanov's and Pavel's earlier inability to undermine Bazarov's rhetoric, Turgenev now leaves it to a woman to demolish the nihilist position adopted by the up and coming 'sons'. But we later find that Odintsova was also capable of selling herself through marriage, when we are told, as regards to her late husband, 'she had married him for his money' (p.88). Turgenev is letting us know that she may be a capable woman and in control but this does not mean that she is highly principled. What we find is that like many a woman before and since she had taken the practical step of trading, as a commodity, looks and sex for security and wealth.

In the end the archetypal rebel in Bazarov, who fights against political orthodoxies, is shown by Turgenev to reside side by side with his 'romantic' views and is in fact bowled over by a 'romantic' or sexual attraction to Odintsova. It is not the 'calm' Odintsova who loses 'control' but Bazarov, when he declares, 'I love you, stupidly, madly' (p.103) leaving him '[H]is whole body was visibly quivering'. Here Bazarov the new male reverts to type causing Turgenev to effectively torpedo his own argument in scientific materialism's belief that somehow 'a "new man" could be created' (p.xi), if only we were to change society 'on rational, socialist lines'. That Bazarov cannot change himself subverts any hope that he or anyone else could change the world in general. Turgenev can also be seen to be making the point that human beings carry within them determinist forces that may never be completely overcome. In the face of the chaos of uncontrollable male passion Odintsova's 'control' never cracks as she opts for '[P]eace of mind is still the best thing on earth' (p.104). She refuses to give up her still calmness, and her individualism, for the uncertainties surrounding an attachment to Bazarov. Her character's intellectual qualities, and practical managerial abilities, can be perceived as a metaphor for the way forward for Russia. But similarly we can see that Bazarov's, and the Kirsanov's, frailties present difficulties that could oppose Russia's chance of progressing to a more modern manageable state.

In conclusion, Turgenev makes clear that whatever the views of the nihilists on the way forward society is going to have to go beyond the utilitarian needs of people. In fact he takes a balanced line between the aesthetic needs of the individual and Russian society's need to modernize. The question is how can the theory of scientific materialism, espoused mainly through the character Bazarov, be tailored to take into account such a fragmented society inhabited by characters that are themselves fragmented? Pavel's confrontation with Bazarov brings to the fore splits between different layers within society. What we see is a Russia with a heritage that is both European and 'Mongol' Asiatic, and the aesthetic needs of the individual. Throughout the work Turgenev is giving the Russian people a realistic assessment of the difficulties that lie ahead. In fact Kirsanov's bid to modernize agriculture on his estate betrays the lack of skills within the Russian workforce and the inability of parts of the ruling elite to manage even the simplest of tasks at this level.

By comparison, with such as Kirsanov, Odintsova acts as a metaphor for the way forward. Her estate is built in good taste, in good order, and is run in an efficient manner. In contrast to the effete males speaking to each other in foreign tongues she can get by speaking in 'good Russian'. In effect Turgenev is bringing into the equation feminist issues by including qualities that might lie in the other half of the Russian nation to help to solve problems brought on through modernization. Also, to run her estate there is less regard for importing foreign ideas in the form of scientific materialism or the nihilistic beliefs that Bazarov brings along with it. Through the character Odintsova what Turgenev is saying is that although there may not be a definitive answer to the way forward, and that the future may be difficult, there is no need to raze everything to the ground in an attempt to get there.

Part Four

By the early part of the 20th. Century writers had to some extent become less and less direct and therefore less inclined towards the didactic in their works. A good example of this approach is in the work of the New Zealand born writer Katherine Mansfield. In her *Introduction* to *Selected Stories*, [Mansfield, K. (2002), Oxford University Press. Oxford. (All references are from this novel unless otherwise stated)], Angela Smith gives us Mansfield's thoughts, in her own words, written to 'Virginia Woolf in 1919: "what the writer does is not so much to *solve* the question but to *put* the question. There must be the question put. That seems to me a very nice dividing line between the true & the false writer" (p.xvi). In other words, in a world of fragmented multiplicity there may be multiple solutions to the questions '*put*' and implicit in this is the active participation of the individual reader. Also, despite her support for the modernist aesthetic of this period, and its belief in the pleasures inherent in art for art's sake, Mansfield emphatically asserts '[T]here must be the question put'.

This allows such social criticisms as gender and class to rise gently to the surface while at the same time staying within the confines of the aesthetic. In other words, on the whole Mansfield does find fault, indirectly, in the organization of society and mutual relations of people and classes. Although Mansfield does not take a particular side, in a political sense, in either of the stories chosen she would be conscious of the part her work would play in the political realities outside of her writing. For instance any subversion of the male identity or the class system can be seen to resonate beyond the aesthetic and have some effect on reasons supporting male authority in institutions as diverse as marriage or even the Parliament of the land. As one would expect, Mansfield's aestheticism is ambiguous and multi-layered but indirectly a pattern of meaning emerges that gives the reader a glimpse of literary purpose through such as the issues already mentioned.

Mansfield establishes gender issues from the opening words of 'Mr Reginald Peacock's Day' (first published in 1917) that in this case are presented to the reader in a third-person voice, using the narrative technique of free indirect discourse, that at times slides into modernist 'stream of consciousness'. 'If there was one thing that he hated more than another it was the way she had of waking him in the morning. She did it on purpose, of course. It was her way of establishing her grievance for the day' (p.121). In several short distilled sentences Mansfield brings to the surface the image of a narcissistic, hysterical male internalizing a dislike, or even a hatred, for what could be a servant but in fact turns out later to be his wife. Readers also get a sense of a realization on his part of passive resistance aimed 'on purpose' at him by this servant-wife. This brings into play a major theme within Mansfield's work of women using this form of resistance against the assumed power of the patriarchy.

In her *Introduction* Angela Smith believes Mansfield's works to be 'incisive interrogations of patriarchy' (p. xiv) but as can be seen later this interpretation requires to be considerably expanded. Throughout the narrative the 'she.... her...wife' remains nameless. Her role as a drudge is further emphasised through appearing 'buttoned up in an overall, with a handkerchief over her head' (p.121). Although the narrative is written in third-person that is focalized mainly through Peacock it is not omniscient. What adds to the image of the containment of women within the institution of marriage is that Mansfield never presents us with the inner feelings of the nameless 'wife'. It suggests a metaphor for the restrictive codes imposed by society as a whole on women and can be seen in social terms as an indirect criticism of this containment of women.

This point is emphasised later when the young son's feelings are presented to us, by means of free indirect discourse, with the words 'why did his father always sort of sing to him instead of talk?...' (p.123). In this case the contrasting of the bleak world of the 'wife' as an unfeeling object is set against her son starting out in life with at least some inner life that holds out potential for him to be seen as a more rounded individual. Using short clauses, well suited to stream of consciousness that in a sense signify thoughts appearing or disappearing and even spilling over, Mansfield gives us Peacock questioning himself as if nobody else is allowed to. 'What was the matter with her? What the hell did she want? Hadn't he three times as many pupils now as when they were first married, earned three times as much, paid for every stick and stone that they possessed, and now had begun to shell out for Adrian's kindergarten?...' (p.121). Mansfield's use of ellipsis can be interpreted as a pause in his thought processes or Peacock veering off in a change of direction as he now criticizes her for 'not having a penny to her name' when they married. Without plot, action, or event, Mansfield gives her readers a virtuoso display of the sheer venom that can reside in the male character within the institution of marriage. Also, that 'she' is paid, through her keep, brings to the fore male payment for services rendered and the lack of financial independence for women in society. The critical social issue of male control of women's lives through money is later emphasised when 'she' has to more or less beg for money to 'pay the dairy' bill (p.125).

Again through free indirect discourse Mansfield indirectly undermines Peacock's character through his own voice with the words, 'But really, really, to wake up a sensitive person like that was positively dangerous! It took him hours to get over it – simply hours' (p.121). Through the use of repetition, 'sensitive person', and exclamation mark, readers again get a sense of the male as hysterical. An image much more associated with the female of the species. Also, the symbolically and literally 'buttoned up' nameless 'she' is again contrasted but in this case with the ironically named Peacock's view of himself as a 'sensitive person'. It is easy to see this image of the 'wife' as an indirect social criticism of the division of labour, and prevailing relations, between men and women within marriage. Mansfield's detached narrative is aesthetic in this sense while the pruned down prose also conflates such issues as female drudgery in the form of the servant-wife, their appearance, and the male ego. The form of the narrative mimics this 'conflation' through a single day in the life of the narcissistic character Peacock that is highly condensed, and also modernist, by means of its use of short story technique. Through the perspective of the male character the reader goes through a process of illumination of the condition of an individual woman within the institution of marriage. Mansfield can also be seen as discrediting male power through the character Peacock's own mind. Paradoxically, what sometimes might appear to be first person perspective indirectly attacks the dominant male position within institution of marriage out of his own mouth or, to be more accurate, the insight into his own consciousness.

In 'Peacock's Day' Mansfield utilizes the modernist technique of flashback to introduce us to Peacock's class ambitions through the use of third-person voice. We are 'directly' told that '[A] few months ago Reginald had spent a weekend in a very aristocratic family, where the father received his little sons in the morning and shook hands with them' (p.123). Mansfield paints a sterile, loveless image, of family life that suggests a 'father' conditioning the next generation to his view of human relationships. Repetition is an important theme in the narrative as it shows society's willingness to repeat past mistakes. Peacock 'thought the practice charming, and introduced it immediately'. This brings to the fore the willingness of the lower classes to ape the actions of their so-called betters making the point of how difficult change may be. Elsewhere we are informed by, free indirect discourse, of his meeting with Lord Timbuck. 'What a triumphant evening!' and later repeated 'triumph upon triumph! And Lord Timbuck's champagne simply flowed' (p.128). He was called 'Peacock, you notice – not Mr Peacock – but Peacock, as if he were one of them'. This was all because '[H]e was an artist'. The conversation with himself not only portrays Peacock as the supreme narcissist but Mansfield also manages to give us the man as an unmitigated snob. In this scene her outsider colonial eye subverts character through his repetitive language. By his repeated use of the words 'triumph' and 'Peacock' Mansfield also entices the reader into seeing the real banality of his world. The ordinary is utilized to subvert both his social climbing ambitions and the male narcissist within him but all of this can also be seen as a social criticism of a layered class system within this society.

Furthermore, Peacock's repeated use throughout the narrative of 'Dear lady, I should [or shall] only be too charmed' to his various female students and friends adds to the image of 'an artist' lacking originality (p.p.125/6/7). His 'charm' with his 'dear ladies' is never taken beyond his banal language. Also, the ironically named and heavily alliterated 'dear ladies' in the form of 'Miss Betty Brittle, the Countess Wilkowska and Miss Marian Morrow' (p.124) also serve to pinpoint the view that some women see their role in life as pleasuring the male ego. Throughout the work Mansfield gently satirizes her own sex by means of breathless prose and typical of this is the letter written in 'violet ink' by his friend 'Aenone Fell', another name that doesn't leave a lot to the imagination. For her the 'wonderful joy' of his singing was '[Q]uite unforgettable. You make me wonder, as I have not wondered since I was a girl, if this is *all.* I mean, if this ordinary world is *all.* If there is not, perhaps, for those of us who understand, divine beauty and richness awaiting us if only we have the *courage* to see it. And to make it ours...'. The double indenting through italics, the short clauses, the trailing off into ellipses all serve to undermine the women outside of his marriage.

Throughout the narrative Mansfield allows these female characters to condemn themselves out of their own mouths through nothing less than gushy prose. Here readers are presented with a world where Peacock and his adoring women deserve each other. While his students are portrayed as more than willing to service Peacock in a physical sense he is portrayed to us as being incapable of actually rising to the occasion. Throughout Mansfield erotically dangles before the reader the pleasure of physical seduction for it to only to end in the anti-climax and impotence of his clichéd language, at the same time further emasculating Peacock in the process. Like each and every one of these women, even 'his wife', he can only 'try to treat as a friend' and this also collapses into the final banality of 'Dear lady, I should be so charmed – so charmed' (p.128). While giving us the male singularly lacking in sexual potency this epiphanic moment also nails the image of a man caught in a slightly mad circular existence. As a metaphor it also shows our ability to repeat what went before making a critical point about the generality of human relations.

Peacock's aping of upper-class mores also suggests a metaphor for the artistic community's willingness to shed their artistic independence for their approval. The repetition within repetition of Peacock's language mirrors his daily routine of waking, bathing and student's lessons. Linguistically and routinely this 'sensitive artist' appears to be on an endless loop. This symbolist patterning can be seen as a comment on the 'artist' in society who repeats what went before making their art as impotent and narcissistic as Mansfield's own creation. A healthy cutting-edge art that questions what went before could be regarded as a necessity in a 'healthy' social system. Pater saw repetition in the arts as '[F]ailure is to form habits; for habit is relative to a stereotyped world', and furthermore, '[W]hat we have to do is to be ever curiously testing new opinions and courting new impressions' instead of pursuing 'a facile orthodoxy' (*A Twentieth-Century Literature Reader,* Gupta & Johnson p.37). Mansfield's impressionistic narrative technique certainly leans more towards Pater's vision of literature than the more obviously didactic and romantic practitioners of the art. Another suggested metaphor is Peacock's 'repetitions' can also be seen as a warning to any society reluctant to bring about socio-political changes and, more importantly, in the way people think as individuals. This symbolist patterning of repetition allows for ambiguity in the text that is an important aspect of the modernist aesthetic project. This same ambiguity also allows meaning to emerge giving literary and social purpose to Mansfield's work but this requires the active participation of the reader's interpretive skills to illuminate issues buried within the text.

The bathroom scene in 'Peacock's Day' also suggests emasculation of the male image while approaching the issue of pleasure for pleasure's sake. Mansfield gives the text emphasis through the aesthetic of poetic technique using alliteration, personification, ambiguity and metaphor. Peacock starts out with the slow build-up of 'nursing his voice' that is then followed by the climactic 'he burst into such a shout of triumph that the tooth-glass on the bathroom shelf trembled and even the bath tap seemed to gush stormy applause...' (p.122). Again Mansfield's use of ellipses allows the reader to add their own interpretations. Is this the anti-climax that follows the climax or just a gap deliberately left in place for the reader to interpret? The point is that the personified surrounding objects and the use of 'nursing...trembled...gush' is a scene that can easily be interpreted in terms of male masturbation, adding to Peacock's narcissistic image.

Barthes makes the point that "hedonism has been repressed by nearly every philosophy" (*A Twentieth-Century Literature Reader* p.44). Furthermore he relates hedonistic pleasure to what Bennett's and Royle's essay calls the 'pleasure in reading'. In their view Barthes conflates hedonistic pleasure and the 'pleasure in reading' that in his opinion also has the effect on the reader of being the cause of "discomforts" that "unsettles the reader's historical, cultural, psychological assumptions". The fact that religions and political elites in many parts of the world to this day still attempt to censor most forms of hedonistic pursuits shows a fear of their ability to subvert the moral and social order they wish to impose. At the time of publishing Mansfield would be well aware of censorship laws and her ambiguous aesthetic style allows her to push up against these limits surrounding hedonistic pleasures that disturb all of these "assumptions". Also, the bathroom scene is part of a process within the narrative to again reduce Peacock to an androgynous figure that in turn ridicules male potency and their dominance of every important institution from marriage up to, and including, the body politic.

In 'The Stranger' (first published in 1921) Mansfield takes up the issue of the class-system again but in this case introduces colonial connotations. Early on in the work she alludes to a colonial willingness to mimic the mother country's class-system. The leading character Hammond's use of '[D]ashed annoying' and later '[B]y Jove' can be seen as a linguistic attempt to set himself above his fellow citizens while putting him on a par with a distant metropolitan upper-class group (pp.214/215). Mansfield also seems to be satirising Hammond's aping of this class by placing him in the incongruous surroundings of a colony at the other end of the world. The class issue is further emphasised by his wife's accommodation on board the incoming vessel in 'her state-room' (p.218). Also, we are informed 'she was surrounded. The whole first-class seemed to want to say good-bye to Janey' (p.217). What tells us that this is not quite third-person narrative is the way Mansfield focalises through Hamilton by slipping in the words 'seemed' and, his name for her, 'Janey'. As in Peacock narrative perspective is slippery, can contain simultaneous views and is unsettling for the reader. We can also see that her status is paid for and grafted on to his and this can be seen as a comment on the male view of reducing women to the role of a trophy. Also, Mansfield seems to suggest a propensity in societies to transplant aspects of social systems over vast distances that works against some people's beliefs in a more egalitarian society. It is a bleak view of any hope for real political and social change when new countries, with new opportunities, repeat what is worse of what they left behind. As with 'Peacock's Day', Mansfield is again suggesting an idea of societies being fated to repeat their previous mistakes. This less than utopian insight into the way of the world suggests an intrinsic political awareness within the work.

Mansfield indirectly examines the role of children in marriage through the relation between Hammond and his wife. The reader is made aware of his erotic anticipations through his seeing her as 'watching him, ready for him' (p.216). This is reinforced later with '[S]he was just the same. Not a day changed. Just as he'd always known her' (p.217). Despite her journeying to the other end of the planet and back for this individual every aspect of her character is expected to be in stasis. But change has come about for his 'Janey' as barriers start to fall into place when she asks '[H]ow are the children, John?' The maternal concern for her children is deliberately contrasted with Hammond's internalised, duplicitous, '(Hang the children!)'. All of this is further emphasised when she later 'tucked' the letters from the children 'into her frilled blouse' (p.221). It is easy to see that through the 'letters' the children become both a physical and a symbolic barrier to Hamilton's sexual ambitions. She apparently wants the letters more than she wants him as unlike Hamilton they are allowed direct contact with her body. As well as a comment on ownership of women within marriage the letter incident also suggests his Janey's priorities now lie elsewhere. What readers begin to see is what Hamilton is too blinkered to see that is that this woman has moved on.

This notion of male ownership is exemplified through his ability to see his 'Janey' as an extension of the male self. She is "Mrs John Hammond!" He gave a long sigh of content and leaned back, crossing his arms. The strain was over. He felt he could have sat there forever sighing his relief – the relief of being rid of that horrible tug, pull, grip on his heart. The danger was over. That was the feeling. They were on dry land again' (p.218). Again readers are required to fill in the gaps in the text. Once he gets her back into his presence he is 'content' but all of the past feelings are not explained. What has caused the 'strain', the 'horrible tug, pull, grip on his heart' and exactly what was the 'danger'? Here Mansfield seems to be undermining ownership of a woman by adding the element of hysteria to male possession by instilling within it the possibilities of loss. Also, the fact that this woman has taken his name, exaggerated through exclamation mark, again indents the notion of woman as a prize won against others. But the use of the word 'feeling' leaves doubt in the reader's mind that the 'danger' may not end there. Making a more universal point, having no more than a 'feeling' where his Janey's loyalties lie raises a question mark over how much anyone might know about any person, close to them or otherwise.

Mansfield reiterates the point of all change and everything the same within Hammond's world view. After her travelling to the other end of the world his concern is '[N]o more going without his tea or pouring out his own. She was back' (p.219). As in 'Peacock' her role is that of the servant-wife but in this case she is also the prized trophy servicing his sexual needs. He then 'turned to her, squeezed her hand, and said gently, teasingly, in the special voice he had for her: "Glad to be home again, deary?" She smiled; she didn't even bother to answer, but gently she drew her hand away as they came to the lighted streets.' The teasing 'special voice' of the male in full seductive mode is ridiculed by the sheer crassness of Hammond's use of "deary". Her silent rebuttal of his entreaties is again a form of passive resistance, supported by her body language, as 'she drew her hand away' in the public domain of 'the lighted streets'. Also, within the small act of drawing 'her hand away' we find his 'Janey' resisting not only the idea of ownership but this man's need to parade his ownership of her in public. Readers can begin to see that 'pouring out his own' tea just might turn out to be the least of his worries.

Throughout 'The Stranger' Mansfield forensically examines desire, both male and female, within the state of marriage. While dialogue and body language describes his

'Janey' as prevaricating, the third-person voice gives us Hammond as 'flushed' with his 'eager gaze upon her' (p.220), and later he 'drew her into the deep, ugly chair' (p.221). It is physical love painted predatorily in terms of the male 'gaze' and physical ownership of the woman. Mansfield's use of 'deep, ugly chair' only exemplifies the crudity of Hammond's intent but there is also the thought of the chair and man enveloping the woman in their grip. Again Mansfield brings to bear stream of consciousness ushering into the text male uncertainties, desire, ownership and the sexual commodification of women. Images follow one another fusing symbolism and realism as Hammond 'embraced her he felt she would fly away, so Hammond never knew – never knew for dead certain she was as glad as he was. How could he know? Would he ever know? Would he always have this craving – this pang like hunger, somehow, to make Janey so much part of him that there wasn't any way of her to escape? He wanted to blot out everybody, everything'.

Here we find his right to appropriate his 'Janey' body and soul is deliberately circumscribed with doubt and question marks. Hammond can only rely on impressions as he tries to come to grips with the actuality of what is going on within this woman. His world has now become, as Pater remarks, 'impressions unstable, flickering, inconsistent... Every one of those impressions of the individual in his isolation, each mind keeping as a solitary prisoner its own dream of a world.' (*A Twentieth-Century Literature Reader* p.36) He is a man out of his depth, he wants to be 'part of' what he does not know. Furthermore, Mansfield's use of 'craving ... pangs ...hunger' reduces his needs to nothing better than the basic instinct of sexual desire. In contrast to Hammond's inner declaration of his needs, Janey's physical contact with him is described in a third-person authorial voice as 'so lightly, so remotely' (p.222).

Like Peacock's 'wife', the character 'Janey' is never given an inner voice at any point in the narrative. Also, in neither case are these women portrayed as having feelings amounting to pleasure. This can be seen as the ultimate image of the female stunted and stranded in an uncaring male dominated existence. In fact their role in life is to service the needs, one way or another, of the man nearest to them. Also, the character's 'remoteness' towards Hammond again suggests feminine use of body language as a tactical resistance towards male dominance, sexual or otherwise. Agreeing, Kaplan takes the view that 'a counter process of resistance and rebellion is always at work' towards these forces that affect women's lives but the use of passive resistance shows us just how limited are the options available to women (*A Twentieth-Century Literature Reader* p.30). The 'stranger' in the title is ambiguous as we begin to question whether it is the wife who has been alienated by her contacts with a 'Europe' at the other end of the world or is it the husband who she now sees in a new light. There is also a question of how close Hammond is to his children and that adds another meaning to the word 'stranger'. Throughout both works stereotypical images of family life are critically examined all without straying from Mansfield's modernist aesthetic mission.

Mansfield deals with the stereotypical male identity and its fragmentation through Hammond's physical relationship with his 'Janey'. She comments indirectly on male expectations within marriage. Hammond's required pleasure is sexual and this is emphasised with poetic alliteration, assonance and repetition of 'A slow, deep flush flowed into his forehead' (p.222). Added to this is the instruction '[K]iss me, Janey! You kiss me!' The repetition with the addition of 'You' smacks of an order and a sign from her of compliance and subservience to his needs. Her silent resistance is conveyed through 'there was a tiny pause'. This is further emphasised later by the kiss being given 'firmly, lightly' and being reduced to her having, what he saw as, 'signed the contract'. But his thoughts 'that wasn't what he wanted; that wasn't at all what he thirsted for' shows a divergence of interpretation of exactly what the 'contract' demands. Here Mansfield conflates male sexual needs within the institution of marriage and the law of 'contract' that in this sense can be seen as having political connotations. Hammond's conjugal rights actually hinge on Janey's acquiescence to his order and her acceptance of his interpretation of the marriage 'contract'. Something we can see that there is a certain resistance towards on the part of the woman.

In what can be described as an epiphanic moment his desire then collapses under the effect of his wife's compassion, or maybe love, for another man who died aboard ship. This is all conveyed symbolically through the image of the 'fire had gone red. Now it fell in with a sharp sound and the room was colder. Cold crept up his arms. The room was huge, immense, glittering. It filled his whole world. There was the great blind bed, with his coat flung across it like some headless man saying his prayers' (p.223). Mansfield's use of poetic technique, short clauses and stream of consciousness gives more than the collapse of desire; it is a man undergoing psychological fragmentation. A man who had been introduced to readers earlier as a 'strong – looking' man (p.213). Here the environment becomes an important spatial representation of the inner man but he also feels, sees, hears and imagines as if on the verge of a nervous breakdown. Also, the 'headless man' image of a prostrate truncated male clinches the narrative's movement towards a collapse in Hammond's power over to his 'Janey', making the emasculation of him complete. Throughout 'The Stranger' the reader is presented with multiple viewpoints of the masculine character with the woman in the final analysis actually appearing to be the stronger force that also helps to undermine any general belief that might support male dominance over a woman.

In conclusion, Mansfield puts forward a devastating critique of relationships between men and women, within or without marriage. With Peacock we have the extremes of idolatry on the part of his female students and his servant-wife's role within the marriage. With Hammond we have a woman who has changed and his total inability to deal with this leading eventually to his psychological disintegration. Both women adopt the position of passive resistance towards their respective husbands giving readers a hint of just how far they are allowed to go. Also, by giving neither woman an inner voice Mansfield emphasizes how women are stunted by these patriarchal forces surrounding them. Even so throughout both narratives Mansfield's emasculation of the two main male characters and their consequent reduction to an androgynous state is the method used to undercut male ascendancy of no matter what type. To merge the stereotypical images of male and female can be seen as a hollowing out from the inside any support for inequality between the sexes. Mansfield's subtle raising of issues as diverse as class, gender, children in marriage, the role of the artist in society, and hedonism, gives her work literary purpose but is contained by a self-imposed discipline of the aesthetic project. Her use of poetic technique, ambiguous condensed prose, and a detached style of writing, gives her work its aesthetic qualities. All of this also diminishes the temptation towards polemics that can date an artist's work and allows readers of each generation to bring their own particular interpretations to bear on her work.

Bibliography

De Laclos, C. *Dangerous Acquaintances,* Translated by Richard Aldington. (1987), Ark Paperbacks, London (Reprint of 1924 Edition).

Bibliography

Wollstonecraft, M. (2001), *A Vindication of the Rights of Woman*, New York, The Modern Library.

Further Reading.

The Enlightenment Texts, II Edited by Simon Elliot and Keith Whitlock (1998), The Open University, Milton Keynes (Reprint of first 1992 edition).

Bibliography

Turgenev, I (1998*). Fathers and Sons*, Oxford, Oxford University Press.

Further Reading.

Walder, Dennis (2000). *Approaching Literature, The Realist Novel*, London: Routledge-Open University.

Bibliography

Gupta, S. and Johnson, D. (2005) *A Twentieth - Century Literature Reader,* Abingdon, Routledge. Mansfield, K. (2002) *Selected Stories,* Oxford, Oxford University Press.

Further Reading.

Brown, R.D. and Gupta, S. (2005) *Aestheticism and Modernism.* Abingdon, Routledge.